DEPOSITORY LIBRARY USE OF TECHNOLOGY: A PRACTITIONER'S PERSPECTIVE

Information Management, Policy, and Services
Charles R. McClure and Peter Hernon, Editors

DEPOSITORY LIBRARY
USE OF TECHNOLOGY:
A PRACTITIONER'S PERSPECTIVE

Edited by

Jan Swanbeck
University of Florida,
Gainesville

Peter Hernon
Simmons College,
Boston

ABLEX PUBLISHING CORPORATION
NORWOOD, NEW JERSEY

Printed in the United States of America

Library of Congress Cataloging-in-Publication Data

Depository library use of technology : a practitioner's perspective /
    edited by Jan Swanbeck, Peter Hernon.
      260 p. 24 cm. -- (Information management, policy, and services)
      Includes bibliographical references and index.
      ISBN 0-89391-908-X. --ISBN 0-89391-999-3 (pbk.)
      1. Depository libraries--United States--Data processing.
    2. Information technology--United States.   I. Swanbeck, Jan.
    II. Hernon, Peter.   III. Series.
    Z675.D4D45   1992
    021.8--dc20
                                                            92-40351
                                                                CIP

Ablex Publishing Corporation
355 Chestnut Street
Norwood, NJ 07648

Contents

List of Figures

List of Tables

Preface

Documents librarianship of today and tomorrow sharply differs from that of yesterday. Present and future documents librarians need a solid understanding of management, decision making, planning and evaluation, collection development and management, and the application of information-handling technologies to depository collections and services. Technology has produced the most dramatic change in documents librarianship.

The central theme of this book is change. Change "is any planned or unplanned alteration in the status quo that affects an organization's structure, services, programs, or allocation of resources" (Hernon and McClure, 1990, p. 224). Technology is a major change agent. Documents librarians, as well as other librarians working with government publications/information and students preparing to enter that field, must be able to negotiate different technologies and feel comfortable with their use. Technology enables librarians to better manage collections and services, as well as to increase the opportunities for library staff and users to negotiate a diverse set of information resources to find those most pertinent to resolving particular information needs.

Documents librarians can now negotiate more of the information environment that is technologically based. This capability will undoubtedly increase in the future. A central question becomes "What information-handling technologies and electronic resources can depository libraries absorb or tap effectively and efficiently in times of fiscal stringency?"

More depository libraries will supplement their collections by taping bulletin boards and other sources to provide their clientele with perishable information and data that are not locally available. Most importantly, this information and data will be in a format that users can download or upload, and manipulate. Such activities have both advantages and disadvantages for libraries. One definite benefit is the opportunity to partner with academic computing facilities and other information facilities and providers.

As government bodies, such as the U.S. Department of Agriculture, entertain pilot projects to get electronic information and data directly to their primary clientele, there are increased opportunities for libraries to supplement their print collections and to forge new partnerships. Undoubtedly, the depository library program of the Government Printing Office (GPO) will undergo dramatic change as it redefines its role in an electronic and information age and as it attempts to better meet the expectations of 1,400 different libraries.

The literature of documents librarianship provides piece-meal coverage of the use of technology for GPO depository services and collections. *Depository Library Use of Technology* fills a noticeable void in the published monograph literature of documents librarianship by updating and expanding Hernon (1982) and McClure (1982).

There is a definite need for a work which draws together the published literature (Chapter 1), provides a brief introduction to the importance of information policy (Chapter 2), and offers the viewpoints and experiences of practicing documents librarians involved in the incorporation of technology into their daily routines (Chapters 3–14). Chapter 5, for instance, advises libraries planning to load GPO records into a library's online catalog, while Chapters 7 through 12 contain case studies profiling libraries at different stages of using or planning the use of technology to meet their role as depository libraries. Chapter 11 offers an important perspective, that of a library struggling to preserve its status as a depository library in a new age.

The coverage is practical. The book shows what libraries are (or could be) doing as part of the GPO depository library program. The specific objectives of this work are to provide a state of the art analysis reflecting some uses of technology for GPO collections and services, to present a diverse set of viewpoints and practices, and to identify present and future trends (see Chapters 1, 3, 13, and 14).

Depository Library Use of Technology should appeal to libraries participating in GPO's depository library program and to students enrolled in library science courses needing an introduction to the applications of technology for depository collections, services, and management. Libraries and individuals associated with other depository programs and countries will find it useful to learn what some libraries are doing and the direction they are going.

The book also identifies a number of individuals at the forefront in the application of technology to documents librarianship. By so doing, *Depository Library Use of Technology* takes on added significance for those libraries wanting to expand their technological uses and needing expert advise on the loading of GPO records in online catalogs and so forth.

Jan Swanbeck and Peter Hernon
December, 1991

REFERENCES

Hernon, Peter (ed.). *New Technology and Documents Librarianship* (Westport, CT: Meckler Publishing, 1982).

————— and Charles R. McClure. *Evaluation & Library Decision Making* (Norwood, NJ: Ablex, 1990).

McClure, Charles R. (ed.). "Special Issue: Technological Applications for Government Document Collections," *Government Publications Review*, 9 (July-August 1982): 253–352.

INTRODUCTION

Chapter One

Use of Technology as Depicted in the Literature

Peter Hernon

By highlighting the published literature, this chapter provides a framework from which the rest of the book builds. The chapter identifies an extensive and growing literature on technological applications to depository collections, services, and managerial practices. Clearly, the depository program must evolve structurally and otherwise to keep pace with an electronic and information age.

This chapter discusses the use of technology in those libraries participating in the depository library program administered by the U.S. Government Printing Office (GPO). The discussion focuses on those uses presented in the literature of library and information science. Subsequent chapters relate the views and perspectives of librarians who have actually incorporated the use of technology into their planning, decision making, collection development, and public and technical services. These perspectives complement and expand the published literature, and indicate the problems, challenges, and opportunities that depository libraries face within an information and electronic age in which the U.S. government produces *more* records, information resources, and data than at any time in the history of the nation.

ABSORPTION OF TECHNOLOGY IN DEPOSITORY LIBRARIES

The literature indicates the extent to which depository libraries have absorbed information-handling technology. For example, a 1988 survey of 403 responding

Federal depository libraries reported that 283 of them have access to microcomputers without modems, 337 to microcomputers with modems, and 169 to CD-ROM reading equipment (Congress. Office of Technology Assessment, 1988, p. 133; see also General Accounting Office, 1988).[1] The technology second in importance to the use of CD-ROM in depository libraries may well be FAX services, which allow libraries to receive promptly information and some data not held in their collections. At the same time, a growing number of librarians use electronic bulletin boards and electronic mail; e-mail is the process of sending text from one computer to another over a network. Some libraries download datasets for manipulation by their clientele.

In fall 1988, Smith (1990) surveyed 93 academic libraries having membership in the Association of Research Libraries (ARL). "Of the respondents with [online public access catalogs] OPACs only a minority had entered a sizable percentage of their collections into the catalog"—11 percent entered "all documents" (p. 305). Furthermore, "only 18 percent of the respondents had loaded either GPO or vendor produced tapes, with 45 percent relying solely on OCLC data. The other...[36] percent had used a surprising combination of OCLC, RLIN, Marcive, Brodart, and GPO tapes" (Ibid.). "Of those libraries reporting online use, 65 percent employed bibliographic vendor services and 48 percent reported using vendor numeric files. In providing these services most of the libraries passed along a portion of the costs to the patron, usually the vendor's online charges and telecommunication costs (p. 307).

Smith (Ibid.) also discovered that:

- A few libraries downloaded data from bulletin boards for patrons [12 or 20 percent]; some used campus electronic mail systems to advertise the collections and answer reference questions, but overall the data were disappointing, showing very little use of technology or innovation (pp. 307–308).
- One library had established an electronic bulletin board on the institution's main computer and was using the board to advertise the holdings and services of the depository collection. Finally, a few mentioned the use of an automated item file in their collection development activities (p. 310).

Table 1-1 reproduces her findings related to the availability of equipment in the reference area.

GPO's 1989 *Biennial Survey* queried depository libraries about the number and type of hardware possessed by the entire library. Figure 1-1 summarizes the responses. Clearly, significant differences among the states and territories exist.

---

[1] See also Congress. Joint Committee on Printing (1984).

Table 1-1.   Equipment Available within the Reference Area*,**

	Staff Use #	Patron Use #
OPAC	38	37
OCLC access	42	11
RLIN access	18	5
PC	28	10
PC/modem	46	6
Videodisk	5	—
FAX	13	—
CD-ROM	43	40
Computer Center access	30	2

*Not necessarily mutually exclusive.
**Source: Smith (1990), p. 309.

Kessler and Daniel (1989) surveyed regional depositories in the spring of 1989. Eighty-seven percent of the responding libraries have access to a personal computer, which was most frequently housed in the documents area. Only six respondents did not have microcomputers with CD-ROM drives. Some 53 percent of the respondents could access a mainframe computer, while 71 percent had access to an electronic mail network. And, finally, the regionals tended to make heavy use of OCLC and Dialog services.

Clearly, data on the number and types of equipment that depository libraries possess are extremely fluid and sketch a portrait of the program at one point in time. Perhaps future surveys might produce trend data and disclose patterns over time, while making short-term projections.

The Depository Library Council to the Public Printer, at its fall 1990 meeting, requested the GPO to establish minimal technical guidelines for the depository program. "Recommended Minimum Technical Guidelines for

Figure 1-1.   Hardware (Average Per Depository).*

State	FAX	Online Services	Readers	Microfiche Reader/Printers	Duplicators
AK	0.67	1.78	5.22	3.00	0.44
AL	0.88	2.40	4.96	3.28	0.24
AR	0.56	1.78	4.61	1.89	0.11
AS	1.00	0.00	1.00	2.00	0.00
AZ	0.93	2.13	8.13	3.33	0.20
CA	0.49	2.95	6.95	2.81	0.20
CO	0.12	1.92	5.08	2.12	0.20
CT	0.50	1.91	4.14	2.64	0.09
DC	0.72	6.62	2.34	3.08	0.22
DE	0.40	2.20	6.60	3.20	0.40

Figure 1-1.   (Continued).

FL	0.73	2.65	5.76	2.97	0.08
FM	1.00	0.00	3.00	0.00	0.00
GA	0.46	2.57	6.93	2.68	0.18
GU	0.00	0.00	3.50	2.50	0.00
HI	0.36	0.73	4.55	2.73	0.18
IA	0.29	2.33	3.90	1.67	0.05
ID	0.55	2.36	8.00	2.36	0.27
IL	0.72	2.14	4.79	2.68	0.14
IN	0.72	3.14	7.22	2.28	0.17
KS	0.71	2.18	4.94	2.41	0.24
KY	0.43	2.38	5.38	2.10	0.10
LA	0.27	2.46	6.54	2.31	0.31
MA	0.64	3.09	6.39	2.88	0.45
MD	0.79	12.83	8.08	3.08	0.38
ME	0.58	2.42	4.75	2.75	0.17
MI	0.85	3.33	4.90	2.42	0.23
MN	0.42	3.15	9.12	2.00	0.19
MO	0.78	2.28	5.78	2.31	0.25
MP	1.00	1.00	4.00	2.00	0.00
MS	0.75	20.17	4.58	2.50	0.17
MT	0.86	3.57	7.29	2.00	0.57
NC	0.79	1.76	5.42	2.61	0.18
ND	0.10	1.40	8.20	1.80	0.10
NE	0.50	1.57	6.07	1.50	0.21
NH	0.56	2.44	6.00	2.44	0.00
NJ	0.79	2.21	4.42	2.60	0.19
NM	1.00	3.36	7.36	2.27	0.18
NV	0.33	2.56	7.33	3.78	0.11
NY	0.53	7.19	8.55	3.53	0.42
OH	0.65	3.31	5.27	2.94	0.15
OK	0.70	2.75	12.10	3.20	0.40
OR	0.48	3.52	5.19	2.00	0.10
PA	0.75	2.54	64.24	2.21	0.16
PR	0.00	1.00	5.50	1.25	0.00
RI	0.25	1.67	4.00	3.33	0.08
RP	1.00	2.00	7.00	3.00	0.00
SC	0.50	2.28	4.78	2.33	0.11
SD	0.30	31.90	3.90	2.00	0.10
TN	0.20	2.68	5.36	2.44	0.00
TX	0.62	2.48	9.51	2.70	0.28
UT	0.73	4.36	14.00	2.36	0.27
VA	0.35	2.70	5.57	2.78	0.16
VI	0.67	0.33	3.67	1.00	0.00
VT	0.50	2.62	3.38	1.88	0.12
WA	0.52	3.14	6.71	1.81	0.29
WI	0.58	2.58	6.87	2.42	0.32
WV	0.20	1.73	4.27	3.13	0.13
WY	0.90	1.80	3.00	2.00	0.10

*Source: "Hardware (Average Per Depository) ..." (1990).

Federal Depository Libraries" (1991), which discusses workstation configurations and software, suggest an IBM compatible 386SX operating at 20 Mhz having hard disk capacity, a CD-ROM drive, a printer, and a modem. As for software, the recommendation includes dBase, Lotus 1-2-3, wordprocessing, and communication software. Of course, such recommentations apply only to those depositories selecting CD-ROM and electronic information resources, and lack a base in statutory law (44 *United States Code*, Chapter 19).

Barriers

Zink (1990) and Sanchez (1989) provide excellent overviews of planning issues and problems encountered in managing CD-ROM collections. One issue is that some depository library staff have inadequate time and expertise for loading, maintaining, and effectively using databases in CD-ROM[2] or other electronic formats. Such expertise may reside outside the documents department and be difficult to tap. A library may have to wait weeks, for example, before being able to install disks or even to have malfunctioning hardware evaluated for repair.

Simple user aids are often nonexistent and must be created by local staff or copied from other sources known to exist. While most users seem eager to use compact disks and are familiar with their advantages over printed sources, many lack the experience necessary to make optimal use of them and need a good deal of personal guidance, at least initially. This is especially true of statistical data on CD-ROM, the *Congressional Record* on CD-ROM, and some other products. Some users seem ignorant of or reluctant to utilize downloading capabilities, and printer maintenance may present a major problem for attendant staff. Hardware security is another access barrier in most libraries. Whereas printed sources remain on the shelves and available for use during all the hours the library is open, a library may lock its CD-ROM workstations up when staff leave for the night.

Another barrier to rapid absorption of new technologies in depository libraries is lack of support—both in terms of software and staff time and expertise— for effective application of these technologies. The wide variety of software packages available, their costs, and GPO's (or the issuing agency's) unwillingness or inability to provide adequate software and/or documentation so that information in electronic format may be easily used creates a barrier to utilization. Software packages for gaining access to currently available census products provide good examples of this type of problem. The Census Bureau has selected dBase as the format for its most recent CD-ROM products, but has also developed simpler, public domain software that is available at nominal cost

---

[2] CD-ROM (Compact Disk—Read Only Memory) is a type of optical disk. One 4-3/4 inch CD-ROM can hold the contents of 1,600 flexible disks or 3 to 4 high-density tapes.

through a clearinghouse operated by the University of Tennessee or which may be downloaded directly from a Census Bureau computer.

Three other issues might also be noted. First, some products can do real harm. For example, the recent episode with the CD-ROM of the *County and City Data Book* involved an accompanying floppy disk contaminated with a "deadly" virus.[3] This can ruin not only the specific product but also attack a whole system. Libraries obviously do not encounter such problems with print products.

Second, clients, either accidentally or intentionally, can cause problems and generate expenses for libraries through the misuse of products. End-user online searching can be very expensive, especially if done by untrained searchers, while "hackers" can destroy files or even whole systems.

Still another issue to be addressed is the client who knows how to program and who wants to do his or her own programming, downloading, etc., to improve the information or data found in electronic products. If the library cannot provide this service, should it prohibit knowledgeable patrons from making their own arrangements?

Conceivably, researchers might extract data or information on individuals in violation of that person's privacy rights. Whose responsibility is it to safeguard against inappropriate use of a dataset distributed by the GPO as a depository publication—the library or the researcher? The question arose, on January 23, 1991, when the Library Programs Service distributed a pamphlet containing a data use agreement and the 1987 National Health Interview Survey CD-ROM on shipping list 91-0011-E to depositories selecting item number 0500-E-01. On April 23 of the same year, the National Center for Health Statistics requested that the libraries either sign the agreement acknowledging compliance with the law or return the CD-ROM.

The Center was bypassing GPO's authority to order the withdrawal of publications from depository libraries. To resolve the dilemma, the General Counsels of the GPO and the Center agreed that the libraries could post a statement near the CD-ROM informing users about the uses and misuses of the data. "By attaching this notice to the CD-ROM, the responisbility is that of the user, rather than that of the library" ("1987 National Health Interview Survey: Guidelines for Use of CD-ROM," 1991, p. 7).

Figure 1-2 represents some of the "considerations for implementation of CD-ROM technology in the library." Attention to these considerations will reduce some, but not all, of the "perils" noted by Zink (1990, pp. 51–55).

---

[3] Jerusalem-B virus infects any .COM or .EXE program on MS-DOS personal computers and increases program size by approximately 1,800 bytes. Other programs are infected when they are executed in an infected system. The virus can cause significant damage on an infected computer. It generally slows down the system and some versions destroy all data on the hard disk. .EXE files continue to grow in size until they become too large to execute.

Figure 1-2. Considerations for Implementation of CD-ROM Technology in the Library.*

IV. Management Aspects
  A. Collection development criteria
    (Some suggested questions to ask)
      1. Is this database appropriate for your user group? Is it consistent with your library's collection development policy (if they have one)?
      2. How comprehensive is the database? Will it replace or supplement existing services?
      3. Will you need to retain hardcopy, or is retrospective data available on CD-ROM? How expensive is it? Can costs be offset or justified given these considerations?
      4. Is CD-ROM copy going to be better quality for preservation purposes?
      5. Will substantial shelf space savings result: i.e., can expensive binding costs be eliminated if full text journals are offered on CD-ROM?
      6. How will technical services handle this new technology? How will subscriptions be handled? Will they circulate?
      7. What, if any, are the advantages of CD-ROM over online searches?
  B. Product selection criteria: suggested considerations:
      1. How accurate is information retrieval?
      2. Are the content and approach relevant for intended users?
      3. What kind of quality control is used by the publisher and/or vendor? Is the publisher reputable? Are bibliographic records consistent?
      4. Can you review the product in the literature or can you have it for a trial period in your own library?
      5. How is subject indexing handled: i.e., is there a controlled vocabulary which must be explained to the user?
      6. Is software included? Can you use the software on more than one product?
      7. How often is the database updated? is it timely?
      8. Will you buy or lease discs?
      9. What are the licensing requirements regarding networking? You cannot usually modify this agreement after you open the package.
      10. Can you get a quantity discount for multiple subscriptions? Can you negotiate a better price for a long-term contract? Can you get a discount by making one yearly payment? Is the cost guaranteed for the life of the contract or can it increase?
      11. Can you subscribe to the product only or must you lease equipment? Is maintenance of hardware included in the agreement or available at extra cost?
      12. Who is responsible for installation? Is there a cost?
      13. Will cost adjustments be made if the equipment fails?
      14. Is there a replacement policy for lost or stolen discs? How easily are they replaced?
      15. Is the product immediately available for shipment? is there a guaranteed shipping date?

Figure 1-2. (Continued)

16. Is training offered as part of the contract?
17. Under what conditions can the contract be terminated? Who can terminate it and what [is the] cost? Will cost adjustments be made?
18. Will the company supply names of satisfied customers? Call them. Also call your colleagues and ask their opinions; nothing is better than first-hand experience in determining the quality of a product.

C. Evaluation of products and use
   1. How user friendly is the product? For example: is the system menu-driven, command-driven, or both? If you do not know what these terms mean, find out. How difficult are the commands?
   2. Are directions and help screens clear to users? Can you easily move from screen to help screens?
   3. Is there enough search support given, on disc and in print?
   4. Is there a manual? How comprehensive is it? Use it yourself and ask others to use it.
   5. How clear are directions for installation and trouble-shooting?
   6. How much documentation is provided? Are help-lines available: when; who can call?

D. Staff considerations
   1. How much staff time is needed to instruct patrons in the use of CD-ROM's? (Lots). In view of the fact that there is little standardization in the software, much instruction is needed. In the absence of good documentation, most librarians say one-on-one, hands-on experience and training...[are] best. Computer trained library assistants and aides have worked well for many libraries.
   2. How much staff time will be required to service equipment, i.e., replace ink and paper, etc.? This does not have to be done by librarians.
   3. Will staff be responsible for checking out CD's to patrons? Will they circulate? (Not many people have access to video CD players.)
   4. Will patrons be able to download information onto floppies easily? How? This is a very big question, and one that has not yet been adequately answered.
   5. Will outside technical assistance such as computer programming and technical assistance with hardware for setup, breakdowns, downloading, etc., be available? Unless the librarian is a programmer or hardware specialist, inevitably expert assistance will be needed.
   6. Technical processing considerations: Who will order, pay invoices, check-in, claim?
   7. How will the databases be publicized? Who will provide "cheat-sheets" or simple handouts for patrons?
   8. Will there be an increase in demand for services of interlibrary loan and document delivery?

Pros and Cons of CD-ROM Technology:
   Pros:
   1. Added value of sophisticated searching capabilities.
   2. User does not have to worry about cost, and can spend time searching.

   3. Expenditure is up front (for hardware) rather than per search.
   4. Huge capacity for storage, excellent clarity for reading of data. relatively low cost.
   5. User can practice online searching at leisure.
   6. The technology and interfaces attempt to be user friendly and are being improved for customer satisfaction.
   7. Reliability of products from familiar vendors to the library community.
   8. Patrons love it! (It helps them to be more self-sufficient in searching.)
Cons:
   1. Slow retrieval of data.
   2. Lack of common search interfaces.
   3. Static database that cannot be changed or interacted with.
   4. Does not hold as much information as an online database.
   5. Equipment is costly.
   6. Networking is problematic and expensive.
   7. CD-ROM requires lots of staff time and patience in training users.
   8. How to recover costs to users?
V. Networking and multiple access considerations (and questions):
Of interest to user groups with large sums of money at their disposal are LAN's, or Local Area Networks. CD-ROM drive "towers" or "jukeboxes" have been set up by a few libraries to access a number of CD-ROM stations simultaneously. This will not be explained in detail here.
   1. Can patron access be simplified (expanded?) if only one PC is available?
   2. Can all government documents software be uploaded to the hard disk?
   3. How can you expand RAM on hard disk?
   4. Can government documents CD-ROM's be networked?
   5. Where can one get information about putting CD's on a Local Area Network?
   6. What hardware is required?
   7. Can we demonstrate products at no cost to us?

---

*Excerpted from "Electronic Corner" (1991). Other parts of this article cover hardware, software needs, and vendors and their products.

WIDER USE OF TECHNOLOGY

Several of the solutions to the problem of slow absorption of new technologies among depository libraries will be found in the technologies themselves. Compact disk sources, for example, will continue to gain in popularity as both multiple and remote (dial-in) searching of CD-ROM databases becomes a practical reality. Advances in software applications will also speed acceptance of new technologies.

The development of inexpensive, user-friendly, standardized access programs that are easy to install and that are accompanied by simple user aids will certainly make implementation of new systems more palatable to a wider depository library clientele.

Decreases in the capital and operational costs of the newer technologies (hardware, software, and telecommunications, primarily) will also facilitate their acceptance and effective use in depository libraries. Yet, cheaper and easier availability of electronically formatted materials will never entirely obviate the disparities that exist between different depository libraries and their ability to utilize these materials effectively: there will always be the "haves" and the "have nots", and undoubtedly many "have somes" as well.

Just as there are wide gaps among depository libraries in their capacity to acquire and utilize CD-ROM (as well as other recent technological innovations), there are great disparities among depository librarians in their awareness of electronically formatted sources and their expertise in installing, maintaining, and making use of them. Certainly greater personal initiative in seeking solutions to these problems would be helpful, but individual librarians can only do so much with the time and resources made available to them.

Greater institutional support is certainly needed. Whether technological expertise is viewed as appropriately residing at the departmental level or beyond, librarians must begin diverting resources currently spent on collection building or other activities to the support of electronic information services if these services are to be effectively utilized. *Sufficient* workstations must be available, software installations and maintenance must be timely, hardware repair and/or backup systems must be handy, and librarians must be afforded opportunities and encouraged to take advantage of these opportunities if they are to increase their skills in the use of different systems and offer instruction to make new technologies widely accessible to end users. The efficacy of a depository library's training and instructional infrastructure will become increasingly important as new formats and technologies proliferate.

In summary, "the recent influx of electronic publications into depository libraries has created something of a management nightmare" ("CD-ROM Software & Policy on Assistance to the User," 1991, p. 18). These problems include, for instance, the necessity of acquiring new equipment in times of financial retrenchment and "the lack of established policies that define how electronic publications fit into depository library operations" (Ibid.);

> Without definite policies, the documents department staff will experience significant stress generated by the uncertainties of functioning in a new work environment. In particular, policies must be established that define for staff members precisely what level of reference service they are expected to provide to library patrons on electronic products. Once such policies have been clearly established, the staff must be trained to provide that service. (Ibid.)

Finally,

> To cope with electronic publications, many depository librarians have initiated a simple unwritten policy—ignore them, find a deep drawer, don't even load them on microcomputer workstations. At the other extreme, some libraries have attempted to provide intensive service wherein library staff have used dBase or other database software to generate customized tables for patrons. While many librarians will entertain ethical objections to the first tactic, few will have adequate staff to even consider the second. (Ibid.)

A basic question becomes "How can a depositroy library identify and maintain a middle ground between the two extremes?"[4]

FORMATS IN WHICH GOVERNMENT INFORMATION RESOURCES APPEAR

Microforms

Libraries have absorbed microforms for years. Hernon and McClure (1988) discuss the emergence of the GPO as a micropublisher/microprinter. Figure 9-1 of their work offers a "conceptual model for interpreting the reasons for

---

[4] The Government Publications Department at the University of Nevada, Reno, has "established a written policy that identifies three levels of access to electronic information products housed in the department, whether the products are depository, non-depository, or commercial. The policy delineates which of the three levels of service the...staff is expected to provide and, by default, defines what level of competency is expected of patrons" ("CD-ROM Software & Policy on Assistance to the User," 1991, p. 18).

The three levels are:

- *Thorough knowledge* ("competency in using these tools and the ability to introduce patrons to their use"), which applies to "electronic bibliographic tools in the...reference area." Thorough knowledge also applies "to some specific databases distributed through the depository library program.... In this case, 'thorough knowledge' is defined as the competency to instruct users in the major software features available in each product."
- *General knowledge* ("knowing what electronic products are available in the Department, and the ability to identify for patrons databases that may be appropriate for their research needs"), which applies to nonbibliographic databases in the department. General knowledge "may also be expected on specific products or software." In this case, the term applies to CD-ROM products for the *Congressional Record* and the *Foreign Trade Data Bank.*
- *Rudimentary knowledge* ("knowing where the product and its documentation are located, knowing which microworkstation to use, knowing how to boot the product, and knowing how to exit from the product"), which applies to non-bibliographic products not covered by the first two levels (Ibid., p. 19).

acquiring microformatted government publications" (p. 198). Despite patron dislike for microforms and the necessity for having a diverse assortment of microform reading devices, many libraries have extensive holdings of microforms. Space savings, cost, unavailability of paper counterpart, preservation of fragile volumes, and longevity are all reasons for choosing microforms. Microform is useful for storage of large amounts of older, less frequently used materials. The infrequent consultation of these publications offsets the inconvenience of usage.

Microfiche, one type of microform, is not as highly regarded today among depository librarians, as it was in past years. The reasons are twofold:

- There is great variation in the legibility of the microfiche (due to the quality of the printed source document or tape product); and
- Librarians are distrustful of microfiche as a means of disseminating publications through the depository program. The default of the GPO contractor in the mid-1980s and the inability of the GPO to curtail the microfiche backlog underscore depository librarian dissatisfaction with microfiche emanating from the public sector and its private sector contractors.

An assumption in the literature is that micrographics technology will not improve that much or that if it did, libraries might not commit that many resources to it. Perhaps microfiche might be a more attractive alternative if the technology improves. Three problems, however, are:

- Discrete items cannot be easily identified and retrieved;
- Reading, printing, and duplication equipment, plus cabinets and environmentally controlled storage areas, are necessary for efficient use of microform materials (see Hernon and McClure, 1988); and
- The datasets cannot be manipulated and downloaded.

A final issue concerns the longevity of microfiche. This issue has been extensively investigated (see Hernon, 1981). Longevity, however, varies according to factors such as storage conditions, amount of use, and composition of the microfiche product itself.

Magnetic Tapes

The literature discussing the use of magnetic tapes, a type of machine-readable data file (MRDF), tends to revolve around the collection and servicing of tapes at the University of Florida Libraries, Gainesville (e.g., Jones, 1982; Pope, 1984; Jones and Kinney, 1988; Kinney and Jones, 1988). Many nonresearch (non-ARL) libraries might not be able to handle such tapes, or if they can, the collection and servicing of the tapes reside with the academic computing center. Such tapes require the use of mainframe computers, special storage, programming, etc., that limit their utility to many depositories.

For access to magnetic tapes, many depositories might refer their users to State Data Centers, in the case of academic depositories, or use the resources of the Inter-University Consortium for Political and Social Research (ICPSR), a partnership among more than 300 universities and colleges in the United States and elsewhere. Housed in the Institute for Social Research at the University of Michigan, Ann Arbor, it provides a central repository and dissemination service for machine-readable social, economic, and political data on national and international levels.[5]

CD-ROM

CD-ROM is a most important evolving technological application for depository libraries. These datasets can withstand extensive use and library clientele can consult them either for reference purposes (look up a statistic) or engage in research (data extraction, manipulation, and comparison). Census products on CD-ROM provide users with information, such as zip code, so that they can make more detailed analyses and comparisons than they readily can from paper copy.

According to Carl C. Abston, Chief, National Oceanic and Atmospheric Administration's Systems Integration and Planning Office, "if you believe the value of CD-ROM is in the delivering of massive amounts of data to massive numbers of users, you are wrong." Rather, "the correlation of previously unrelateable data is likely to be the main benefit" ("Feds Have Big Plans for CD-ROM," 1991, p. 6).

The longevity of CD-ROM is unknown. If an individual CD-ROM got lost or damaged, libraries would lose much valuable data. The GPO's Library Programs Service, however, provides replacement copies for mutilated or missing publications from the *original shipment only*. Regarding replacement, availability perhaps more than cost is the central issue. The GPO does not have a fulfillment role. It neither presses copies of CD-ROM nor maintains archival copy. However, it does obtain extra copies of CD-ROM, but only for filling

---

[5] In 1990, the Research Libraries Group, Inc. and OCLC announced plans to exchange cataloging data for computer files of the ICPSR. As a result, users of OCLC and the RLIN system will have access to the complete holdings of the ICPSR. Such a service benefits academic libraries. An important issue relates to the general public and what are the public's needs for data contained on magnetic tapes. Presumably such people would have to rely on State Data Centers and perhaps pay a fee. Nonetheless, here is a topical area requiring further research and discussion.

claims. This policy meets short-term, rather than long-term, needs. The availability of replacement copy might change in the future when technology permits easier copying of CD-ROM. It is important to emphasize that this solution only applies to public domain software.

As technology continues to advance, the equipment of tomorrow may no longer be able to read the CD-ROM products of today. Libraries, therefore, could house census material that is inaccessible.

It should be noted that in October 1989, the GPO surveyed depository libraries (special survey 89-300) about CD-ROM and selected microfiche products. In particular, the GPO queried the libraries about their wanting the *County and City Data Book* on CD-ROM (item 0151-D), which is the equivalent to the print source, and *County Business Patterns* (item 0133-E), which is *not* the same as the print counterpart. Item 0154-B-01 has become a catch-all class for miscellaneous CD-ROM products from the Census Bureau. By establishing this item, the GPO is prepared to order copies of future CD-ROMs as they become available. The other items in the survey pertained to the *Toxic Chemical Release Inventory* on CD-ROM and state, District of Columbia, U.S. summary, and outlying areas on microfiche.

Some 700 libraries opted for the "catch-all class," 740 for *County Business Patterns*, and 772 for *County and City Data Book*. Expressed another way, at least half of the depository libraries have selected at least one census CD-ROM product from the GPO.

It is estimated that the Federal government will produce more than 500 new CD-ROMs in 1991. "The massive output... will have the... government single-handedly increasing by half the number of English-language [CD-ROM] titles worldwide" ("Feds Have Big Plans for CD-ROM," 1991, p. 1). The National Aeronautics and Space Administration (NASA) will produce more than 100, half of which will be images of Venus. The Patent and Trademark Office will produce "more than two new disks per week," while the Bureau of the Census will offer more than 45 CD-ROMs (Ibid., p. 6). The National Oceanic and Atmospheric Administration has stored so much data on tapes that it "would take 1,100 years to publish it all" (Ibid.).

In the case of documents librarianship, online searching may be losing its importance in comparison to CD-ROM searching. Many users want to search for information themselves as opposed to having a librarian conduct an online search. Online searching can be costly and requires the use of trained staff. End users often can only conduct simple searches, such as through the files available on "BRS after Dark."

Perhaps the amount of online database searching performed might increase if telecommunications and online access costs were lower. Nonetheless, online searching does not have the mass appeal of CD-ROM searching, in which end users may not have to make appointments and go to special locations.

Flexible Diskettes

"While the distribution of government information on diskette is a relatively recent development, there is already a significant amount of government information available in this medium" (Kinney and Jones, 1988, p. 148). The National Technical Information Service (NTIS), as well as agencies such as Bureau of the Census, sell diskettes of statistical data and textual material. Some of these sources have a print counterpart, whereas others do not. However, the storage capacity of flexible diskettes may be too limited for reproducing census and other files. Agencies might find that they can distribute smaller files more efficiently through bulletin boards. A possible exception to this rule are diskette products that involve data and software combined in a "turnkey" application.

Floppy disks are aimed more at end users than libraries (see Kinney and Jones, 1986), and may require special configuration to work on certain microcomputers. Often libraries would have to obtain vast numbers of disks and written documentation. Furthermore, the staff would have to learn different packages, show users how to manipulate the data, and enter data into hard disk drive memory. In addition, disks only provide data, without corresponding access software to manipulate datasets. In the case of census products, floppy disks often correspond to printed publications. They do not contain additional data; for this reason and because of their format, many floppy disks have limited value to depository libraries.

Electronic Mail (E-mail)

Electronic mail provides a means whereby libraries can transmit and receive messages. They can also upload, download, and transmit datasets. Such a capacity enables a library to increase its access to statistical data and to replace small datasets that have been mutilated or misplaced.

A 1988 survey of members of the Association of Research Libraries (ARL) discusses the use of e-mail for interlibrary loan, administrative purposes, and communication with users through an online catalog. The report identifies both the strengths and weaknesses of e-mail (*Electronic Mail*, 1988), and notes that the use will increase.

In 1989, GovDoc-L, an electronic network conference, began operation over BITNET.[6] Participants in this electronic "invisible college" can share information, experiences, and procedures "in a timely and efficient manner" (Kovacs, 1990, p. 411). Apparently, depository librarians—especially those in academic institutions connected to BITNET and the INTERNET—are making greater use of this communications network.

---

[6] See "Govdoc-L: Online Discussion of Government Documents Issues" (1990).

Electronic Bulletin Boards

Bulletin boards provide perishable, not permanent, data. The data are timely, often released that day or very recently.[7] The Department of Commerce's Economic Bulletin Board (EBB) is one of the electronic pilot projects for the depository library program. The EBB provides statistical press releases generated by various agencies, including the Bureau of the Census. Press releases convey timely information and may be available from issuing agencies in limited quantity. Subsequent attempts to acquire them can be costly and futile.

The only equipment required to access EBB is a PC terminal, modem, and communications software. Subscribers, however, may use personal computers to download data to floppy disks for subsequent review and manipulation. As more libraries experiment with EBB, the popularity of such a resource might increase. Some libraries have lost paper publications that contain the same (or similar) information that appears on EBB. Academic libraries can upload (and some have done so) bulletin boards for campus-wide use.

Libraries, according to Hernon and McClure (1991), need to address questions related to who pays, user training, user-friendly searching software, and staff support. Some services bear no user charge other than telecommunications fees; perhaps, in some cases, reduced rates or a minimum level of free service for depository libraries could be negotiated.

CENDATA™, an online service began in 1984 and available through Dialog and CompuServe, offers current economic, agriculture, and demographic data. CENDATA also offers textual information—press releases, area profiles, and up-to-date information about census product availability.

According to Jacobs (1990, p. 393), a number of Federal agencies:

> have established electronic computerized bulletin boards as a means for distributing information that they collect and create. The establishment of these bulletin boards has met important needs of many users of government information, but it has also left unmet the needs of other users and depository libraries.

The technology for gaining access to bulletin boards includes a microcomputer, modem, phone line, and commercial "off-the-shelf" software. In some cases, access depends on having a password. Some agencies will provide libraries with a password; in some instances, libraries have to set up prepaid accounts. Clearly, some libraries find that the value of the information and data exceed the costs and other barriers inhibiting the use of this information and data.

---

[7] For a list of government bulletin boards see "Bulletin Boards Give Users the Line on Federal Info" (1990).

TYPES OF GOVERNMENT INFORMATION RESOURCES AVAILABLE ONLINE

Although a number of databases already exist, both the public and private sectors are creating new ones and modifying present ones. The population of databases differs by type, content, subject, scope, coverage, periodicity of release of new information and data, frequency of updating, and the presence of value-added features. Figure 1-3, which identifies different types of reference and source databases, offers examples of the formats in which these databases appear. Such

Figure 1-3.   Types of Databases (Examples).*

REFERENCE DATABASES

Bibliographic (Citations to the literature). Examples include:

CD-ROM:	Monthly Catalog (GPO), GRA&I (NTIS), ERIC, and CIS's CIS Index and American Statistics Index
Magnetic Tapes:	Monthly Catalog (GPO)
Online:	Monthly Catalog (GPO), GRA&I (NTIS), ERIC, CIS's CIS Index and American Statistics Index, Publications Reference File (GPO), TOXLIT (NLM), and TOXLINE (NLM)

Referral (These databases contain references to nonpublished information and offer referral to individuals, organizations, and information resources). Examples include:

Online:	Federal Election Commission Direct Access Program (Federal Election Commission), and The Technical Logistics Reference Network (Innovative Technology Inc. and U.S. Naval Sea Systems Command)

SOURCE DATABASES

Numeric (Statistical data, including survey data). Examples include:

Bulletin Boards:	Economic Bulletin Board (NTIS and Department of Commerce), and State Data Center bulletin board (Bureau of the Census)
CD-ROM:	Census products (e.g., County and City Data Book and County Business Patterns) and World Factbook (CIA). See also NTIS's annual Directory of Computer Software and Directory of Computerized Databases
Floppy Disks:	Some census products as County and City Data Book. See also NTIS's annual Directory of Computer Software and Directory of Computerized Databases

Figure 1-3.   (Continued)

Magnetic Tapes:	Census products, public health data from the Centers for Disease Control, and data from the National Center for Health Statistics. See also NTIS's annual Directory of Computer Software and Directory of Computerized Databases
Online:	National Fire Incident Reporting System (NTIS and FDIC (Federal Deposit Insurance Corp.)

Textual-Numeric (Records contain various data elements or fields, some of which provide numeric data). Examples include:

Bulletin Boards:	Bureau of Labor Statistics, Department of Commerce, and Customs Service (Customs Electronic Bulletin Board)
CD-ROM:	Registry of Toxic Effects (NTIS), patents, Geological Survey, National Oceanic and Atmospheric Adminstration, and Toxic Release Inventory (EPA)
Floppy Disks:	See NTIS's annual Directory of Computer Software and Directory of Computerized Databases
Magnetic Tapes:	TR-20 Project Formulation (NTIS), FCC Datafiles, and Nutrition and Food Composition Data (NTIS). See also NTIS's annual Directory of Computer Software and Directory of Computerized Databases
Online:	Cendata and USDA EDI Service (USDA)

Visual (The display of digital mapping and visual images). Examples include:

CD-ROM:	TIGER (digital mapping from the Census Bureau), Geological Survey, National Aeronautics and Space Administraiton, Defense Mapping Agency

Full-Text (Records contain complete text of an item). Examples include:

Bulletin Board:	Project Hermes Bulletin Board (opinions of the Supreme Court) and FDA Electronic Bulletin Board
CD-ROM:	Code of Federal Regulations, Federal Register, and Congressional Record
Online:	Westlaw

Software (Software contains computer programs that enable downloading and use with local computers). Examples include:

Floppy Disks:	Grateful Med (National Library of Medicine), AutoMan: Decision Support Software for Automated Manufacturing Investments (NTIS), and USDA Dietary Analysis Program (NTIS)

*Adapted from *Directory of Online Databases* (1990), pp. vii-viii.

databases are available from the GPO and its sales program (i.e., some CD-ROM), NTIS, other government agencies, and the private sector (e.g., Slater Hall Information Products). Users may need special assistance and equipment to use some of the source databases, such as those displaying digital mapping.

Some of the databases comprise *products* or *electronic publications*, whereas others may be characterized as services. Based on the aborted attempt to reauthorize the Paperwork Reduction Act in 1989-1990, Congress might differentiate between the two and confine depository distribution to *products*. A number of *services* may be too expensive to distribute on a large scale, and their distribution as depository items may impinge on the role of government clearinghouses and the private sector. However, the Office of Management and Budget's (OMB) revised draft Circular No. A-130, in 1992 (57 *FR* 18296-18306, April 29, 1992), does not distinguish between products and services. It does differentiate between electronic and nonelectronic products; the former may be optional for depository distribution, and the GPO may not have sufficient funds for the printing and distribution of electronic products. In the view of this author, OMB's interpretation violates the spirit, if not the intent of 44 *USC*, Chapter 19.

Both regional and selective depository libraries already find it difficult to cope with the amount and diversity of CD-ROM forwarded by the GPO. Some of them store these products and do not promote their availability. There may not be the time, staff expertise, or resources to make CD-ROM products user friendly and to lessen the need for staff intervention. Complicating matters, many depositories may not have more than one or two microcomputers for public use. Key questions become "What should be available and when?" and "What are the costs as well as the strengths and limitations of different products?" For example, the *Congressional Record* on CD-ROM, one of the GPO pilot projects, only covers 1985. Yet, tracing a legislative history often requires the use of different years of this one source.

ROLE OF BIBLIOGRAPHIC UTILITIES

The inclusion of bibliographic records from the *Monthly Catalog of United States Government Publications* in OCLC, which began in 1976, represents a milestone in improving bibliographic control over publications distributed by the GPO. A bibliographic utility may engage in cataloging and provide current and retrospective conversion for the archival tapes resulting from cataloging in OCLC. It may also engage in interlibrary loan, reference and bibliographic verification, and the processing of GPO tapes for inclusion in local circulation and online catalog systems.

Walbridge (1986) discusses OCLC and its uses for shared cataloging and resource sharing. Since October 1980, the GPO has cataloged in the "master mode," which means that it can change the database record when another source has done the original cataloging. All cataloging done under GPO contract is verified as meeting GPO standards before it is entered into OCLC.

GPO serial records that were previously available only to OCLC users are now available through the Library of Congress. This distribution means that these records are available to other networks, including the Washington Library Network (WLN) and the Research Libraries Information Network (RLIN) (see Ernest, 1988). Serial records in the *Monthly Catalog* tapes contain issue-specific bibliographic information, while the OCLC cataloging record describes a serial in its entirety. Non-OCLC users can obtain "pure" GPO serial records through the Library of Congress as well.

Some depository libraries have entered their *Monthly Catalog* holdings in their own online catalogs, while other libraries have relied on the services of a commercial vendor for the preparation of catalog card sets, obtaining computer-readable tapes for loading into their online catalogs, or developing COM (computer output microfilm) catalogs for their holdings of GPO publications. Marcive, Inc. (San Antonio, Texas), for example, matches item numbers against the GPO tapes and produces card sets, COM, and/or tape records for its subscribers (see Mooney, 1990; Bolner and Kile, 1991).

Library staff members interested in the placement of records for GPO publications in online catalogs should review Bowerman and Cady (1984). They constructed a cost-effectiveness model for obtaining bibliographic records, comparing the costs and quality of cataloging, and evaluating choices among the alternatives.

According to Mooney (1989, p. 268), "there is a significant time lag between the receipt of U.S. depository publications by libraries and the availability of GPO's cataloging data for these titles in the printed *Monthly Catalog* and in GPO data tapes from which the *Monthly Catalog* is generated." Powell, Johnston, and Conrad (1987) explored the use of the OCLC database for cataloging the documents collection of The College of Wooster Library, a selective depository. They examined the availability and quality of records for current U.S. government publications on OCLC; the time lag between the date of the receipt of a document and the appearance of its OCLC record; the time necessary to search the data, attach holdings, or catalog the publications on OCLC; procedures, such as the mechanics of follow-up searching; staff needs; and the costs of implementing such a project. They tested the feasibility of attaching library holdings to only slightly modified records in the OCLC database. Their aim was to devise a cost-effective method for including the records of depository publications in an online public access catalog for the library as a whole. Such a system, they suspected, would result in increased circulation of depository holdings.

Libraries acquiring additional Federal publications, those not contained in OCLC, would have to explore methods for including these other records in their online catalog. Unless they do so, the online system is not comprehensive;

however, users and general reference staff might presume comprehensiveness. Depositories might also consider a cooperative project aimed at adding records to the OCLC database for pre-1976 documents.

The OCLC database provides bibliographic access to some NTIS distributed publications. However, neither the *Monthly Catalog* nor the database can serve as a replacement for use of *Government Reports Announcements & Index (GRA&I)*. Overall, McClure, Hernon, and Purcell (1986, Chapter 7) discovered that approximately 10% of the sample *GRA&I* entries were duplicated in the *Monthly Catalog* and 30% were duplicated in the OCLC database. Further, the most effective strategy for searching for NTIS publications in both OCLC and the *Monthly Catalog* is a title search.

In February 1990, OCLC introduced a new cataloging service for depository libraries. Called GOVDOC, it is designed to enable depository libraries to use GPO machine-readable cataloging records for their own local depository holdings (see Dobbs, 1990). OCLC can provide MARC records of government publications at an affordable price to many depository libraries. Each month, OCLC produces OCLC-MARC tapes or catalog cards for items distributed through the depository program. Libraries can use a customized order form to indicate which item numbers they want and whether they need tapes, cards, or both. Regardless of whether the library is a member of OCLC, the organization will attach an OCLC institution holdings symbol to the record in the database. This facilitates interlibrary loan of government publications, thus undoubtedly producing a multiplier effect regarding use.

Summary

The dissemination of government information in machine-readable form creates problems for libraries in making that information and data usable. In other words, a key question becomes "How can they convert what is in machine-readable form to 'human-readable' form" (Kinney and Jones, 1988, p. 152)? Kinney and Jones (Ibid., p. 150) suggest that libraries can provide various services to assist users in gaining access to government information in "microcomputer-accessible formats." According to them, libraries could (Ibid., pp. 150–152):

- Query online government information sources for users;
- Provide bibliographic access to government information on diskette and optical disk, and assist users in obtaining items from outside sources;
- Assist library users to do their own searching of online government information databases and bulletin boards;
- Acquire, maintain, and provide access and reference assistance with government information on diskette and optical disk;

- Provide in-house microcomputer workstations for users for access to government information on diskette, optical disk, and/or online;
- Reformat machine-readable data and/or create machine-readable or printed subsets of data for users; and
- Maintain in-house online government information databases.

And, finally (Ibid., p. 154),

A library with users who do not generally have access to microcomputers and are not familiar with them might provide in-house workstations with easy-to-use software for retrieving information. A library with a small budget but with "microcomputer-rich" users might concentrate on helping users do their own online searching and on locating and obtaining data from outside sources. Large libraries with a diverse user group, including academic research libraries, will need to support users at as many levels as possible.

ONLINE BIBLIOGRAPHIC DATABASE SEARCHING

Online searching of government documents databases can provide increased access to specific types of government information resources not indexed elsewhere, reduce the time lag between availability of the document and its bibliographic access, reduce library expenditures by eliminating the need for infrequently used printed indexes, reduce time needed for actual searching, improve search strategies and effectiveness of searches because of Boolean and proximity operators (among other techniques), increase access to documents because they have been tagged by search fields unique to government information resources, and reduce search problems. Further, online searching can assist collection management by utilizing information in various search fields, such as publication year, format, and issuing agency, and by showing the titles in demand.

However, difficulties regarding staff training, access to appropriate computer equipment, the possibility that the library may not own many of the titles identified (Hernon, 1979), and online search costs can limit the application of this technology to government information collections.

As Murphy (1985, p. 169) indicates,

documents librarians must consider the advantages and disadvantages of online searching. Do online bibliographic databases duplicate the citations found in printed index equivalents or do these two mediums complement each other? Is one method of searching less labor intensive than the other? Which format is more cost effective?

Furthermore (p. 178),

> As access to computerized bibliographic retrieval systems at library reference desks increases, it may become easier to search online without considering the specific needs of the information seeker. Certainly, online bibliographic databases are a useful resource for reference librarians. However, it is important to remember that an online search cannot substitute for a manual search and vice-versa; the two search methods complement each other.

Yet, according to the literature (which is now very dated), many depository personnel infrequently engage in database searching of any kind. Further, they may lack formal training in searching protocol. Regional depositories in the GPO program do not conduct more database searching, or make greater use of technology, than do selective depositories (Hernon, McClure, and Purcell, 1985).

As Walsh and Stark (1990, p. 359) point out, the *Monthly Catalog* appears in "many versions: paper, microform, online, CD-ROM, and computer tape." They assess the different products and note that documents librarians face a "dilemma: a choice of products, publishers, and formats" (p. 360). Furthermore (Ibid.),

> many questions...[have] to be answered that were never asked before. What format(s) of the *Mo Cat* do I want? What format(s) of the *Mo Cat* do I need? What format(s) of the *Mo Cat* can I afford? What type of computer hardware do I need? The list goes on.

Stand-alone services do not displace other library resources. Rather, they comprise one step in the process of information gathering and may only duplicate coverage of the printed *Monthly Catalog*. Both *PAIS Bulletin* and *Government Reports Announcements & Index*, for example, supplement the *Monthly Catalog* and are available on CD-ROM. If anything, the cost to libraries of providing library users with access to government information and data will increase.

AUTOMATED SYSTEMS

For purposes of this chapter, an automated system is a computer-based system which accomplishes specific goals related to the access, organization, or dissemination of information in a documents collection; and/or provides management information that assists librarians in making decisions related to the collection. Typical information in an automated system can include bibliographic information, textual information, circulation data, acquisitions information, user information, and a host of management information including budgets, personnel, inventories, and more.

Automated systems for government information collections can be developed under any of the following approaches (Corbin, 1981, pp. 15–18):

- *Purchase or lease a turnkey system.* A turnkey system is one that is ready to be installed as a complete package by a vendor or contractor. Usually, it is intended to address a specific function or area of functions, such as acquisitions, circulation, and serials control.
- *Share an automated system with another library via a network or through a formal cooperative agreement.* Such approaches rely on an online time sharing mode of operation, in which the libraries either share a basic system and apply it to meet their own purposes, or actually input and manipulate the same primary database and supporting system software.
- *Modify a system from another library.* The library purchases programs and appropriate hardware and adapts the programs to meet the specific needs and objectives of the library. Typically, the modifications are done on the software of the system to be adapted.
- *Piggy-back the system onto existing and available institutional hardware and software.* This approach assumes that the library has access to institutional computer services—either the computer services of the university or local government. The documents collection typically accepts some "constraints" in the software rather than making significant changes.
- *Develop the system locally.* Here the documents staff, perhaps with the assistance of a library systems analyst, designs, programs, tests, de-bugs, and implements the system. Although this approach allows for greater control over the system and ensures its appropriateness for the local library, it assumes the availability of expert staff, significant time commitments, and knowledge of sophisticated issues related to both equipment and programming.

Although these approaches are presented individually for purposes of illustration, in practice they are often combined and used in conjunction with each other to develop the final product.

Writings by Morton (see chapter Appendix) offer one example of a local system that has been "piggy-backed" on a commercial software package—in this case DATATRIEVE. He identifies the benefits of having an automated shelflist for documents, but also indicates the need for having some in-house expertise related to the development of automated systems. Using such a system as the one developed at Carleton College (Morton and Cox, 1982),[8] access to and

---

[8] Three selective depositories in Richmond, Virginia, use GOVDOX offered by Mecklersoft, Westport, Connecticut (Walters, 1990). For a discussion of a different GOVDOX, one written in dBase and compiled through Nantucket's CLIPPER, see Kiser and Grotophorst (1988).

control of the depository collection might increase significantly, and management information for collection development (e.g., serials control and collection review) is readily available. At the same time, staff can use the system for producing labels and lists of specialized holdings, and maintaining a title or Sudocs number file.

Stephenson and Purcell (1986) have discussed "the potential advantages that sophisticated automated records systems offer for both the control of government documents and the integration of the documents function into other automated library systems" (p. 191). They "identified the functional requirements for automating documents collections" (1985, p. 57) and listed selected serials software control systems potentially useful in automating documents collections. As demonstrated at Carleton College Library, impressive use of a software program for the management of documents collections can be accomplished without staff needing to acquire sophisticated programming skills (since the software is "canned") and without significant cost. The critical ingredient for success, it appears, is the desire and dedication of documents librarians who attempt to develop such systems.

Perhaps it might be useful to conclude this section of the chapter with a few examples. Using DATATRIEVE, Paradox, INMAGIC, or other software, libraries could enter data for the following fields into a management database:

- Level of government;
- Issuing agency;
- Type of publication;
- Format;
- Distributor (GPO, NTIS, etc.);
- Individual title;
- Series title and number;
- Sudocs, NTIS, etc., number;
- LC or Dewey number;
- GPO item number;
- Date surveyed (GPO);
- Date published;
- Date selected/ordered;
- Date received;
- Received as depository or nondepository item;
- Subjects/descriptors; and
- Notes.

Libraries could enter such information for every government information resource received as of a certain date. Such a database enables staff and users to identify and retrieve resources regardless of level of government, format, and distribution source. They can then combine search fields and generate data and statistics useful for evaluation and decision making. For example, they might locate all *microfiche* pamphlets received more than five years ago. They could then review these titles and make decisions about their retention.

To assist libraries and their collection development decision making, the library of the University of California, Riverside, has captured information about depository item numbers in machine-readable form (dBase III for use on IBM PC, or compatible hardware, with hard disk capacity). The database includes all active item numbers available for selection since September 1984. The staff assign "broad subject or discipline concepts to each record to further enhance the utility of the database as a collection development and management tool" (Mooney, 1986, p. 3).

The collection development staff at Ball State University has also reviewed the GPO item number list and imposed a general subject classification upon it (Hodge, Calvin, and Rike, 1989). The purpose is to identify which government bodies issue source material of value to each academic department. Such information is then included in the written collection development policy statement and guides the library in the level of intensity that it collects from each government body.

EXPLOITING OTHER TECHNOLOGIES

Stephenson and Purcell (1984) discuss the benefits of using technology for making collection development, reference, cataloging, circulation, and managerial decisions. To assist library clientele in discovering the types of government resources appropriate to their information needs, Smith (1986) reports on the development of menu-driven microcomputer software that defines selected search questions through a series of sorting sequences. This precursor to an expert or knowledge-based system simulates some of the actual steps of a reference or search query. Students and other library users may, therefore, be able to locate some potentially useful source material without needing the intervention of staff.

Harley and Knobloch (1991) report on Government Documents Reference Aid (GDRA), a prototype expert system "developed to aid government documents reference service in the Stanford University Libraries" (p. 15). As they conclude, "technological innovations, in appropriate contexts, can enhance the quality of both the library workplace and government information services offered by library staff" (p. 29).

DOWNLOADING DATA

Regardless of the electronic format, it is likely that more people will download statistical data and manipulate those data to study specific hypotheses and research questions. Most depository libraries, including regionals, are unlikely to have the staff time to act as intermediaries in assisting patrons with downloading and the resources to provide such individualized services themselves. However, some libraries already do this. Those needing replacement copies or part of a dataset not locally held might download the data, and perhaps enter them into their own online catalog.

NETWORKING

Libraries participate in a number of formal and informal networks, including BITNET and INTERNET. At the same time, the use of libraries will change as homes and office are connected to libraries over local networks via wide-band channels, such as an optical fiber or a cable TV conduit. People external to libraries can already gain access to library online catalogs, and libraries are expanding the diversity of resources contained in these catalogs. From remote sites, people can review library holdings and check for and request specific titles. In the near future, they will search numerous bulletin boards and list-serves available through libraries, and use various CD-ROM products and selected magnetic tapes included in online catalogs.

With appropriate technology, libraries will be able to create local area networks (LANs) that provide multiple access to CD-ROM products. The diversity of library services will continue to expand and provide library users with increased opportunities for linkage to resources available from other information providers.

The State Data Center program of the Bureau of the Census represents one example of a network linking libraries to other information providers as well as print and electronic information and data. The National Research and Education Network (NREN) may ultimately create a high-speed-computer-network linking government, industry, and educational institutions, and making electronic data and computing resources more widely available to the research community. Apparently, the Government Documents Round Table (GODORT), American Library Association, favors depository library participation in NREN as a means to ensure that the general public has access to the information and data carried by the network (*National Research and Education Network and the Federal Depository Library Program*, 1991).

GODORT's position paper recommends that regional depositories, "academic research libraries with the computing facilities, and large libraries with special electronic resources" would serve as "original nodes for the network. They could then provide access for the smaller libraries and selective depositories within their regions through dial-up facilities or local area networks" (Ibid., p. 7).

Such recommendations represent a misunderstanding of NREN, even within the educational role envisioned (see McClure, Bishop, and Doty, 1989; McClure, Bishop, Doty, and Rosenbaum, 1991) and the capabilities of the depository library program, as presently constituted, to realize GODORT's expectations. There is great variation among regionals and "large libraries," whatever that term means, to serve as effective network nodes. Suffice to say, it is time to review the depository library program within the context discussed in the next section and in Hernon and McClure (1988, Chapter 17). As well, restructuring the depository program in an electronic and information age is a theme of the Fall 1992 meeting of the Depository Library Council to the Public Printer. Clearly, restructuring will become more of a key issue as the library community plans its service roles for an electronic and information age.

ELECTRONIC INFORMATION REQUIRES A NEW FRAMEWORK

Technology & U.S. Government Information Policies (1987), a report of the Association of Research Libraries' Task Force on Government Information in Electronic Format, identifies certain issues related to depository distribution of electronic government information. The report emphasizes that document delivery systems and library resource sharing may undergo fundamental change. Electronic distribution may have an impact on the budgets of government agencies, libraries, and users, as well as the services offered by the public and private sectors. Equally as important, since libraries and the government incur costs, some form of cost recovery may be required (e.g., see *Government Printing Office Improvement Act of 1990*). Cost recovery must be examined in the context of *value-added* enhancements provided to electronic government databases and files.

As the report correctly notes (p. 16),

> Evolving patterns associated with electronic information will have a significant impact on the role of research libraries in the provision of national information services. Catalogs of research libraries could serve as regional or national gateways that contain references to information in electronic as well as printed formats whether held locally or elsewhere. This could lead in turn to an increased emphasis on linkages with state-wide and regional systems through advanced telecommunications networks. It is unlikely, however, since the use of electronic sources requires large capital and personnel investments, that sharing will necessarily lead to a reduction of current expenditures for any individual library.

Clearly, there is need to reexamine the depository program and its component parts prior to the introduction of electronic information, other than through bibliographic databases available from Dialog and other vendors, on a large scale.

The reexamination might explore removal of the depository program from the GPO and the legislative branch of government. The new home might be, for instance, in the Department of Education or the National Archives and Records Administration. Part of the reason for the new location might be to obtain more funding for an information and educational program that requires full technological and other support. Clearly, Congress is unwilling to devote sufficient funds for the depository program to reach its potential as a legislative branch agency (see Hernon and McClure, 1988, Chapter 17).

Change in the depository program "may lead to a redefinition of depository library service responsibilities in which government documents and gateways to government information will be focused along... [three] lines..." (p. 21). These are (p. 22):

- *Basic services*: This level of depository library would serve as an information center in which there would exist a small government document collection and a computerized gateway to electronic government information located elsewhere. The service might be focused more on self-help and on-demand levels. There would be a high cost per transaction but a small fixed cost.
- *Intermediate Services*: This level of depository library would maintain a larger government document collection and some electronic information and gateways to other electronic information located elsewhere. This library might devise products which would work well through the gateways and might invest in developing value-added approaches to the government information. The service would include more mediation and synthesis than the Basic level.
- *Full services*: This level of depository library would contain research level government documents and a full range of electronic information and the most sophisticated gateways to other electronic information. The depository collection would be supplemented by related, locally available databases. The level of service would include the highest levels of value-added characteristics. There would be developed software packages and other approaches which would change wholesale government information into retail government information. The cost per transaction would be low and the fixed cost high.

Electronic dissemination through the depository program will have a profound effect on the role that the government fulfills. The report suggests five scenarios (pp. 11–12).

The supplying of government information in electronic format to libraries requires fundamental changes on the part of both government and libraries, in terms of cooperation and resource sharing. At the same time, change requires a reassessment of the legal framework under which the government operates.

Information policies take on added significance because they shape the information environment, the format in which government information is produced, and whether the government even collects information. For the government to manage the life cycle of government information suggests that greater attention will be given to cost-effectiveness (see Smith, 1990), or more precisely cost curtailment and control over what is produced, distributed, and disseminated.

The amount of electronic information will continue to expand and the number of print titles distributed may decline. Libraries realize a number of benefits to the incorporation of technology into reference and other departments. Now the depository program must be reevaluated and better prepared for resource-sharing, cooperation, the electronic dissemination of government information, and functioning as an effective *safety net* for making government information publications and *products* available to the public (see Hernon, 1990).

A key issue will become the extent to which the GPO can and should provide depository libraries with electronic information products and *services*. According the GPO's General Counsel, "the Government is required to fund electronic access charges for the depositories to the extent that Congress has appropriated monies for such purpose." The GPO must also factor in "program priorities" (Zagami, 1991, pp. 2, 6).

On July 11, 1991, Congressman Charlie Rose, Chairman of the Joint Committee on Printing, introduced H. R. 2772, the "GPO Wide Information Network for Data Online Act of 1991." Popularly known as the "GPO WINDO," the bill, together with susequent legislation, proposes to make the GPO into a disseminator of a wide range of electronic databases and to supply depository libraries with free access. The result might be a more technologically oriented depository library program. However, the legislation has met opposition from the private sector and other groups. It may be inappropriate for the GPO to serve as a distributor of databases, many of which are already available elsewhere, for which its staff may lack the technical expertise. Indeed, it may make more sense to use databases directly from the National Library of Medicine (NLM) and other groups; the NLM, however, exercises tight control over the dissemination of its services. Such legislation provides the legislative branch with centralized authority over the other branches of government. Why should only depository libraries have free access to a wide assortment of databases? And, finally, how will GPO products and services accommodate inclusion on the INTERNET and NREN? How will this inclusion and remote access to government information impact on the in-person use of depository libraries?

Clearly, increased opportunities for the inclusion of more government publications, products, and services within the realm of the depository library program directs attention away from important issues, such as whether or not regionals really need to retain everything, especially when the National

Archives retains a complete set of GPO publications forever; and the location and structure of the program.

To repeat, there needs to be an objective study of the depository library program, with the goal of making it more relevant to today's and tomorrow's world. The evolving networked environment, such as that represented by NREN, may be the most important issue facing libraries this decade. This environment and NREN will increase in importance and impact more directly on libraries. Future planning and funding must address such challenges and opportunities.

OTHER CHAPTERS

Figures 1-4 and 1-5 identify sources for keeing abreast of recent developments within the published literature of library and information science, and thereby updating the information content of this book. At the same time, librarians and library school students must supplement the literature by turning to conferences, other libraries using particular technologies, and private sector services. Such avenues provide access to information not found in the present literature as well as recent developments—those of the past six (or so) months.

Figure 1-4.   Appropriate Indexing and Abstracting Services.

Title	Coverage
Library and Information Science Abstracts, 1969-*,†	Books, periodical articles, dissertations, reports, and conference proceedings on an international basis.
Library Literature, 1921/32-†	Journal articles, books, pamphlets, and research papers.
Monthly Catalog of United States Government Publications, 1895-*†	Government publications printed and procured by the GPO. Includes, for example, publications of the Office of Technology Assessment, the GPO, and the Joint Committee on Printing. Individual GAO reports appear in the agency's "Reports Issued in _____" and its "Index of Reports and Testimony: Fiscal Year _____."
Resources in Education (RIE), 1966-*,†	Reports and other sources accepted by an ERIC clearinghouse. These reports include internal evaluation studies conducted by libraries. ERIC's *Current Index to Journals in Education* (*CIJE*) tends to duplicate *Library Literature* in its coverage of depository library use of technology. *CIJE* (1969-) covers education-related periodicals.

*Available online.
†Available on CD-ROM.

Figure 1-5. Key Journals and Newsletters.

Administrative Notes, 1980– . A newsletter produced by the GPO on an irregular basis.

Documents to the People, 1972– . A quarterly newsletter of the Government Documents Round Table, American Library Association.

Government Information Quarterly, 1984– . An international and scholarly journal published by JAI Press.

Government Publications Review, 1973– . An international and scholarly journal published bi-monthly by Pergamon Press.

The following chapters identify libraries and librarians actively involved in specific uses of technology for public services and managing depository collections and services, and providing their clientele with electronic information and data. By checking chapter appendices and references, readers can identify others at the forefront in applying technology to depository library services and collection management.

Perhaps others will produce companion volumes covering library holdings of government information resources for state and local governments, international organizations, and other countries. Ultimately, a more complete picture of technological uses worldwide might emerge. Nonetheless, practice will always advance faster than the literature. In this regard, e-mail, electronic bulletin boards, and the invisible college will continue to play a vital role in answering the questions raised in this book and elsewhere.

REFERENCES

Bolner, Myrtle Smith and Barbara Kile. "Documents to the People: Access through the Automated Catalog," *Government Publications Review*, 18 (1991): 51–64.

Bowerman, Roseann and Susan A. Cady. "Government Publications in an Online Catalog: A Feasibility Study," *Information Technology and Libraries*, 3 (December 1984): 331–342.

"Bulletin Boards Give Users the Line on Federal Info," *Government Computer News*, 10 (May 27, 1991): 38–40, 42.

"CD-ROM Software & Policy on Assistance to the User," *Administrative Notes*, 12 (July 31, 1991): 18–19 *(GP3.16/3–2:12)*.

Congress. Joint Committee on Printing. *Provision of Federal Government Publications in Electronic Formats to Depository Libraries*. Joint Committee Print, 98th Cong., 2nd sess. (1984) *(Y4.P93/1:P96/2)*.

Congress. Office of Technology Assessment. *Informing the Nation* (Washington, D.C.: GPO, 1988) *(Y3.T22/2:2In3/9)*.

Corbin, John. *Developing Computer Based Library Systems* (Phoenix, AZ: Oryx Press, 1981).

Directory of Online Databases (New York: Cuadra/Elsevier, 1990).

Dobbs, Christopher C. "Quality Control in Implementing OCLC GOVDOC Current Cataloging Service," *Documents to the People*, 18 (September 1990): 166–167, 170.

Electronic Mail. Spec Flyer 149 (Washington, D.C.: Association of Research Libraries, Office of Management Services, 1988).

"Electronic Corner," *Administrative Notes*, 12 (January 15, 1991): 3–9 *(GP3.16/3–2:12)*.

Ernest, Douglas J. "Accessing Federal Government Publications with RLIN," *Government Publications Review*, 15 (1988): 237–244.

"Feds Have Big Plans for CD-ROM," *Government Computer News*, 10 (April 1, 1991): 1, 6.

General Accounting Office. *Federal Information: Users' Current and Future Technology Needs. GAO/GGD–89–20FS* (November 1988).

"Govdoc-L: Discussion of Government Documents Issues," *Administrative Notes*, 11 (November 15, 1990): 15–18 *(GP3.16/3–2:11)*.

"Hardware (Average Per Depository): Based on 1989 Biennial Survey," *Administrative Notes*, 11 (April 13, 1990): 8–9 *(GP3.16/3–2:11)*.

Harley, Bruce L. and Patricia J. Knobloch, "Government Documents Reference Aid: An Expert System Development Project," *Government Publications Review*, 18 (1991): 15–33.

Hernon, Peter. "Government Information *Safety Nets*," *Government Information Quarterly*, 7 (1990): 249–257.

————. *Microforms and Government Information* (Westport, CT: Microform Review, 1981).

————. *Use of Government Publications by Social Scientists* (Norwood, NJ: Ablex, 1979).

———— and Charles R. McClure. "Electronic Census Products and the Depository Library Program: Future Issues and Trends," *Government Information Quarterly*, 8 (1991): 59–76.

———— and Charles R. McClure. *Public Access to Government Information*. 2nd ed. (Norwood, NJ: Ablex, 1988).

————, Charles R. McClure, and Gary R. Purcell. *GPO's Depository Library Program* (Norwood, NJ: Ablex, 1985).

Hodge, Stanley, Diane Calvin, and Galen E. Rike. "Formulating an Integrated Library Government Documents Collection Policy," *Government Information Quarterly*, 6 (1989): 199–213.

Jacobs, Jim. "U.S. Government Computer Bulletin Boards: A Modest Proposal for Reform," *Government Publications Review*, 17 (1990): 393–396.

Jones, Ray. "The Data Library in the University of Florida Libraries," *Library Trends*, 30 (Winter 1982): 383–396.

———— and Thomas Kinney. "Government Information in Machine-Readable Data Files: Implications for Libraries and Librarians," *Government Publications Review*, 15 (1988): 25–32.

Kessler, Ridley R., Jr. and Evelyn H. Daniel. "A Survey of United States Regional Government Depository Libraries," report to the Council on Library Resources for a Faculty/Librarian Cooperative Research Grant (October 1989).

Kinney, Thomas and Ray Jones. "The Distribution of Federal Statistical Data on Microcomputer-Readable Media: Implications for Academic Research Libraries,"

Proceedings of the American Society for Information Science Annual Meeting, 23 (1986): 138–142.

_____ and Ray Jones. "Microcomputers, Government Information, and Libraries," *Government Publications Review*, 15 (1988): 147–154.

Kiser, Chris and Clyde Grotophorst. "GOVDOX: A Government Documents Check-in System," *Library Software Review*, 7 (January/February 1988): 42–43.

Kovacs, Diane K. "GovDoc-L: An Online Intellectual Community of Documents Librarians and Other Individuals Concerned with Access to Government Information," *Government Publications Review*, 17 (1990): 411–420.

McClure, Charles R., Ann P. Bishop, and Philip Doty. *Impact of High-Speed Networks on Scientific Communication and Research: Final Report to the U.S. Office of Technology Assessment.* Syracuse, NY: Syracuse University, School of Information Studies, 1989 [mimeograph].

_____, Ann P. Bishop, Philip Doty, and Howard Rosenbaum. *The National Research and Education Network (NREN).* Norwood, NJ: Ablex, 1991.

_____, Peter Hernon, and Gary R. Purcell. *Linking the U.S. National Technical Information Service with Academic and Public Libraries* (Norwood, NJ: Ablex, 1986).

Mooney, Margaret T. "Automating the U.S. Depository Item Number File," *Administrative Notes*, 7 (November 1986): 2–4 *(GP3.16/3–2:7)*.

_____. "GPO Cataloging: Is It a Viable Current Access Tool for U.S. Documents?," *Government Publications Review*, 16 (1989): 259–270.

_____. "Matching Library Holdings against GPO Tapes: Issues, Concerns, and Solutions," *Government Publications Review*, 17 (1990): 421–428.

Morton, Bruce and J. Randolph Cox. "Cooperative Collection Development between Selective U.S. Depository Libraries," *Government Publications Review*, 9 (1982): 221–229.

Murphy, Cynthia E. "A Comparison of Manual and Online Searching of Government Document Indexes," *Government Information Quarterly*, 2 (1985): 169–181.

National Research and Education Network and the Federal Depository Library Program. A position paper from the American Library Association/Government Documents Round Table, Federal Documents Task Force. By Herb Somers, Michele Ruhlin, and Judith Rowe, March 1991 [unpublished paper].

"1987 National Health Interview Survey: Guidelines for Use of CD-ROM," *Administrative Notes*, 12 (June 30, 1991): 6–7 *(GP3.16/3–2:15)*.

Pope, Nolan F. "Providing Machine-Readable Numeric Information in the University of Florida Libraries: A Case Study," in *Numeric Databases*, edited by Ching-chih Chen and Peter Hernon (Norwood, NJ: Ablex, 1984), pp. 263–282.

Powell, Margaret S., Deborah Smith Johnston, and Ellen P. Conrad. "The Use of OCLC for Cataloging U.S. Government Publications: A Feasibility Study," *Government Publications Review*, 14 (1987): 61–73.

"Recommended Minimum Technical Guidelines for Federal Depository Libraries," *Administrative Notes*, 12 (August 3, 1991): 1–3 *(GP3.16/3–2:12/19)*.

Sanchez, Lisa. "Dissemination of United States Federal Government Information on CD-ROM: An Issue Primer," *Government Publications Review*, 16 (1989): 133–144.

Smith, Diane H. "Depository Libraries in the 1990s: Whitner, or Wither Depositories?," *Government Publications Review*, 17 (1990): 301–324.

Smith, Karen F. "Robot at the Reference Desk?," *College & Research Libraries*, 47 (September 1986): 486–490.

Stephenson, Mary Sue and Gary R. Purcell. "Application of Systems Analysis to Depository Library Decision Making regarding the Use of New Technology," *Government Information Quarterly*, 1 (1984): 285–307.

————. "The Automation of Government Publications: Functional Requirements and Selected Software Systems for Serials Control," *Government Information Quarterly*, 2 (1985): 57–76.

————."Current and Future Direction of Automation Activities for U.S. Government Depository Collections," *Government Information Quarterly*, 3 (1986): 191–199.

Technology & U.S. Government Information Policies: Catalysts for New Partnerships (Washington, D.C.: Association of Research Libraries, 1987).

Walbridge, Sharon. "OCLC and Improved Access to Government Documents," *Illinois Libraries*, 68 (May 1986): 329–332.

Walsh, Jim and Mallory Stark. "The Monthly Catalog of United States Government Publications: One Title, Many Versions," *Government Information Quarterly*, 7 (1990): 359–370.

Walters, John. "Using Automated Item Files as the Basis for Effective Collection Management and Cooperative Collection Development: A Note," *Government Publications Review*, 17 (1990): 251–256.

Zagami, Anthony J., General Counsel, "'Cost Sharing' for the Dissemination of Government Information in Electronic Formats," Memorandum to the Public Printer, March 25, 1991.

Zink, Steven D. "Planning for the Perils of CD–ROM," *Library Journal*, 115 (February 1, 1990): 51–55.

APPENDIX: SELECTED WRITINGS ON TECHNOLOGICAL APPLICATIONS FOR DEPOSITORY COLLECTIONS AND SERVICES (ONES NOT LISTED IN CHAPTER REFERENCES).

"Accessing Government Documents," *Illinois Libraries*, 71 (November 1989): 449–526 [entire issue].

"Automatic Bibliographic Control of Government Documents: Current Developments," *Documents to the People*, 15 (December 1987): 224–246.

Bahr, Alice H. "Cataloging U.S. Government Depository Materials: A Reevaluation," *College & Research Libraries*, 47 (November 1986): 587–595.

Becker, K. A. "Getting Documents to the People: Using Finder for an Automated Solution," *Illinois Libraries*, 71 (November 1989): 513–516.

————. "Using Finder Information Storage and Retrieval Software for Government Documents," *Library Software Review*, 9 (1990): 14–17.

Bortnick, Jane, ed. "Electronic Collection and Dissemination of Federal Government Information," *Government Information Quarterly*, 5, no. 3 (1988), entire issue.

Bower. Cynthia. "OCLC Records for Federal Depository Documents: A Preliminary Investigation," *Government Information Quarterly*, 1 (1984): 379–400.

Case, Donald and Kathleen Welden. "Distribution of Government Publications to Depository Libraries by Optical Disk: A Review of the Technology, Applications, and Issues," *Government Publications Review*, 13 (1986): 313–322.

Congress. Joint Committee on Printing. *An Open Forum on the Provision of Electronic Federal Information to Depository Libraries* (Washington, D.C.: GPO, 1985) *(Y4.P93/1:El2/4)*.

Cornwell, Gary. "GPO Cataloging Records: Background and Issues," *Documents to the People*, 17 (June 1989): 83–85.

Dossett, R. "For Those Few of You Who Still Aren't Confused: An Introduction to Government Information and CD-ROM," *Illinois Libraries*, 71 (November 1989): 492–494.

Ernest, Douglas J. and Fred C. Schmidt. "Computerized Access to Government Publications at Colorado State University Libraries," *The Reference Librarian*, 32 (1991): 277–278.

Gassman, M. "Government Information: Getting It Online," *Illinois Libraries*, 71 (November 1989): 500–505.

"Government Documents and Reference Services," *The Reference Librarian*, 32 (1991), entire issue.

Harley, Bruce L. and Patricia Knobloch. "Government Documents Reference Aid: An Expert System Development Project," *Government Publications Review*, 18 (1991): 15–33.

Hernon, Peter, ed. *New Technology and Documents Librarianship* (Westport, CT: Meckler, 1983).

Higdon, Mary Ann. "Federal Documents Processing with OCLC: The Texas Tech Experience—Planning, Utilization, and the Future," in *Government Documents and Microforms: Standards and Management Issues*. Proceedings of the Fourth Annual Government Documents and Information Conference and the Ninth Annual

Microforms Conference, edited by Steven D. Zink and Nancy Jean Melin (Westport, CT: Meckler Publishing, 1984), pp. 89–97.

Jamison, Carolyn C. "Loading the GPO Tapes—What Does It Really Mean?," *Government Publications Review*, 13 (1986): 549–559.

————. "Planning for Documents Automation," *Documents to the People*, 15 (December 1987): 247–252.

Kadec, Sarah T. "The U.S. Government Printing Office's Library Programs Service and Automation: An Insider's Commentary," *Government Publications Review*, 12 (1985): 283–288.

Kahin, Brian. "Information Policy and the Internet,: Toward a Public Information Infrastructure in the United States," *Government Publications Review*, 18 (1991): 451–472.

Kinney, Thomas and Gary Cornwell. "GPO Cataloging Records in the Online Catalog: Implications for the Reference Librarian," *The Reference Librarian*, 32 (1991): 259–275.

Lewis-Somers, Susan. "Who Uses Project Hermes?," *American Association of Law Libraries Newsletter*, 22 (July 1991): 1, 436–437.

Lynch, Frances H. and Charles Lasater. "Government Documents and the Online Catalog," *Bulletin of the Medical Library Association*, 78 (January 1990): 23–28.

MacGilvray, Marian W., Joseph P. Paskoski, and John M. Walters. *Electronic Bulletin Board System for the Federal Depository Library Program: A Study* (Washington, D.C.: GPO, Library Programs Service, 1991) *(GP3.2:El2)*.

Maclay, Veronica. "Automatic Bibliographic Control of Government Documents at Hastings Law Library," *Technical Services Quarterly*, 7 (1989): 53–64.

McClure, Charles R. "Online Government Documents Data Base Searching and the Use of Microfiche Documents Online by Academic and Public Depository Librarians," *Microform Review*, 10 (Fall 1981): 245–259.

————. "Provision of Federal Government Publications in Electronic Format to Depository Libraries...," *Government Information Quarterly*, 3 (1986): 113–116.

————. "Technology in Government Documents Collections: Current Status, Impacts, and Prospects," *Government Publications Review*, 9 (1982): 255–276.

———— and Peter Hernon. *Academic Library Use of NTIS: Suggestions for Services and Core Collection* (Springfield, VA: NTIS, 1986, PB86–228871).

Morton, Bruce. "Attitudes, Resources, and Applications: The Government Documents Librarian and Computer Technology," in *New Technology and Documents Librarianship*, edited by Peter Hernon (Westport, CT: Meckler Publishing, 1983), pp. 43–59.

————. "Implementing an Automated Shelflist for a Selective Depository Collection," *Government Publications Review*, 9 (1982): 323–344.

————. "An Items Record Management System: First Step in the Automation of Collection Development in Selective Depository Libraries," *Government Publications Review*, 8A (1981): 185–196.

Musser, Linda R. and Thomas W. Conkling. "Impact of NTIS CD-ROM on the Use of a Technical Report Collection," *College & Research Libraries News*, 52 (February 1991): 111.

Myers, Judy E. "The Government Printing Office Cataloging Records: Opportunities and Problems," *Government Information Quarterly*, 2 (1985): 27–56.

Olivia, Victor T. and Michael K. Reimer. *Using INNOVACQ to Process G.P.O. Titles* (Garden City, NY: Adelphi University Libraries, 1989) (ED 316 195).

Plaunt, James R. "Cataloging Options for U.S. Government Printing Office Documents," *Government Publications Review*, 12 (1985): 449–456.

Redmond, Mary. "From Backwater to Mainstream: Government Documents in the Online Catalog," *Bookmark*, 47 (Spring 1989): 161–165.

Regueiro, Judith E., Margaret L. Breen, Kathleen Knox, and Susan Williamson. "Creating a U.S. Government Documents Database from an Online System: The Tri-College Project," *Government Publications Review*, 19 (1992): 59–73.

Scott, Jack William and Anne Marie Allison. "United States Documents in an On-line Catalog," *The Serials Librarian*, 1 (Summer 1977): 365–371.

Smith, Karen F. "POINTER: The Microcomputer Reference Program for Federal Documents," in *Expert Systems in Libraries*, edited by Rao Aluri and Donald E. Riggs (Norwood, NJ: Ablex, 1990), pp. 41–50.

―――――. "POINTER vs Using Government Publications: Where's the Advantage," *Reference Librarian*, 23 (1989): 191–205.

Stanfield, Karen. "Documents Online: Cataloging Federal Depository Materials at the University of Illinois," *Illinois Libraries*, 68 (May 1986): 325–329.

Swanbeck, Jan. "Federal Documents in the Online Catalog: Problems, Options, and the Future," *Government Information Quarterly*, 2 (1985): 187–192.

Tull, Laura. "Retrospective Conversion of Government Documents: Marcive GPO Tape Clean-up Project," *Technicalities*, 9 (August 1989): 4–7.

Turner, Carol and Ann Latta. *Current Approaches to Improving Access to Government Documents*. An OMS Occasional Paper Produced as Part of the Collaborative Research-Writing Program. Washington, D.C.: Association of Research Libraries, Office of Management Studies, 1987.

Tyckoson, David A. "Appropriate Technologies for Government Information," *RQ*, 27 (Fall 1987): 33–38.

Veatch, James R. "Automating Government Documents Orders with a Microcomputer," *Government Publications Review*, 12 (1985); 137–141.

Walbridge, Sharon. "OCLC and Government Documents Collections," *Government Publications Review*, 9 (1982): 277–287.

Chapter Two

Government Information Policy and Its Implications for Depository Services and Collections

Harold B. Shill and Peter Hernon

This chapter introduces government information policy and key policy instruments that impact the depository library program and the availability of government publications through that program (44 USC 1901). Current developments and possible future ones will shape the depository program for future generations.

The United States has neither a national information policy nor a Federal government information policy. Instead, the existing policy structure is a fragmented jumble of specific legislation, Executive Branch regulations and guidelines, bureaucratic compartmentation, rulings of agency legal counsels, long-standing practice, and "turf" protection by agencies and congressional committees. In addition, the political agendas of various presidential administrations have had a profound impact on Federal agencies' collection, processing, distribution and dissemination, and retention of the information they have gathered and processed.

Given the government's historic lack of a coherent approach to information policy development and implementation, it is little wonder that agencies have been unable to integrate electronic products and services smoothly into existing dissemination channels, including the depository library program of the Government Printing Office (GPO). This inability of policy making and dissemination structures to adapt to technological change has far-reaching implications for public access to government information, since agencies are increasingly stressing the use of electronic formats for managing agency records and disseminating government information and data. This adaptive failure also has important implications for depository libraries and their ability to serve as access channels to government information. This chapter, therefore, places libraries in a broad policy context—as one of several information safety nets providing access to government information/publications.

In a recent examination of United States information policy, Hernon and McClure (1991) identified 79 fundamental policy issues, which they subsequently grouped into 13 categories: Federal organization for information policy making; freedom of information; secrecy, security, and protection of information/records; the economics of government information; information technology; standards; licensing; the relationship between the government and other stakeholders in the information sector; public access to, and availability of, government information; role of depository library programs; the National Research and Education Network (NREN); and information policies for other levels of government in the United States. These issues are not an exhaustive inventory of policy questions. Furthermore, the categories and issues are not mutually exclusive.

The recently completed White House Conference on Library and Information Services generated 97 recommendations calling for action on part of executive agencies, the President, and Congress ("Recommendations," 1991). These recommendations tend to be disappointing in that they are sweeping, overly general, and simplistic; many of them deal in generalities and ignore specific policy instruments and accomplishments. The list of resolutions neither makes specific policy recommendations nor provides a realistic framework for guiding Congress and agencies in making information policy decisions. Most damaging, perhaps, they do not provide a useful framework for consensus development and producing change.

This chapter discusses selected policy issues, ones that focus on the types of information resources that the depository library program receives or is likely to receive. At the same time, the chapter encourages readers to become familiar with policy questions and to realize that issue resolution involves negotiation and compromise among competing stakeholders within and outside government. (Figure 2-1 identifies selected works on government information policy.)

The GPO plays an important role in the printing and binding of government *publications* and, to some extent, in the distribution of publications appearing in electronic formats. However, the nature and extent of this role have not been fully defined or universally accepted. Moreover, some within government recognize that the GPO, as well as the Joint Committee on Printing (JCP), its primary congressional oversight committee, want to stake out a preeminent role in the rapidly emerging information and electronic ages.

Figure 2-1.   Selected Works on Government Information Policy.

Flaherty, David H. *Protecting Privacy in Surveillance Societies.* Chapel Hill, NC: University of North Carolina, 1989).

Hernon, Peter and Charles R. McClure. *Federal Information Policies in the 1980s* (Norwood, NJ: Ablex, 1987).

McClure, Charles R., Ann Bishop, Philip Doty, and Howard Rosenbaum. *The National Research and Education Network.* Norwood, NJ: Ablex, 1991.

McClure, Charles R. and Peter Hernon. *United States Scientific and Technical Information Policies* (Norwood, NJ: Ablex, 1989).

————, Peter Hernon, and Harold C. Relyea. *United States Government Information Policies* (Norwood, NJ: Ablex, 1989).

McIntosh, Toby J. *Federal Information in the Electronic Age: Policy Issues for the 1990s* (Washington, D.C.: Bureau of National Affairs, 1990).

Office of Technology Assessment. *Informing the Nation: Federal Information Dissemination in an Electronic Age* (Washington, D.C.: GPO, 1988).

Shapley, Deborah and Rustum Roy. *Lost at the Frontier: U.S. Science and Technology Policy Adrift.* Philadelphia, PA: ISI Press, 1985.

POLICY ISSUES

This section discusses eight issues that have not been permanently resolved: government organization for information dissemination, the extent of government publishing activity, inclusion of materials in GPO's depository library program, public access, public versus private sector roles, costs of dissemination, inclusion of electronic information in the depository program, and American competitiveness. The discussion identifies relevant policy instruments, while the chapter conclusion stresses the importance of monitoring planned and future policy instruments and participation in their formulation.

Government Organization for Information Dissemination

More than 100 Federal agencies collect, process, and disseminate information and data (Office of Technology Assessment, 1988). Some agencies, such as the departments of Defense and Energy, the National Aeronautics and Space Administration (NASA), and the Environmental Protection Agency (EPA), maintain extensive dissemination programs. Such dissemination programs channel agency publications directly to agency personnel and outside individuals/organizations having an ongoing relationship with that agency, such as scientific research institutes, some universities, and contractors performing research for the agency.

It has been optimistically estimated that only one-half of all Federal publications enter the depository library program (Ibid.). However, this estimate does not take into account the vast number of publications printed at the GPO regional facilities and the impact of desktop publishing. Many agencies fail to consider that wordprocessed reports may comprise a government publication eligible for depository distribution.

The government's primary counterweight to this centrifugal tendency among agency publishing programs is the maintenance of three governmentwide dissemination agencies: the GPO, the National Technical Information Service (NTIS), and the National Archives and Records Administration (NARA). It is extremely significant that both NTIS and NARA have an explicit archival function. Some, but not all, librarians believe that the depository program does as well. Furthermore, the GPO is a legislative agency accountable to Congress, NTIS is an executive agency within the Department of Commerce's Technology Administration, and NARA is an independent executive agency. This dispersal of dissemination responsibilities prevents any one executive order, Office of Management and Budget (OMB) directive, or act of Congress from altering the entire dissemination apparatus. Since both the executive and legislative branches want to protect their own "turf" (i.e., maintain or increase power) in the information arena, proposals to consolidate dissemination responsibilities tend to be resisted by both the branches themselves and outside interest groups. In addition, as noted earlier, many agencies, such as the Bureau of the Census, assume dissemination roles and only use the GPO and the other governmentwide dissemination agencies selectively. Since NARA's dissemination role is small, this discussion will focus on the GPO and NTIS.

In addition to being located in different branches of government, the GPO and NTIS:

- Disseminate significantly different types of materials;
- Finance their dissemination programs in radically different manners; and
- Have very different relationships with depository libraries. Each of these differences is important.

The publications printed by the GPO include congressional hearings, reports, documents, prints, the *Congressional Record*, and other Legislative Branch documents. The agency also prints publications of executive agencies and the judiciary. The GPO identifies materials for the depository library program, in large part, by *riding* (e.g., monitoring) print orders for agency and congressional publications. With certain exceptions, 44 *USC* 501, 502, and 504 require agencies to use the GPO for printing all their publications. This requirement is a major source of resentment for many agencies, which believe that they can get publications printed more quickly and inexpensively in-house or through commercial printers. Agency officials reinforce this resentment with a frequent perception that agency personnel and certain outside persons/organizations, not the general public, comprise their primary clientele. As a result, a number of agencies frequently attempt to evade the printing requirements of title 44 and print their publications in-house or with a private printing firm. Publications not printed by the GPO, as well as many titles printed at GPO's regional facilities, are likely to remain *fugitives* from the depository library program.

In contrast, NTIS primarily acquires and disseminates technical reports of research done under government contract or within government agencies, computer software, and government databases. NTIS also publishes its own current awareness newsletters. In addition, NTIS operates a patent information/licensing clearinghouse, acquires foreign technical reports through international agreements, and permanently archives the technical reports that it disseminates. Some high-demand reports acquired by NTIS are offered for sale through the GPO sales program. NTIS uses GPO's printing services for most of its printing activity.

GPO operations are financially supported through a combination of legislative appropriations and printing charges to executive agencies. The depository library program is funded through annual appropriations currently in the $25 million range. Fees are recovered from the public only through its small sales program of high-demand materials, while access to publications disseminated to depository libraries is required to be free (44 *USC* 1911).

NTIS, on the other hand, receives appropriations only for the patent licensing service and for acquiring/translating Japanese technical literature. The remainder of its operations are designed to be self-supporting through publication sales under legislation enacted in the later 1970s. Unfortunately, NTIS has had to increase document prices steadily through the 1980s and its effectiveness in disseminating scientific and technical information has been reduced as sales to the public have declined.

Since NTIS lacks mandatory deposit legislation, such as the GPO has in 44 *USC*, Chapter 5, agencies (the EPA, in particular) frequently fail to make copies of their technical reports available to NTIS. NTIS also archives the reports it receives on a permanent basis, thereby both preserving valuable scientific and technical information for future users and incurring additional costs that must be passed on to users. The GPO avoids archiving expenses by printing only the number of copies it expects to sell or disseminate, but potential users may later find a much-needed report to be "out of stock." They must, therefore, attempt to locate a copy elsewhere.

Some NTIS publications appear in the depository library program, thereby further undercutting NTIS's revenue base. However, most NTIS publications must be acquired directly from NTIS or through libraries with significant NTIS document collections. There is no formal depository library program for NTIS publications, however, although NTIS maintains a moderately active library liaison program. Significantly, many libraries are now cataloging NTIS publications, and an OCLC/EPIC search by one of the authors in April 1990 revealed the presence of bibliographic/location information for 72,000 NTIS publications in the OCLC database. As a result, there is a nascent network for the sharing of NTIS reports coming into existence as libraries catalog individual documents. This distributed access system, however, is far less extensive, in scope or breadth, than the depository library program with its 1,400 member institutions. Moreover, no NTIS library resource-sharing network has been formally articulated.

The GPO maintains a close relationship with the depository library community through the Depository Library Council to the Public Printer, an advisory body consisting of librarians and representatives from the private sector and government. GPO staff members also attend national library association meetings. NTIS, in contrast, sees its primary users as the business community and has ceased to prepare exhibits for American Library Association conferences, though it does so for Special Libraries Association meetings. An NTIS Advisory Board, created by the National Technical Information Act of 1988 (P. L. 100-519), was formed in early 1991 after considerable political maneuvering within the Commerce Department. The initial board includes three librarians and a technology transfer expert from large corporations and one librarian from a university library. Ironically, no small business representatives were included.

The issue of an all-encompassing "government information agency" was raised several times in the past decade, particularly by Representative George Brown of California, a long-time member of the House Science, Research and Technology Subcommittee. However, the proposal generated little enthusiasm in Congress, among executive agencies, or from major interest groups monitoring Federal information policy decisions (e.g., American Library Association and Information Industry Association). As a result, the information dissemination apparatus is likely to remain fragmented along legislative-executive, fee versus free access, cost recovery versus appropriations, and type of material lines for years to come.

An increasingly important policy issue is the proposed creation of a Federal Information Locator System (FILS) that could serve as a governmentwide information inventory/locator system (GIILS) and, thereby, supersede the system currently operated by OMB. Successful management of government information resources requires agencies and users to know what information is available and where it is located. The GIILS would list information resources across the span of government agencies. It would be a pointer system and direct users to offices, libraries, and archives where the information could be obtained; the system would not actually contain the information.

The GPO, NTIS, Library of Congress, NARA, and the General Services Administration have all been suggested as possible lead organizations directing agencies in supplying information to the central database. Apparently, the Library of Congress would like to be the lead agency for scientific and technical information, whereas Congress and the Commerce Department might consider NTIS as a more logical lead agency. It might not be desirable from a public access standpoint to divide the GIILS into scientific and technical (STI) and non-STI systems, with different lead agencies. Equally as important, lead status in a GIILS will expand the power, prestige, and resources of an agency in the electronic dissemination of government information.

Government Publishing Activity

The Federal government is the largest publisher in the world. Despite the efforts of the Reagan administration to manage Federal information resources, the government does not know exactly how many publications it generates annually. That administration did claim a reduction of recurring publications from 16,000 to 12,000 between 1981 and 1984, however. The government produces 22 types of government publications (Hernon and McClure, 1988, Chapter 4), and from 1981 through 1990, the GPO distributed 514,054 titles to depository libraries; 56.2 percent of these were in microfiche. The number and percentage of microfiche, undoubtedly, would have been greater if the GPO's contractor had not defaulted (Hernon, 1992).

Desktop publishing and the current and planned release of electronic publications in CD-ROM and other formats are, at the same time, expanding the actual number of government publications and making central identification of those publications increasingly difficult. *Government Computer News* (see Chapter 1) has published several articles on the number of publications that NASA and other agencies might release annually and over time. Clearly, if even a fraction of these electronic publications entered the depository program, many regional and selective depositories would be overwhelmed and find it difficult to absorb more print titles as well as CD-ROM and other electronic formats.

An emerging issue for both government and nongovernment publications is whether it is more important to have publications on library premises or electronically accessible. The latter alternative includes more opportunities for (and expectations that) depository libraries will engage in referral and becomes nodes in a networked environment. As discussions in *The Chronicle of Higher Education* illustrate, humanists and some social scientists in academic institutions prefer immediate access to paper copy publications on campus, whereas some scientists and other social scientists favor electronic access.

The Office of Management and Budget has played an increasingly important role in government publishing activity and the overall direction of information policy since 1980. Two OMB circulars, A-3 and A-130, have been especially important vehicles for expanding OMB's activities in the area of government publications. One major piece of legislation, the Paperwork Reduction Act (P. L. 96-511), is also cited as giving OMB statutory authority for some of its policy initiatives. OMB has also issued a series of more specific bulletins and memoranda addressing particular aspects of government publishing and information collection/dissemination activities during the 1980s.

Circular A-3, "Government Periodicals," is intended to establish both bibliographic and fiscal/policy control over periodicals by requiring that agencies annually submit to OMB an inventory of their periodical publications. Originally published by the former Bureau of the Budget in 1922, Circular A-3 was modified in 1972 and 1985 to require advance OMB approval of certain recurring publications and to stipulate that OMB must approve the expenditure of agency funds for the printing of periodicals. While similar to the GIILS proposal in its potential to provide bibliographic control over government periodicals, A-3 can also be used to impose the political preferences of a particular administration on government publication activities, as was done by OMB during the 1980s.

The Paperwork Reduction Act, passed during the final year of the Carter administration, was intended to reduce the paperwork burden of Federal regulations on businesses, universities, and other organizations. The Act was also designed to promote the efficient and economical use of Federal information resources and to encourage the development of coordinated Federal information policies. The legislation provided that an Office of Information and Regulatory Affairs (OIRA) would be created within OMB to carry out these activities. The Act was twice reauthorized for three-year extensions by Congress in 1983 and 1986, but it expired in September 1989, despite vigorous reauthorization efforts. Despite the Act's expiration, OMB has continued to regard the Paperwork Reduction Act as Congress's basic statement of its intent and may continue to do so until new or alternative legislation passes.

Circular A-130, "The Management of Federal Information Resources," became the Reagan administration's policy on information and publishing activities in December 1985, after two years of discussion. This policy directive emphasized that agencies should publish only those materials specifically required by law, should rely on the private sector for information dissemination wherever possible, should avoid unfair competition with the private sector, should apply cost-benefit analysis considerations in deciding whether or not to publish, and should publish only materials needed to further the agency's own mission. This directive placed a strong burden on agencies to demonstrate that existing and proposed publications met the criteria of A-130 and encouraged reliance on the private sector, rather than existing Federal mechanisms, such as the depository library program, for information dissemination.

OMB published two "Advance Notices" of intent to revise Circular A-130 to accommodate electronic information and publications in January and June 1989, respectively. Furthermore, OMB admitted that A-130 does not adequately address the importance of government information as a public good, places too much reliance on the private sector, and provides insufficient coverage of information dissemination. Preparation of a new draft of A-130 was delayed pending the clarification of congressional intent in a reauthorized Paperwork Reduction Act. Since Congress did not reauthorize the Act, OMB has continued to treat the existing Circular A-130 as its primary policy instrument. In Spring 1992, OMB did release a draft revision of A-130 for public comment (see Chapter 1).

OMB appears to accept that, under title 44, the GPO has a role in printing executive agency publications and that the agencies must abide by the requirement of depository distribution for publications having educational value and not intended as internal working documents. However, some agencies, such as the Department of Defense, challenge the role of the GPO as a centralized printer.

Inclusion of Publications in Depository Program

Section 1901, title 44 of the *United States Code,* defines a government publication, for this chapter, as "informational matter which is published as an individual document at government expense, or as required by law." The legislative history of that definition fails to define key terms: "informational matter," "published," and "as an individual document." It would seem that "information matter" includes electronic resources, whereas "published" and "as an individual document" could be more restrictive. Since the definition is not all-encompassing, there is room for the GPO and agencies to maneuver.

More agencies are beginning to consider CD-ROM products as publications, in part because this technology provides a means to distribute information at a lesser cost. Depository distribution of products (tangible materials which can be "placed in a box") has proven less controversial than the distribution of services. Services involve telecommunications and other costs, in addition to possible competition with major database vendors. The central question becomes "who pays?"

In March 1991, the General Counsel of the Government Printing Office issued a memorandum entitled " 'Cost Sharing' for the Dissemination of Government Information in Electronic Formats" (1991). He made the following observations:

- "Depository libraries are prohibited under existing law from charging the public for accessing government information supplied under the aegis of the depository library program" (Ibid., p. 1);
- "The depository library program was not intended and has not been operated to fill the totality of the depositories' needs for government information" (Ibid., p. 4); and
- "When a Federal agency publishes a government publication exclusively in an electronic format, the agency is responsible for the costs of furnishing access to the data base and GPO is obligated to pay the costs of conveying that government information to the depository libraries in an electronic format or in such other format(s) as may be produced and made available under the program. This would include the payment of telecommunication costs for the transmission of online publications when published only in that

format. *However, such obligation may be limited, and must be viewed in the context of available funds and program priorities, as determined by the Government Printing Office, the Joint Committee on Printing and the congressional appropriations committees"* (italics added) (Ibid., pp. 5–6).

The memorandum is an important reminder that the appropriations committees play an important oversight role. Both the GPO and JCP may declare a proactive policy but the appropriations committees may refuse to provide funding to support that position. The GPO, therefore, must carefully negotiate within the policy framework set by title 44, the JCP, and the appropriations committees. Section 1902 of title 44 specifies that:

> government publications, except those determined by their issuing components to be required for official use only or for strictly administrative or operational purposes which have no public interest or educational value and publications classified for reasons of national security, shall be made available to depository libraries through the facilities of the Superintendent of Documents for public information.

Section 1903 excludes cooperative publications (the results of a joint project between different agencies or organizations) from the depository program because they are expensive to produce and "must necessarily be sold in order to be self-sustaining." They are not paid for with federally appropriated funds and are sold to recover their cost.

Agencies, as a result, determine what they want published as a government publication. Once they make that decision and rule that the publication does not comprise an exemption (sections 1902 and 1903), the JCP expects the publication to enter the depository program.

Complicating matters, given the heavy volume of annual publication and variations in agency practices, it is impossible for the JCP, GPO, and library community to identify and monitor all publications and ensure their entry into the depository program.

Public Access to Government Publications/Information

Access and availability to government publications are not always the same as access and availability to government information. Numerous examples exist where the identification of and access to a specific government document did not uncover the necessary government information. Access to, and availability of, government publications are a prerequisite for access to government information.

Discouraged from taking a proactive dissemination stance by Circular A-130 and other OMB policies, agencies have sometimes equated access with availability in a public reading room in Washington, D.C. While such minimal efforts may technically meet statutory requirements for public access, they do not place information and publications in a physical location where public use for all citizens is really facilitated. Availability in a public reading room in Washington, D.C. may provide reasonable access to a person in rural Chevy Chase, Maryland, but it does little for an interested observer in Missoula, Montana. Depository libraries are an example of one type of safety net that has historically provided members of the public in all 50 states with local access to Federal government publications.

The issue of public access is complex and must address whether the information is *public* or *protected* (private or classified) (see Hernon and McClure, 1987, Chapter 1). "A truly sovereign people must be able to obtain information, of their own volition, from their government for minimal reasons of protecting their individual rights as well as preserving the well-being of the larger community or society" (Relyea, 1987, p. 52).

OMB Circular A-130 regards government information resources as a commodity requiring management. That circular equates distribution and dissemination, while encouraging agencies to take a more passive role, one of information availability upon request. Dissemination was recognized as a costly activity and best performed by one of the dissemination agencies, such as NTIS.

Neither the Paperwork Reduction Act of 1980 nor its 1986 reauthorization emphasized dissemination. However, dissemination is now becoming more in vogue. *Informing the Nation* (Office of Technology Assessment, 1988) underscored both the opportunities for enhanced information dissemination and the threats to public access provided by the Federal government's ongoing adoption of electronic information formats. The long-delayed GPO electronic pilot projects, two online databases and three CD-ROM products, were made available to depository libraries in 1990 and 1991 to gauge the effectiveness of electronic dissemination through the existing depository library infrastructure. For the EPA, the placement of government data into the public's hands has become a major senior management concern ("Interagency Conference on Public Access," 1992). And, as noted earlier, OMB is revising Circular A-130 and addressing electronic dissemination needs.

With growing attention being accorded to dissemination and use, Thompson (1991) of the General Accounting Office questioned if the public is receiving its "money's worth from the Federal government" and, by extension, its publicly generated information. He encouraged agencies to define *service quality* as "meeting the public's expectations." The challenge, as he noted, "is to meet the rising demands for public services in an environment of continual revenue shortages." In effect, he advocated the adoption of performance measures as a means for holding agencies accountable and ensuring the effective dissemination of government information.

The Public Printer is suggesting that he might ask Congress to reconsider parts of title 44. The presumption is that his plan will address the depository program and the types of *publications* eligible for depository distribution. Undoubtedly, he will allude to GPO's pilot projects and the dissemination of CD-ROM products and services (bulletin boards, databases, etc.). It is impossible to predict at this time the amount of support within Congress for revision of title 44.

Other anticipated policy developments relate to the Freedom of Information Act (5 *USC* 552) and privacy protection. The Act may be amended so that it applies more directly to electronic records. Legislation might advocate greater privacy protection given the electronic environment and the possible inadvertent release of information on individuals. Access must also be provided to information maintained in electronic form only as Federal recordkeeping becomes increasingly automated.

The Glenerin Declaration (National Commission on Libraries and Information Science, 1987), a joint British-Canadian-American statement, encourages each government to take a proactive approach to national information policy, to promote access to information for all citizens with each country, and to reduce barriers to the transnational flow of information. Yet, the White House Conference failed to acknowledge this declaration as a central principle. Furthermore, the declaration has failed to gain widespread support and attention. It has probably become a historical document objecting to the Reagan administration's market-oriented approach to information policy.

Public and Private Sector Roles

Both the public and private sectors have important and legitimate roles in the bibliographic control, distribution/dissemination, and use of government publications/information. Government, however, cannot totally abdicate a leadership role in product development and utilization.

Discussions of privatization tend to focus on cost reduction and presume that privatization results in high-service quality and program/service effectiveness. The presumption may not be totally accurate; in fact, cost reduction may shift costs to other categories and programs, as well as provide less service quality and effectiveness. This is especially true when government privatizes libraries, information centers, and other information and referral services (see Shill, 1990).

Clearly, partnerships between the public and private sectors may serve the public's interests. Nonetheless, government must ensure its commitment to information dissemination and meeting the information needs of the public. The public must hold government accountable and tap into the vast array of information products and services supported by the government.

With all the problems facing society and the enormous price tags for resolution of long-standing problems, government must neither abandon legitimate responsibilities nor more narrowly define its responsibilities. Cost reduction, while important, must be balanced against other considerations. However, mandates that government balance the budget and not incur further debts mean that sacrifices must be made. Information and social programs should be accorded more importance and not be the first items cut. Government officials need a balanced perspective and must place information and social programs in proper perspective.

Two important information policies relating to the private sector are OMB Circulars A-130 and A-76, which encourages the government to use commercial sources to supply the products and services the government needs. As noted earlier, A-130 treats government information as a commodity and favors use of the private sector. The circular also does not adequately treat government information as a public good. (The 1992 draft revision of the circular partially remedies these shortcomings; however, that draft has not yet replaced the original circular.) Circular A-76 has been used to privatize several major agency libraries, including the Department of Energy and National Oceanic and Atmospheric Administration (NOAA) libraries. This critical policy instrument discourages those agency dissemination initiatives which have been viewed as private sector commercial activities that should not be performed by Federal agencies unless the private sector cannot perform them more economically.

Costs of Dissemination

Typically, this issue examines the costs of agency dissemination programs and emphasizes the need to reduce or control costs and to provide indicators of cost effectiveness. An important aspect from the vantage point of libraries is limiting the cost to users.

Recently, a new aspect of the issue has emerged. As tax dollars have become scarce and the size of the Federal deficit has grown, Federal agencies are seeking alternative sources of revenue. One possible source is the sale of government information to the private sector and the citizenry. The Library of Congress has proposed legislation "for the provision of fee-based library research and information products and services" (S. 1416). "In other words, the user fees were to be a revenue source for financing certain LC programs and might even turn a handsome profit" (Sprehe, 1991, p. 10).

Sprehe (Ibid.), a former OMB official, has observed that

The lure of selling government information products may be irresistible for cash-starved agencies. We may be witnessing the rise of an entrepreneurial spirit at all levels of government, a mentality that, seeing the fiscal crisis as blotting out all other considerations, is determined to initiate user fees for information products— and damn the torpedoes.

As more state and local governments face dramatic losses of revenue, they are doing the same (see Allen, 1992). Because of this, Sprehe (1991, p. 10) also asserts that

> Ultimately, the local, state and federal electorates will have to decide whether profit making from government information resources is compatible with their concepts of the business of government.

Another OMB Circular A-25 (user fees), promulgated in 1958, encourages Federal agencies to charge fees for users of Federal services deriving a specific benefit which is not simultaneously provided to the general public. Coast Guard rescues, entry fees for national parks, and other services for which a specific beneficiary can clearly be identified are among the types of services for which user fees have historically been charged. NTIS's sale of documents to specific individuals or organizations is also rooted in this specific-benefit philosophy. The expansion of this practice more broadly to government publications and information, together with possible government copyrighting of information and software, would clearly challenge the public's right to equal access to publicly available government publications/information.

" 'Cost Sharing' for the Dissemination of Government Information in Electronic Formats" (1991, p. 1) underscores that depository libraries cannot "impose library user fees upon depository library patrons who desire to obtain government information which is available in electronic format." However, depository libraries will definitely be faced with added hardware, software, and personnel costs. At minimum, should they make a genuine effort to provide broad user access to government information in electronic formats? The GPO General Counsel's opinion indicates that Federal support for depository library online (not necessarily CD-ROM) access will be minimal. Clearly, depository libraries will have to assume a greater proportion of costs if they intend to provide the public with extensive access to electronic government information.

With a greater focus of attention on costs, accountability also becomes a more important issue. Undoubtedly, library managers and users will compare information costs to the value of information they receive/use. Depository librarians will have to become more adept at the conduct of research and evaluation studies so that they can demonstrate the cost effectiveness and cost benefit of programs, services, and collections.

Inclusion of Electronic Information in the Depository Program

Other chapters in this book discuss the topic. Suffice it to say, the number and diversity of electronic *products* entering the depository program will greatly expand, while electronic *services* will be introduced on a highly selective basis. Passage of the proposed GPO WINDO legislation (see Chapter 1), however, would expand the number of electronic services eligible for depository distribution. That legislation would make the GPO into a disseminator of electronic services (e.g., the *Federal Register, Congressional Record,* and selected databases) and, thereby, a competitor with other distributors of these databases. Yet, budgetary restrictions would likely limit the ability of the GPO to distribute a large number of electronic services, since there is no evidence that appropriations committees will increase funding of the depository program beyond $25 million.

The National High Performance Computing Act of 1991 (P.L. 102-194) will ultimately create a national network of *information superhighways* designed to transmit billions of bits of data per second. That network, known as the National Research and Education Network (NREN), has great opportunities for the gathering and transmission of knowledge, information, and data on a worldwide basis. Speaking from a private sector perspective, Allen (1992) asks: "Will the price of NREN be that the government can monitor public use of information in exchange for the right of access?" Another question is "What role can/should/will depository libraries play in such a networked environment?" The answer to the second question might require revision of the printing chapters of title 44 and restructuring of the depository library program. Furthermore, Hernon and McClure (1991, p. 26) caution:

> The view that the NREN will lead to significant increases in productivity, enhanced national competitiveness, and upgraded educational infrastructures, and that everyone can be a better researcher, educator, student, etc., must be tempered by awareness of the various issues yet to be resolved. Indeed, the technical issues associated with the development of the NREN may be easier to resolve than the social and behavioral ones. The development of the NREN, however, may recast both governmental and non-governmental information policy-making into very different contexts than policy-makers currently consider.

American Competitiveness

"Discussions of U.S. competitiveness typically are dominated by the international economic dimension" (Office of Technology Assessment, 1990, p. 7) and "by increasing innovative capacity," or "bringing the benefits of new technology more quickly and broadly to...[the Nation's] manufacturing firms" (Branscomb, 1991, p. 52). Congress has seen technical information as a resource promoting local economic development and enabling firms to compete more effectively with foreign business, as demonstrated in the passage of the 1986 Japanese Technical Literature Act (P. L. 99-382).

Other nations have assumed more of a leadership position in the development of information technology standards among Third World countries in the belief that their capital investment will expand trade and economic opportunities.

Economic competitiveness, therefore, underscores the necessity of having a supportive infrastructure, one that has yet to emerge in the United States.

Congress has pursued economic competitiveness through the Omnibus Trade and Competitiveness Act of 1988 (P. L. 100-418). Two purposes of competitiveness for Congress are to "ensure that the government sponsors research that industry can use" and "that industry does use that research" (Congress. House. Committee on Science, Space, and Technology, 1987, p. 2).

As the ability of the United States to compete in international markets declined, American business "pressed for relief from [the adoption of] stringent export controls" (Relyea, 1990, p. 37). The dramatic and historical changes taking place in the Soviet Union and Eastern Europe have resulted in some softening of regulatory power as exercised through national security and export controls. As seen in discussions over reauthorization of the Export Administration Act (S. 320), there is bipartisan support in Congress to limit enforcement to "the most sensitive high tech exports," or those relating to the production, transportation, and use of chemical and biological weapons; the release of trade secrets; or the advancement of terrorism ("Senate Approves Export Bill Linking Sanctions, Weapons," 1991, p. 455).

Congress expects NTIS to collect resources that will advance U.S. competitiveness. It would also like libraries to collect and retain more scientific and technical information produced in other countries. Clearly, the emphasis is on quantity of information and the presumption that at some point in time that information might lead to a scientific breakthrough or a competitive edge for U.S. industry in world markets. Despite these expectations, Congress is unwilling to fund libraries to accomplish these expectations.

IMPLICATIONS OF POLICY ISSUES FOR
DEPOSITORY PROGRAM: SUMMARY

OMB Circular A-130 is the closest approximation the United States has to a single all-encompassing information policy. This policy mandates lifecycle information management, but it has many omissions and shortcomings. It does not displace a body of other policy instruments. At times, these instruments are fragmented, overlapping, uncoordinated, and contradictory. No wonder that from the 95th through the 100th Congress, 1977 through 1988, more than 300 public laws dealing with information policy were enacted (Chartrand, 1989, p. 1). Added to this, many authorization and appropriation bills contained provisions that direct agency information policy activities. Furthermore, numerous administrative rules and regulations were proposed and implemented during this time period.

The library community is one of many interest groups participating in information policy formulation and review. The American Library Association (ALA) attempts to speak for the general public interest while also representing the specific interests of depository and other libraries. The Special Libraries Association, Association of Research Libraries, and the American Association of Law Libraries have also been active participants from the library community in information policy deliberations.

The library community, while not always united, has usually found itself in opposition to the Information Industry Association (IIA). Such public interest groups as OMB Watch, the Computer Professionals for Social Responsibility, and Public Citizen have also been active in the information policy debate, usually taking positions somewhere between the ALA and IIA stances. None of these interest groups is sufficiently strong to dominate the policy-making process, by itself, so policy outcomes are normally the result of consensus-building, negotiation, and compromise among the affected groups, plus initiatives by key actors in the Executive Branch (usually OMB) and Congress (usually key congressional staff members with considerable expertise and knowledge of information policy issues). Since legislative and regulatory actions are initiated with the Federal government, however, congressional staff members and agency officials have the considerable advantage of defining the agenda.

Success in this fast-shifting environment for the library community is affected by the:

- Preferences of the Administration;
- Preferences of key committee staff members;
- Ability of the library community to cultivate good relationships with key participants in Congress and OMB; and
- Ability to forge alliances with other interest groups.

Typically, interest groups stake out an initial negotiating position, realizing that that position may change as the policy debate proceeds and new alternatives are presented. Still, both ALA and the IIA have typically brought forward some basic principles and specific arguing points which are not subject to negotiation.

As discussions of a reauthorized Paperwork Reduction Act, a revised A-130, and other policy instruments emerge, the depository library community must participate and work with other stakeholders in the information environment, including the private sector. The depository library program may undergo extensive change as more technological opportunities emerge. Clearly, technology has changed documents librarianship. It is only a matter of time before technology changes the policy instruments directing the depository library program.

REFERENCES

Allen, Kenneth B. "Access to Government Information," *Government Information Quarterly,* 9 (1992): 67–80.

Branscomb, Lewis M. "Toward a U.S. Technology Policy," *Issues in Science and Technology* (Summer 1991), pp. 50–55.

Chartrand, R. L. "Information Policy and Technology Issues: Public Laws of the 95th through 100th Congress" (Washington, D.C.: Library of Congress, Congressional Research Service, 1989).

Congress. House. Committee on Science, Space, and Technology. Subcommittee on Science, Research and Technology. *The Role of Science and Technology in Competitiveness.* Hearings. Washington, D.C.: GPO, 1987 (*Y4.Sci2:100/22*).

" 'Cost Sharing' for the Dissemination of Government Information in Electronic Formats." Memorandum from Anthony J. Zagami, General Counsel, to the Public Printer, March 25, 1991.

Hernon, Peter. "Superintendent of Documents Operates an Outdated Vacuum Cleaner," *Government Information Quarterly,* 9 (1992): 99–105.

_____ and Charles R. McClure. *Federal Information Policies in the 1980s.* Norwood, NJ: Ablex, 1987.

_____ and Charles R. McClure. *Public Access to Government Information.* Norwood, NJ: Ablex, 1988.

_____ and Charles R. McClure. "United States Information Policies," in *National and International Information Policies,* edited by Wendy Schipper and Ann Marie Cunningham. Philadelphia, PA: The National Federation of Abstracting and Information Services, 1991, pp. 3–48.

"Interagency Conference on Public Access," *Government Information Quarterly,* 9 (1992): 187–198.

National Commission on Libraries and Information Science. "Glenerin Declaration: Statement of Policy," *Federal Register,* 52 (December 10, 1987): 46980–46981.

Office of Technology Assessment. *Informing the Nation.* Washington, D.C.: GPO, 1988 (*Y3.T22/2:2In3/9*).

"Recommendations," *Discovery* [newspaper of the White House Conference on Library and Information Services] (August 1991), pp. 5–14.

Relyea, Harold C. "Public Access through the Freedom of Information and Privacy Acts," in *Federal Information Policies in the 1980s,* edited by Peter Hernon and Charles R. McClure. Norwood, NJ: Ablex, 1987, pp. 52–82.

"Senate Approves Export Bill Linking Sanctions, Weapons," *Congressional Quarterly Weekly Report,* 49 (February 23, 1991): 455.

Shill, Harold B. "Privatization of Public Information: Its Impact on Libraries," *Library Administration & Management,* 5 (Spring 1991): 99–109.

Sprehe, J. Timothy. "Government Information Policy: Perspectives on Federal Issues," *Bulletin of the American Society for Information Science,* 18 (October/November 1991): 9–10.

Thompson, Lawrence H., Assistant Comptroller General, Human Resources Division, General Accounting Office. "Service to the Public: How Effective and Responsive Is the Government?" Statement before the House Committee on Ways and Means. *GAO/T–HRD-91-26,* May 8, 1991, pp. 1, 3, 10, and 13.

Chapter Three

GPO Pilot Projects*

Duncan M. Aldrich
Janita Jobe

Between 1989 and 1991 the United States Government Printing Office (GPO) initiated five pilot projects to assess the viability of distributing Federal information in electronic formats through the depository library program. This chapter discusses the origins of the GPO pilots and examines the implementation of the pilots in depository libraries. Examining the effectiveness of the pilot products from the perspective of depository librarians, the chapter concludes that the pilots will provide GPO with valuable information for future dialog among depository librarians, the GPO, and Federal agencies regarding the design and implementation of future Federal electronic products.

INTRODUCTION

Over the past decade the term "electronic library" has been employed to characterize what libraries are predicted to evolve into as information products and services are increasingly produced and distributed in electronic formats. Indeed, most libraries have come to depend on computerized infrastructures. Card catalogs and journal indexes, traditionally paper products, now reside on

* Special thanks is given to Jane Bartlett, head of the Government Printing Office's Information Technology Program. She provided much information on and many insights into the origins of the pilot projects.

mainframes and microcomputers. Libraries daily transfer massive quantities of digitized information over national networks, and most library office work is performed using microcomputer software. As libraries increasingly depend upon computers to manage their collections, publishers are making an ever-increasing number of information products available in electronic formats. These products range from digitized indexes and bibliographies to full-text electronic versions of books, encyclopedias, dictionaries, and periodicals (Larsen, 1988).

In response to this convergence of publishing trends and library computerization, and under the advisement of the American Library Association and the Depository Library Council, the Joint Committee on Printing (JCP) appointed in 1983 the Ad Hoc Committee on Depository Library Access to Federal Automated Data Bases. In its 1984 report to the Joint Committee on Printing, the Ad Hoc Committee recommended that the United States Government Printing Office (GPO) initiate pilot projects to test the viability of disseminating Federal information in electronic formats through the Federal depository library program (Congress, 1984, p. 10). Between 1988 and 1991, the GPO implemented five pilot projects.

Scope

This chapter provides an overview of the origins of the GPO pilot project program and examines the effectiveness of the pilot projects from the perspective of librarians. Discussion of the first four pilots constitutes a case study of the implementation of the four pilots in the Government Publications Department (GPD) at the University of Nevada, Reno (UNR). The focus of this section is on the day-by-day management decisions that were made as the pilot products were integrated into departmental operations and on the question of how functional the pilot products were in the GPD reference area. Discussion of the fifth pilot project, for which UNR was not a test site, is based on telephone interviews with librarians representing 13 of the 17 DOE test sites. The objective of this discussion is to identify what the librarians involved with the DOE pilot considered to be its strengths and its weaknesses. The telephone interviews were conducted between September 15 and 30, 1991.

The term used in this chapter to provide a context within which to discuss the impressions librarians had regarding the functionality of the pilot products is *usability*. From the perspective of library patrons, the user friendliness of software interfaces is the most significant aspect of usability. When products are user friendly, the average patron should be able to infer from information displayed to the screen how to manipulate the software. Only minimal consultation with paper manuals should be required.

From the perspective of library staff the most significant aspect of usability is the cost that libraries incur in providing service on electronic products.

Electronic products introduce potential cost increases in staff training, in training patrons to use the products, in generating on-demand information for patrons unable or unwilling to learn to use the products, and in managing the products. Equipment and space costs associated with electronic products can also be significant. Electronic products that require significant costs but generate minimal returns are not usable from the librarian's perspective. Assessments of the usability of the first four pilot projects are based on the subjective impressions of librarians at the University of Nevada, Reno.

PILOT PROJECTS

Origins

The Ad Hoc Committee on Depository Library Access to Federal Automated Data Bases was appointed by the Joint Committee on Printing (JCP) in May 1983 to evaluate the feasibility and desirability of providing depository libraries with access to government information in electronic formats. After hearing presentations about electronic information technologies from a number of public and private sector speakers, the committee resolved, on February 2, 1984, that (Congress, 1984, p. 10)

> The Committee unanimously supports the principle that the Federal Government should provide access to Federal information, as defined in 44 U.S.C. 1901, in electronic form through the depository library system. Recognizing that it is technologically feasible to provide such access to electronic information, the Committee recommends that the economic feasibility be investigated through pilot projects.

The Ad Hoc Committee also recommended that the JCP and Superintendent of Documents "together initiate a pilot program, through which depository libraries could access Federal information electronically and provide that information to the general public, free of charge" (Ibid.). In response to this recommendation, the JCP sent a letter asking for proposals for pilot projects to heads of all Federal departments and agencies in June 1986. The letter assured agencies that "every effort will be made to establish a range of pilots that test various methods of electronic dissemination and serve different types of depository libraries (medical, legal, public, etc.). Due consideration will also be given to existing policy guidelines under which participating agencies are required to operate" (Mathias, 1986). Sixteen agencies responded with proposals.

The JCP then charged the Ad Hoc Committee with two tasks. One was to review the proposals and make recommendations about which pilots "would best demonstrate the economic feasibility of regularly providing data in electronic format to the depository libraries" (Congress, 1987, p. 1). The second charge was to identify the steps needed to implement and evaluate the projects. Two subcommittees were created within the Ad Hoc Committee to fulfill these charges; the Technical Subcommittee to review the agencies' proposals and the Criteria Subcommittee to establish the evaluation criteria for the projects.

In January 1987, the Ad Hoc Committee on Depository Library Access to Federal Automated Data Bases (1987) submitted a report to the JCP recommending that the planning, administration, and implementation of the projects be undertaken by the GPO and that a Pilot Projects Office be created within the GPO. In addition to its responsibility for the pilot projects, the Office would also develop plans for the general dissemination of electronic information to depository libraries (Ibid., p. 3). Furthermore, the Ad Hoc Committee recommended that "the Joint Committee on Printing request Congress to provide funding to the Superintendent of Documents for planning in the FY 1987 supplemental and for pilot projects in the FY 1988 budget" (Ibid., p. 2).

The Ad Hoc Committee also suggested criteria for the selection of pilot projects and of test sites for the pilots. The selection criteria for pilot products were many. First, an attempt should be made to identify products for both specialized and general audiences. Specialized products may include technical reports and economic statistics. General products may include tax information, census reports, and legislative information. Second, it was recommended that the pilots compare products in paper, microfiche, and electronic formats. Third, pilots should include a variety of types of data (text, numerical, bibliographic, and graphic). Fourth, data from all three branches of government should be included. Fifth, pilots should involve information previously available only in traditional formats as well as products available only in electronic formats. Sixth, the pilots should test the production and dissemination of publications through a variety of entities, such as the GPO, executive agencies, contractors, and commercial vendors. The final recommendation was that pilots should include both time sensitive and static information (Ibid., p. 7).

Criteria for the selection of libraries included the recommendation that pilot site libraries be geographically dispersed, and that they be of varying type, size, and subject specialty. Participating libraries should include libraries with access to electronic networks and libraries without such access. Further, the recommendation was made that libraries selected as test sites should have sufficient trained (or trainable) staff, complementary subject collections to back up information in the pilot, a plan for public access, sufficient funds to service and house equipment, and access to proper utilities (Ibid., p. 8).

The report estimated that the cost of the pilot projects for a four-year test would be over $5.5 million. Included in the Committee's suggested budget was a recommendation that Congress appropriate funds for equipment for one test library in every congressional district. This recommendation reflected the

Committee's belief that unless comparable equipment was made available to all potential test site libraries, the pilots would concentrate in wealthy libraries and would "not fairly evaluate the needs of the general public" (Ibid., p. 9). The JCP accepted the recommendations of the Ad Hoc Committee in April 1987 and directed GPO to request $800,000 for fiscal year 1988 to fund pilot project activities ("Dissemination of Information in Electronic Format to Federal Depository Libraries," 1988, p. 5). Although Congress did not appropriate money to support the pilots, the JCP instructed the GPO to continue to plan, administer, and evaluate the pilots, and to do so using existing funds.

As a first step in implementing the JCP mandate, the GPO established the Information Technology Program (ITP) within Library Programs Services division, in Spring 1987, and immediately began examining electronic information dissemination technologies. In light of the absence of a budget for the pilots, the GPO abandoned or modified many of the Ad Hoc Committee's more ambitious recommendations. Criteria for selection of pilots were redefined as "costs, willingness of the publishing agency to participate in the planning of the project, value of the information to the public, size of publication, frequency of update, search requirements, and the publishing schedule" (Ibid., p. 8). Costs had become the primary criterion.

Jointly, the JCP and the GPO narrowed the field to five projects. Those selected for implementation were *CD-ROM Test Disc 2*, containing the *1982 Census of Retail Trade by Zip Code* and the *1982 Census of Agriculture*, the Environmental Protection Agency's (EPA) *Toxic Chemical Release Inventory* on CD-ROM, the final edition of the 1985 *Congressional Record* on CD-ROM, the Commerce Department's online *Economic Bulletin Board*, and the Department of Energy's (DOE) online *Integrated Technical Information System*. The projects selected provided a variety of types of information: economic and agricultural statistics, environmental data, bibliographic records of scientific and technical reports, and full-text transmissions of legislative and economic information. The different data products were to be tested in various electronic media.

Setting

The Government Publications Department at the University of Nevada, Reno, which serves herein as a case study for the first four pilots, is a regional U.S. depository, a partial depository for United Nations publications, and a depository for state of Nevada publications. The department also acquires materials from various other international governmental organizations, foreign countries, and states. GPD first acquired a microcomputer workstation in 1982 for online searching and office work. The department's second microcomputer was purchased in 1987 to provide end-user access to *GDCS*, a CD-ROM version of the *Monthly Catalog of United States Government Publications*. Since 1987 GPD has acquired four more public access CD-ROM workstations. GPD is staffed by two librarians, three library technicians, and a weekly average of 100 hours of student assistance. All GPD staff work approximately 12 hours each week on the GPD reference desk. The staff had very little experience with microcomputer applications prior to the arrival of the pilot project products. Knowledge of DOS management was minimal.

The 17 test site libraries for the DOE pilot project were: Cleveland Public Library, College of William and Mary, Denver Public Library, Eastern Washington University, Emporia State University, Louisiana State University, Oklahoma Department of Libraries, Rice University, Texas A & M University, University of Colorado at Boulder, University of Kentucky, University of Massachusetts, University of Minnesota, University of New Mexico, University of Tennessee at Knoxville, Utah State University, and West Virginia University.

CD-ROM Test Disc 2

Census *CD-ROM Test Disc 2* (Bureau of Census, 1989, 1988) was the first nonbibliographic CD-ROM product received in the UNR documents department. As such, *Test Disc 2* presented the first opportunity for GPD staff to manage and provide access to CD-ROM data files. A simple windows software produced by the Census Bureau was distributed with the *Test Disc* on separate floppy diskettes. This software, a prototype that has evolved over the past four years, is generally referred to as the Census GO software. The *Test Disc* files, stored in dBase format, are also accessible through various off the shelf database software packages that can use or import dBase files. Detailed print documentation was distributed describing the Agricultural files on *Test Disc 2*. Printed documentation for the *Test Disc*'s Retail Trade files was less detailed. Documentation did not include instructions on using the GO interface. Equipment needed to run the *Test Disc* is minimal—all that is required is an AT or XT microcomputer with a CD-ROM drive with CD- ROM extensions.

GPO distributed *Test Disc 2* with directions for installing the CD, but with no instructions or recommendations on how documents departments should integrate the product into their collections and service. At UNR the *Test Disc* was installed on the one CD-ROM workstation then available, at that time a dedicated workstation for a CD-ROM version of the *Monthly Catalog*. Installation of the *Test Disc* provided the first of many on-the-fly lessons in managing electronic depository materials. Though GPD staff had sufficient DOS management skills to install the *Test Disc* interface software, the requirement that CD-ROM extensions software be loaded on the workstation was puzzling. The one CD-ROM product then in use automatically loaded CD extensions during installation, so it had been assumed that all CD-ROM interfaces were capable of communicating directly with CD drives. After some investigation, and several weeks wait, CD extensions were acquired and the *Test Disc* was installed.

To determine what level of reference service GPD staff should provide on the *Test Disc*, the GPD librarian responsible for electronic products examined the

GO interface. Owing to GO's simplicity, the librarian decided that no formal staff training beyond a short demonstration on how to load and boot the product would be necessary. Interested staff were encouraged to examine the *Test Disc* more thoroughly. The expectation was that most patrons would not need assistance on GO and that staff, if asked to provide assistance, would quickly infer how to manipulate the software.

Completely menu-driven, GO presents the user with a series of menus which, as the user works through them, progressively narrow the topical and the geographic focus of a search. The Census of Agriculture, for example, initially prompts users to select a topic, then prompts them to select a state. After selecting a state, users are presented a list of counties from which to choose. The next screen displays the data on that topic for the selected county. The GO software for the Retail Trade database works in essentially the same manner— choice of type of business, choice of state, and then choice of ZIP code. At this level, GO is very usable both from the perspective of library patrons and library staff. Most patrons will readily learn to manipulate the software in a few minutes. Libraries will expend minimal time managing the software, training staff, and providing reference assistance.

Unfortunately, patrons seeking even moderately complex data will find GO cumbersome to use. To create multicounty or multi-code datasets, for example, patrons must print data one county at a time, then manually interfile information from the printouts. Furthermore, GO does not allow for downloading. At base, GO is ill suited for more sophisticated users. These limitations within GO, as released on *Test Disc 2*, cloud assessments of the disc's usability from the perspective of many library patrons. A more powerful software is desirable. To partially skirt these limitations of GO, GPD installed a database management software (dBase) for patrons desiring more elaborate *Test Disc* information. However, owing to the significant investment in time that would be required to train the GPD staff to use database management software, GPD staff were not required to learn the database software. Consequently, they were not expected to train patrons to use it. Furthermore, it was presumed that training patrons to use complicated software was not within the scope of the library's overall mission. Other more appropriate agencies are available for patrons desiring instruction in dBase. As with GO, the basic obligation of staff was to load the CD, to boot the software, and to provide the documentation.

Though disappointed with GO's lack of power, and frustrated at being unable to provide more elaborate service on the database software, the electronic products librarian concluded that, with improvement, products like the *Test Disc* could be useful and usable in the documents reference setting.

Toxic Release Inventory (TRI)

The *Toxic Chemical Release Inventory* CD-ROM (TRI) (Environmental Protection Agency, 1990) contains a large body of data on toxic materials released into the environment by private and public organizations. Produced on a single CD, *TRI* data are accessed through SearchExpress, a search software interface licensed to the Environmental Protection Agency (EPA) by Executive Technologies of Birmingham, Alabama. Because the *TRI* data are stored in neither dBase nor ASCII, they are readily accessible only through the SearchExpress interface. The software is distributed with the CD on separate floppy diskettes. The *TRI CD-ROM Users Guide*, a well-designed and usually easy-to-follow manual, completes the *TRI* package. Equipment requirements for *TRI* are minimal, an XT or AT microcomputer with CD-ROM drive and CD-ROM extensions will operate the product.

The GPO distributed the *TRI* disc in June 1990 and, as had been the case with Census *Test Disc 2*, provided no instructions or suggestions for integrating the product into depository reference services. At the time *TRI* arrived, the UNR documents department had acquired an additional CD-ROM workstation on which to run CIS CD-ROM indexes. *TRI* would share the CIS workstation. It was believed that installation of *TRI* would be relatively easy owing to the many DOS management lessons that had been learned while coping with *Test Disc 2*. Unfortunately, the instructions for loading *TRI* software included a confusing discussion of interface options. It was not clear from the instructions what the significance of differences among options were. After pondering the instructions for some time, the decision was made to load the option that appeared to be the more powerful. In the end, installation of *TRI* had led to several more on-the-fly lessons in DOS management.

GPD's electronic products librarian examined the SearchExpress interface and concluded that it was both powerful and functional, but that the interface was not intuitive and was so complex that it would be difficult to integrate into the documents reference setting. He also predicted, in light of the usual sort of reference inquiries received in GPD, that *TRI* would not be much used. Owing to the combination of difficult software and projected low use, it was decided that because training GPD staff to become proficient with the *TRI* interface would divert too much time from ongoing responsibilities, GPD staff would not be trained to provide reference assistance on TRI. GPD staff would be informed that the product was available and shown how to load and boot the CD. Beyond that, patrons wishing to use *TRI* would be given the *TRI CD-ROM Users Guide*, then left on their own.

To fulfill GPO requirements to make depository materials available, it was decided that patrons seeking *TRI* information would be encouraged to use the *TRI* microfiche product, which contains essentially the same information as the CD-ROM. However, patrons occasionally insisted upon using the CD and GPD staff were inevitably called upon to attempt to provide assistance. Each attempt to use the CD-ROM was abandoned in favor of microfiche. The inability of GPD staff to provide effective service on a product available in the department (*TRI*) created feelings of ineffectiveness and ineptness. The prospect of receiving more

CD products as convoluted as *TRI* added fuel to these feelings of inadequacy. It was unofficially decided at that time that if overwhelmed by products as difficult as TRI, GPD would not be able to provide service on the products. In this sense, the products would not only have few qualities of usability, they would simply not be used.

TRI software is difficult to learn primarily owing to its complexity. *TRI* functions are listed in five windows that drop down from a banner crossing the top of the screen. When initially booted, *TRI* automatically displays the functions listed in the FIND window. FIND functions include "Advanced Search," "Word Search," "Search for Similar Objects," and "Search Only Recently Added." Upon first encountering these options it is not obvious which is the most appropriate to use to search the database, so before even a perfunctory search can be performed the user is forced to consult *TRI*'s paper documentation. This confusion regarding terms identifying SearchExpress functions persists throughout the *TRI* interface. For example, users wishing to display a record to the screen may toy around with the READ function for some time before turning to the *TRI CD-ROM Users' Guide* to learn that ZOOM, not READ, is the *TRI* display function. Unfortunately for users depending upon their intuition, most other software products use the term ZOOM to expand or contract the current screen display, along the lines of a zoom lens on a camera. Likewise, most software packages use terms, such as DISPLAY, VIEW, Print-to-Screen, or READ, to display search results. Other software design problems exacerbate this confusion. The most noticeable is that one entire window on the main menu banner, CREATE, does not work at all.

From the perspective of casual or occasional patrons, *TRI* is too difficult to be considered usable in the library reference setting. Patrons who anticipate using the *TRI* data in depth or on a regular basis, on the other hand, may find *TRI* useful and, with considerable self-training and practice, find the software to be usable. However, the amount of time in-depth *TRI* users will require on the CD workstation poses an additional problem from the perspective of librarians. The CD workstation which houses *TRI* also serves as the only access point to many other CD products—bibliographic, full text, and data. Products like *TRI* that may tie up a workstation for hours are obviously an impediment to patrons desiring to use other CD products. The overall assessment of TRI, then, was that the software made it too difficult to use in the library setting, both from the staff and patron perspectives.

Economic Bulletin Board (EBB)

The *EBB* (Department of Commerce, 1988) is a microcomputer-based electronic bulletin board supported by the Department of Commerce's Office of Business Analysis. Information contained in the *EBB* includes current and historical statistical data from the Bureau of Labor Statistics, the Bureau of the Census, the

International Trade Administration, the Bureau of Economic Analysis, and several other Federal agencies. The software selected for the board is TBBS, a widely used shareware software. No paper documentation accompanies a subscription to the *EBB*. Equipment requirements to access the *EBB* are minimal. A microcomputer workstation with at least a 300 baud modem, telecommunications software, and a phone line are all that is required. A faster modem and hard drive are strongly recommended. The workstation need not be based on PC DOS. To become participants in the *EBB* pilot, libraries were required to submit an application to the GPO which included an outline of how the library would use the *EBB*. Owing to the required written application, the *EBB* was the first pilot that required libraries to plan for implementing use of the pilot product before it became available. The GPO selected 100 of the 361 libraries that applied to serve as test sites.

Examination of the *EBB* software interface at UNR required only a few minutes to ascertain that the TBBS software was relatively easy to navigate, though it must be noted that the librarian examining the software had previous experience on similar electronic bulletin boards. Libraries not familiar with bulletin boards will presumably experience a somewhat steeper learning curve. Regardless, most users of the *EBB* should be able to learn the software in an hour or two. The organization of the information on the *EBB* is similar to most bulletin boards. *EBB* data FILES are posted to the board as hundreds of individual FILES. The FILES are sorted into broad subject groupings referred to as AREAS, with each AREA title indicating the general topic of FILES it contains. As of November 11, 1991, the *EBB* is divided into 17 AREAS containing 1,318 FILES comprising 30,739,737 total bytes. Separate from the FILES is a list of bulletins that have been posted to the board. The main shortcoming of the EBB, as with most electronic bulletin board software, is the lack of automated search mechanisms, such as keyword searching. The only subject access to the *EBB* is through the list of FILES. Much like in paper or microfiche documents having tables of contents but no index, users must page back and forth between the list of FILES and actual FILES to determine which FILES meet their information needs.

The first decision made regarding access to the *EBB* at UNR was to download and print a list of FILES. This list would be consulted when *EBB* data were thought to be a potential source to answer patron inquiries. If a likely FILE was identified from the printed list, a GPD librarian would log into the *EBB* and download or print the desired information. End-user access to the *EBB* was not made available. Although the software would be relatively easy for patrons to master, it was believed that librarians trained to use the *EBB* would be more efficient at identifying and downloading FILES than would occasional *EBB* users. Efficient use of the *EBB* was thought important because the board is accessed via a long distance phone call. Extraneous use would incur unwarranted phone bills. The possibility that on-demand service on the *EBB* would impinge upon the librarians work schedule was considered, but the ease of using the *EBB* persuaded librarians that, unless an overwhelming number of requests were received, such demand would not present a problem.

A second decision regarding access to *EBB* information was regularly to download the *EBB*'s CPI.EXE file, which summarizes in considerable detail the current Consumer Price Index. The printout of CPI.EXE was housed at the documents reference desk. Because CPI.EXE is posted to the *EBB* the day of its release, access to CPI information in GPD became significantly more timely than it had been prior to the availability of the *EBB*.

Overall, demand for *EBB* data, even with the printed list of FILES available for consultation, was limited. Undoubtedly, part of the explanation for the low level of demand was that GPD staff, not accustomed to providing full text or numeric data files from bulletin boards, had not yet worked *EBB* into their reference routines. Additionally, when the list of *EBB* FILES was referred to, the brevity of description in the list tended to occasion uncertainty. Furthermore, because *EBB* FILES are not indexed in standard reference sources, such as *American Statistics Index (ASI)*, staff would reasonably tend to turn first to publications that are well indexed. So, though the software was usable and *EBB* FILES were of potential use to patrons, the lack of a search software, in combination with the absence of indexing in standard reference sources, limited actual use of the EBB.

Because the *EBB* was not made available for use by library patrons, the question of its usability can only be assessed from the librarians perspective. At UNR there was little or no difficulty mastering the software. In fact, the *EBB* was the most used, useful, and usable of the pilot projects. Because the *EBB* was accessed online, it was treated much like traditional online bibliographic databases. As with bibliographic databases, only librarians would learn to use the EBB. In fact, most work on the *EBB* would be performed by one librarian. This decision minimized investment in staff training, and, because the *EBB* was not made available to patrons, no time was committed to training patrons to use the product. Furthermore, because the *EBB* was easy to use, little time would be lost learning the software and performing searches. Perhaps because the *EBB* was used in this more traditional mode librarians found it comfortable to work it into their daily routine. Additionally, because the *EBB* was accessed from the same microcomputer workstation that is used in GPD for online searching, the *EBB* did not compete with patron demand for access to other electronic products, and no investment was required for new equipment.

Congressional Record

The *Congressional Record on CD-ROM* (Congress, 1990b) is a two CD product containing the final bound edition of the 1985 paper *Congressional Record*, minus tables and graphics. The *Congressional Record* CD's software interface,

Quantum Leap, is produced by Quantum Access, Inc., of Houston, Texas. The software is housed on the CD and can be booted either directly from the CD or loaded to a microcomputer workstation's hard drive. Specialized indexes traditionally available in the paper *Congressional Record*, such as the History of Bills and Resolutions and the Daily Digest, are contained on the discs. Documentation for the product is attractively packaged and is reasonably easy to follow. Equipment requirements are again minimal, requiring only an XT or AT workstation having a CD-ROM drive and CD-ROM extensions.

As with *Test Disc 2* and *TRI*, the *Congressional Record* CD arrived with no suggestions on how to integrate the product into documents department reference services. To assess how the *Congressional Record on CD-ROM* should be integrated into GPD service, the electronic products librarian installed and carefully examined the CD's software interface. His first observation was that installation procedures for the Congressional Record CD represented a significant improvement over *TRI* and *Test Disc 2*. Because the Record can be run directly from the CD, librarians are saved the time of installing the interface to a hard drive and, more importantly, are saved space on their hard drive.

Beyond installation, however, it was predicted that the *Congressional Record on CD-ROM* would be a catastrophe in terms of usability in the library setting. The primary problem was that the software was not at all intuitive. To perform virtually any function on the *Congressional Record on CD-ROM* the user is forced to consult the *Congressional Record on CD-ROM Tutorial and Reference Manual* (Congress, 1990a). For use in a library setting, where most users seek quick, small segments of information, to be confronted with a product that requires extensive consultation with a manual is extremely frustrating. At first glance the interface for the *Congressional Record on CD-ROM* is remarkably obscure—it does not get much clearer with practice.

As on *TRI*, commands for the *Congressional Record on CD-ROM* are listed in windows that drop down from a banner crossing the top of the screen. Unfortunately, the choice of headers for the windows is not always clear without consulting the *Reference Manual*. The meaning of OUTLINE, NOTE, and QA are particularly obscure. Though the SEARCH function window does clearly indicate the nature of functions available in the window, it is distinctly difficult to figure out how to formulate a search from information provided on the search screen. That users must hit <Control> B rather than hit <Return> to initiate the search is troublesome. The purpose and workings of several functions, such as STICKY NOTE, cannot be fathomed without consulting the users manual.

An additional problem with the *Congressional Record* interface is that searches retrieve an overwhelming number of irrelevant hits. In nearly every search, for example, the first item that displays is the daily prayer. Though further examination reveals that software functions are available to limit the number of hits retrieved in searches, the fact that these functions must be employed for simple searches merely amplifies the impression that the *Congres-*

sional Record interface is too complicated to be considered usable in the library reference setting. A substantial amount of time must be invested to gain a minimal level of competence on the software. From the casual or occasional users' perspective this is unacceptable. To these users the *Congressional Record on CD-ROM* is not usable.

From the librarians' perspective providing staff training on the *Congressional Record on CD-ROM* would be prohibitively time consuming. Consequently, as with *TRI* and with database management software, it was decided not to train staff to provide reference assistance on the *Congressional Record on CD-ROM*. Staff were informed that the CD was available, were shown how to load and boot the system, and were encouraged to examine the interface if they were so inclined. Beyond that, staff were encouraged to advise patrons to use the daily paper copy of the *Record*, which is awkward to use but is much easier to learn to use than is the CD-ROM. Patrons wanting to use the CD rather than paper would be on their own. The bottom line was that the *Congressional Record on CD-ROM* was the CD that broke the librarians back. The arrival of yet another CD product that was too difficult to train patrons to use was exasperating.

DOE Pilot

The Department of Energy (DOE) pilot project was designed to assess ways to improve the dissemination of, access to, and utilization of DOE scientific and technical information. As initially conceived, the pilot would have two phases. Phase I contained two components. The "Information Access" component provided electronic access to DOE's energy database—the Integrated Technical Information System (ITIS). The second component of Phase I, referred to as "Alternative Media for Full Text Delivery," sought input from librarians through a written survey to determine what librarians believed would be the optimum media for distributing the full text of DOE technical reports to depository libraries. Phase II of the DOE pilot, which was intended to select and test a system for delivering DOE reports electronically, was not funded and there are no plans to implement it.

Eighteen libraries were selected for participation in the "Information Access" component of Phase I; one withdrew very early. This component entailed two distinct elements, online searching and uploading bibliographic records. Online searching centered on access to ITIS, which provided participating libraries with access to recent bibliographic records of DOE documents. The ITIS database is equivalent to the paper *Energy Research Abstracts* (Department of Energy, 1976-). A gateway allowed participants to switch to the commercial system (Dialog) to search older energy database materials. Both menu- and command-driven modes were available. Libraries were also given the capability to upload DOE bibliographic records and use a COSATI to MARC conversion utility to transform and transfer bibliographic records from ITIS into their libraries' online catalogs. It was assumed that the libraries could use existing programs to convert the transferred records into a format which would be compatible with their catalogs. Of the 17 libraries involved in the project, only 2 had success loading the DOE bibliographic records into their online catalogs; 1 of the 17 had no online catalog and thus did not participate in that part of the project.

An informal telephone survey of 13 of the 17 sites involved in the DOE pilot suggested several problems in the cataloging component of the project. The primary complaint was that transferring DOE records occupied too much time. The shear volume of records (approximately 18,000 annually) was the principal source of this problem. The initial plan that records would be downloaded via phone lines, in fact, was so time consuming that most libraries opted to receive the records on tapes. Unfortunately, uploading tapes into inhouse systems was also time-consuming. Only one library reported having no problems downloading from ITIS or uploading the records into their local catalogs. Furthermore, the MARC-like records that DOE provided were not compatible with most library systems. The local support and expertise necessary to write programs which could read the records into local databases was not available in most libraries. Costs associated with use of computer time and storage space were yet another problem.

Furthermore, because ITIS records are not in MARC format and do not use Library of Congress subject headings, they created an authority disaster for most library catalogs. Keyword searching was possible and frequently effective, however, because DOE had assigned descriptors. Author and corporate author headings were also unlike LC headings. Basically, most of the pilot libraries found the records unusable in the format offered through the pilot project. Of the sixteen test sites with online catalogs, only two successfully loaded the bibliographic records. Despite these problems with ITIS records and the apparent low levels of success, participants generally concluded that access to ITIS bibliographic records should be available to depository libraries that select DOE reports. Additionally, they believed that the GPO should continue to pursue ways to make these records available in usable and inexpensive formats.

The second segment of the "Information Access" component involved online access to the latest 14 months of records in ITIS. A "gateway" from ITIS to Dialog's DOE database was provided for searching older records. While demand for the database varied among libraries, those who used it found it usable and appropriate for libraries. Access to the ITIS database was appreciated owing to a discount rate that was provided for pilot test sites. The Dialog gateway was less attractive because there was no discount offered. The ongoing commercial rate for Dialog searching of the Energy Science and Technology database is $93.00/ hr and .60¢/citation (*Dialog Database Catalog*, 1991). In fact, test sites having NTIS on CD-ROM reported that they used the CD rather than Dialog as first choice for identifying older DOE reports.

One aspect of the ITIS online searching segment of the DOE pilot that librarians did not welcome was the tight security that DOE required. Generally, only one person per site received training on ITIS and searching was presumably limited to that person. This necessitated that searching be done by appointment, which some librarians felt limited demand for the database by eliminating casual searching in ITIS. Cost associated with this component of the project was also troublesome to some participants. While most libraries did subsidize online searching for patrons on the pilot project databases, others had little option but to pass charges along to patrons. Computation of charges was tedious because the system did not report costs at the end of the search. Searchers had to track logon time and calculate costs based on time and number of citations. Overall, reviews of the ITIS software varied. Many libraries reported that it was more cumbersome and more difficult to use than Dialog; others thought it much like Dialog in difficulty only different in structure. The most frequent complaint was that there was no subject access. Users had to rely on keywords.

Experiences librarians had implementing the DOE pilot prompted several suggestions for future efforts to provide electronic access to DOE bibliographic records. For example, one suggestion was that if dissemination of DOE bibliographic records is to continue along the lines tested in the pilot, DOE or GPO must provide on site technical support. Without such support, many libraries will be unable to use the product. A proposed alternative was that the DOE make the records available to libraries for loading as independent files in their inhouse catalogs. Systems that can house such files are currently available from several vendors. The purchase cost of the system, presumably, would be the responsibility of individual libraries.

A common suggestion was that DOE should develop a CD-ROM version of the energy database for distribution to depository libraries. Though recent DOE records would continue to be available only through ITIS or through commercial database vendors, a well designed CD-ROM would provide all patrons free and ready access to most reports. Prospects of CD-ROM access, however, did not generally dissuade librarians from their belief that inhouse catalogs have the greatest potential for providing widespread access to DOE information. Another proposal was that DOE records be made available to a bibliographic utility (OCLC, RLIN, or WLN) just as GPO records are. Records would then be automatically available to all network users to tag with their holdings identifiers. This option, which would mainstream DOE records, would minimize the need for tape loading and local support associated with other options. Another suggestion involving existing electronic networks was that DOE establish an INTERNET connection. Costs to libraries for transferring records via the INTERNET would be considerably less than transfer by phone line, diskette, or tape. While this alternative is not available to non-INTERNET libraries, it would be efficient for those with INTERNET access.

Yet another suggestion was that a joint GPO/DOE venture along the lines suggested in the GPO WINDO bill be implemented (H.R. 102-2772) (U.S. House, 1991). In this scenario, the GPO would provide a centralized online window to many Federal databases, including the energy database. With the full text of reports available through the WINDO for on demand downloading, libraries would net tremendous savings in space and stack maintenance. Even DOE might net savings under this scheme by having to distribute only those documents that are specifically requested. A final suggestion was that the accession lists to DOE microfiche that were distributed to pilot libraries become depository items. The pilot sites thought the lists extremely useful as current awareness tools. Many libraries found that routing the lists to their clientele noticeably increased demand for current reports. Accession lists would help achieve DOE's objective of increasing use of the collection if made available to all libraries receiving microfiche reports.

CONCLUSION

One specific lesson learned from participating in the pilots was that the level of microcomputer management skills necessary to implement the pilot products was not available in GPD. Though the requisite skills were learned in dealing with the pilots and other electronic products, it quickly became obvious that if libraries are widely to adopt computer products, graduates of library science programs must be equipped with extensive training in microcomputing technology, including DOS management and telecommunication software skills. Library administrators must invest more resources to train staff in the use and management of electronic products. Furthermore, additional staffing may be required at reference desks—or the decision must be made to drop some of the more difficult electronic products. The only viable alternative is for providers of electronic products to produce software that is exceptionally user friendly. Improved software will significantly reduce demands on staff time, which, in turn, will make the products usable in the library setting. This prospect is certainly more palatable to librarians than increasing staff or eliminating electronic products.

Conclusions regarding the viability of the specific products made available through the pilot projects are mixed. *CD-ROM Test Disc 2* was usable at a very simple level but was not useful for sophisticated patrons. The other two CD pilots, *TRI* and the *Congressional Record on CD-ROM*, had interfaces that were too complex and obscure to be usable by most library patrons. The inability of GPD to commit staff time to the training that would be required to operate these products precluded them from regular departmental reference services. Had the software interfaces been friendlier, the decision would have been to make the products available. Of the two online pilot projects, the *EBB* was relatively successful both because it fit readily into existing online bibliographic database procedures and because the software interface was relatively easy to learn. The DOE project was less successful, owing largely to the technical complexity of the project which demanded significant investments on the part of library staff and resources.

These shortcomings, however, are precisely what pilot projects are initiated to identify. Overall, the pilot projects succeeded in exposing librarians to a variety of electronic products and in eliciting responses from librarians (often negative) on the functionality of those products in the library environment. Comments regarding the inadequacy of some pilot project products will provide useful information from the perspective of librarians for future plans to distribute electronic products through the depository library program. That information will become available in the results of follow-up surveys that the GPO conducted on all but the *Test Disc 2* project.

The primary implication of the pilot projects is that input from depository librarians is essential from the ground level in future planning efforts if electronic products are to succeed in depository libraries. The most appropriate forum for this input would be a dialog among depository librarians, Federal agencies, and the GPO—with the GPO presumably assuming the role of moderator. One apparent outcome of this dialog should be a list of criteria suggesting how electronic products might be configured to be considered user friendly in the library setting. The pilot projects also suggest that two criteria for software targeted for depository libraries is that the software be both powerful and easy to use. Some preliminary efforts to suggest standards for CD-ROM software in the library setting have been made (Zink, 1991). The fact that the Depository Library Council to the Public Printer has recently completed a chapter on management of electronic materials for the *Federal Depository Library Manual* (1985) suggests that Depository Library Council would be an appropriate vehicle for developing such a list of criteria.

Lest it appear that the documents department at UNR has simply ignored every CD-ROM product that has arrived, it is noted that many CD products have been integrated into GPD reference service with varying degrees of use and success. One microcomputer workstation is dedicated to *GDCS* (1986–), the *Monthly Catalog* on CD-ROM. Another station has the three CIS CD products, *P.A.I.S.*, and the *Index to United Nations Documents* issued by the READEX corporation. Several Patent and Trademark Office CD-ROMs are available on a third workstation. A fourth workstation is set aside for CD-ROMs containing full-text files, such as *NTDB*, and data files, including the various Bureau of the Census economic, foreign trade, and decennial census CD-ROMs. Because software on these products is more user friendly (particularly *NTDB*'s Browse interface), or because there is constant demand for information on a product (such as *CIS Congressional Masterfile*), the products are regularly used. Those with user-friendly software, such as *NTDB* and more recent versions of Census *GO*, may serve as models for future software interface designs.

REFERENCES

Ad Hoc Committee on Depository Library Access to Federal Automated Data Bases, *Report to the Joint Committee on Printing*, (Unpublished) 1987.

Bureau of the Census. *CD-ROM Test Disc 2* [machine-readable data file]. Washington, DC: The Bureau, 1989.

Bureau of the Census. *CD-ROM Test Disc 2 Technical Documentation*. Washington, DC: The Bureau, 1988.

Congress. Joint Committee on Printing. Ad Hoc Committee on Depository Library Access to Federal Automated Data Bases. *Provision of Federal Government Publications in Electronic Format to Depository Libraries*. Washington, DC: GPO, 1984 *(Y4.P9311:P96/2)*.

Congress. *Congressional Record on CD-ROM Tutorial and Reference Manual: Proceedings and Debates of the 99th Congress, First Session, January 3, 1985 to December 20, 1985*. Washington, DC: GPO, 1990a

Congress. *Congressional Record on CD-ROM: Proceedings and Debates of the 99th Congress, First Session* [machine-readable text file]. Washington, DC: GPO, 1990b.

Department of Commerce. *Economic Bulletin Board (EBB)* [electronic bulletin board]. Washington, DC: Dept. of Commerce, 1988.

Department of Energy. Office of Scientific and Technical Information. *Energy Research Abstracts*. Oak Ridge, Tennessee: Dept. of Energy, 1976-.

Dialog Database Catalog. Palo Alto, CA: Dialog Information Services, Inc., 1991.

"Dissemination of Information in Electronic Format to Federal Depository Libraries," *Administrative Notes*, 9 (July 1988): 1–26 *(GP3.16/3–2:9)*

Environmental Protection Agency. *Toxic Release Inventory on CD-ROM* [machine-readable data file]. Washington, DC: EPA, 1990.

Federal Depository Library Manual. Washington, DC: GPO, 1985.

GDCS (Government Documents Catalog Service) [machine-readable text files]. Pomona, CA: Auto-graphics, Inc., 1986-.

Larsen, Svend. "The Idea of an Electronic Library: A Critical Essay," *Libri*, 38 (September 1988): 159–177.

Mathias, Charles McC., Jr., then Chairman Joint Committee on Printing, Letter to Head of all Federal Departments and Agencies, June 6, 1986.

U.S. House. 102nd Congress, 1st Session. H.R. 2772, *A Bill to establish in the Government Printing Office a single point of online access to a wide range of federal databases*....Washington, DC: GPO, 1991.

Zink, Steven D. "Toward More Critical Reviewing and Analysis of CD-ROM User Software Interfaces," *CD-ROM Professional*, 4 (January 1991), 16–22.

Chapter Four

Electronic Technical Services

Myrtle Smith Bolner

Although the technology for automating technical processing services in libraries has been available for some time, many documents librarians have not availed themselves of its opportunities. Historically, bibliographic control of government documents collections in depository libraries has not kept pace with that of the holding libraries' general collections. This is reflected in the fact that the use of technology in the day-to-day procedures involved in caring for and maintaining a documents collection has lagged behind that of other technical processing units in most libraries. Recent developments in technology are likely to change this.

Some libraries have cataloged their documents holdings through the use of shared cataloging utilities; still others have acquired the enhanced GPO tapes from a commercial vendor. More and more depository librarians are realizing the potential of automation not only to enhance their users' access to materials, but also to improve the procedures associated with collection development, acquisitions, and preparation of materials for use. This chapter will examine the basic tasks involved in maintaining a documents collection, explore ways of automating these routines, and identify some of the documents librarians who have applied computer technology to routine tasks involved in processing documents.

THE STATE OF AUTOMATION FOR TECHNICAL PROCESSING

Background

In agreeing to become a depository for U.S. government publications, a library pledges a level of maintenance of the collection that probably only a few deliver. The regulations for maintaining a depository library are stipulated in the *Instructions to Depository Libraries* (1984, 1988):

> ...the library must ensure that these materials are properly preserved and protected. As a minimum standard for the care and maintenance of depository property, the Government Printing Office insists that the maintenance accorded to depository materials be no less than that given to commercially purchased publications. (Chapter 1-4)

It has long been recognized that library administrators have not, in fact, met this minimum standard;

> A government documents collection is not likely to have even a full-time librarian... this staffing pattern supports the conclusion that depository libraries view documents as not requiring or deserving high levels of professional attention.... All this suggests that most libraries think documents are not particularly unique or as deserving of attention as books, and that they require no more than simple maintenance (i.e., shelving). (Hernon, McClure, and Purcell, 1985, p. 125)

If one compares the cataloging of documents with that of privately published materials in libraries as a measure of the extent to which equal treatment is accorded, documents invariably fall short. Turner and Latta (1987, pp. 10-17) reported that only 23 of 77 responding members of the Association of Research Libraries (ARL) cataloged more than 10% of their government publications. This low level of bibliographical control for government publications is corroborated by Smith (1990), who surveyed 93 ARL libraries. Although only 11% of responding libraries had entered their full documents collections in their online catalogs, 75% provided some measure of cataloging (p. 310). Smith was much more encouraged at the pace at which documents are beginning to see the light of day by way of the online public access catalog (OPAC) than she was by other innovative uses of technology to improve access to and management of Federal documents collections. According to her, the use of technology in depositories continues at a low level. Only one library has developed an expert system for documents reference; a few download information from electronic bulletin boards, and a few use an automated item file. She concluded that the "resulting picture of technology and expertise in the depositary collections at the moment is not positive" (p. 310).

Libraries began developing the capabilities for automating library services in the early 1970s. By the mid-1980s automation was commonplace in libraries and included a wide range of functions, such as acquisitions, cataloging, and circulation. As evident from the literature cited above, a majority of documents libraries were not part of the initial wave to automate and have continued to lag behind the remainder of the library. This may be due in part to the fact that the typical documents collection is housed in a separate department which is responsible for processing all of its own material, including acquisition, inventory control, circulation, maintenance of shelflist holdings, physical preparation, and shelving. Isolated from the rest of the library, documents collections were generally not included in automation plans.

For its part, the Government Printing Office (GPO) has "encouraged," but not required, cataloging of documents. Further, the only tangible support provided by the GPO for automating documents processing is the cataloging of documents in machine-readable format. The GPO began creating machine-readable cataloging records for U.S. government documents in 1976, but it is only towards the end of the 1980s that the use of the GPO/MARC tapes gained widespread use. This was made possible through the efforts of documents librarians and commercial vendors (Bolner and Kile, 1991).

The saga of the GPO/MARC tapes vis-á-vis depository libraries is a long one which is well documented in the literature and will not be discussed here. Later sections of this chapter will discuss the ways that some libraries have loaded the enhanced GPO/MARC tapes and integrated check-in with online catalog records.

The GPO requires that depository libraries maintain an item file and a shelflist as the absolute minimum for bibliographical control. It does not specify a format, but most libraries use the 3x5 card file. Typically, library administrators have accepted GPO's dictum as being the top level of service they needed to support. Consequently, the majority of documents collections rely on the *Monthly Catalog of United States Government Publications* or other bibliographic tools for access to the collection and maintain card files for verification and check-in of receipts.

AVAILABLE TECHNOLOGY

Microcomputers

In the early 1980s, during the first stages of computer development in libraries, most personal computers were expensive, had only small reserves of memory and could not handle database management programs. Libraries used computers primarily for online searching of remote databases or for word processing applications. Because computers contained limited memory they were not suitable for database management, such as maintenance of item record files and shelflists.

The number of computers available in libraries increased rapidly as a result of a reduction in the cost of equipment coupled with technological advances in the numbers and kinds of software programs available for library applications. Some of the hardware advances included the expansion of internal memory, the development of hard disk drives with greatly expanded storage capability, and the development of faster processing units. The availability of software designed for database management also proliferated during this period. Technological advances enabled librarians to use microcomputers for a variety of tasks, including check-in, cataloging, circulation, and collection development. With the proliferation of microcomputer-based technology, electronic processing of library materials became affordable for nearly any library. As a consequence, it is no longer a question of whether microcomputers are necessary in libraries, rather the question now is "How do we expand services through the use computer technology?" According to Jones (1986, p. 17), a microcomputer is necessary

> regardless of collection or budget size, or library type; the uses are limited largely by imagination. The trend toward increased use of microcomputers both in libraries and in society at large, may well combine to force any library to use a microcomputer. In so doing, a library enlarges its potential for resource and information sharing, sets the foundation for more effective and informed decision making, and takes a potential big step toward better serving the community of users.

In spite of the obvious need to make microcomputers standard equipment for collection management, documents librarians have been slow to adopt their use for some of the day-to-day routines. Further, the availability of microcomputers for processing documents was also a matter of administrative decision; documents librarians, traditionally given low priority by library administrators, probably were not in the front line of recipients for microcomputer equipment. Even among research libraries the availability of microcomputers in documents libraries is low as compared to other areas of the library (Smith, 1990, p. 319).

Automated Systems

An automated system, for the purpose of this discussion, is a large scale storage and retrieval system which is configured around a mainframe computer, located at a central site and contains data from multiple users. The system is accessed via terminals and microcomputers connected to the mainframe by phone lines. Typically, large databases and extensive software applications can reside in a mainframe database. Many libraries load their online catalogs on a mainframe computer. Much of the software used to manage library catalogs can perform multiple functions which relate one to another. This is known as an *integrated system*. All of the applications associated with technical processing are performed in the system: acquisitions, cataloging, serials control, check-in, and circulation. The information is then visible to the user in the OPAC. The system can generate reports, keep statistics, and perform other tasks, such as flag items for binding. How have depository libraries taken advantage of online systems? Smith reports that of 93 libraries surveyed, 51 (84%) had an online catalog; of these, 38 (75%) had entered depository holdings (Smith, 1990, p. 319).

Why Automate?

Automating a documents collection is both expensive and time-consuming; during planning and implementation it interrupts ongoing services. Why would documents librarians with limited support from library administrators and from the GPO want to undertake such a project? There are four reasons:

- *Improved Access.* Because electronic databases have multiple access points, there is improved reference service. Patrons and reference staff can have immediate access to information since it is available as soon as the data are entered. Two studies of the online services at The Heard Library, Vanderbilt University, analyze the benefits of an automated system (Getz, 1987). The primary benefit was a decrease in the time required to find materials. In a later study of the circulation mode of the online system, the findings were even more significant (Getz, 1988). Using previously established figures as to the amount of time it takes to fill out a card and charge out a book manually, Getz (Ibid., p. 535) calculated that library users save an average of 78.5 seconds per book because of the automated system.
- *More efficient use of staff time.* Automation can eliminate a number of the more labor-intensive tasks associated with the manual processing of documents such as typing and filing of shelflist cards. With the use of an automated system, information can be entered into an electronic database much more rapidly, thus decreasing the turn-around time between receipt of documents and the time the documents reach the shelves. Although it is to be expected that staff may experience an initial increase in workload as a result of implementing automated procedures, once the procedures are mastered, the routines can be done much faster than with a manual system.
- *Facilitate collection development.* Collection development for selective depository libraries should be based on the needs of the user community. As these needs change so should the selections. An automated item file provides an effective tool for analyzing the collection and for selecting or deselecting those items deemed appropriate. Additionally, an automated file can serve as an effective means for assisting libraries located in the same geographical area to coordinate item selections. Three selective depository libraries in Richmond, Virginia, have successfully used an automated item file to identify those items that were held by all three libraries, those that were not selected by any of the three, and those that were unique to either one or two of the libraries. With these data the libraries developed a policy of collection development that could better serve their respective constituencies (Walters, 1990, p. 222).
- *Assist in compiling statistics and management reports.* The computer can automatically generate statistical data needed for compiling reports used in management and in reports submitted to the GPO on the *Biennial Survey*.

The library can use management reports which are generated electronically to plan for staffing levels, budgeting of resources, and reorganization.

PROCEDURES FOR PROCESSING DOCUMENTS

The systematic processing of materials in any library is necessary for the proper administration of the collections. Processing includes all of the activities that enable users to identify, locate, and use library materials: acquisition, cataloging and classification, marking and preparation of materials, shelving, binding, and weeding. GPO requirements for collection maintenance are (*Instructions to Depository Libraries*, 1988):

- Shipments must be unpacked and processed as they are received;[1]
- Documents must be checked against an item record file to ensure receipt of documents to which the library is entitled and to claim for nonreceipt of documents;
- Records of the library's holdings to the piece level must be provided, either on a shelflist, a serial check-in record, or other appropriate check-in source; claims for documents not received must be made in a timely fashion.
- Documents which are to be withdrawn must be noted on a list sent to the regional library requesting permission to withdraw, and withdrawn documents must be recorded on the library's holding record; and
- Statistics of receipts and discards must be kept for inclusion in GPO's *Biennial Survey*.

The tasks involved in implementing the GPO requirements for maintaining a documents collection are labor intensive; they require typing, filing, and keeping inventories and statistics. These routine tasks consume much of the time that staff might otherwise devote to reference, collection development, and outreach. While the procedures for maintaining a documents collection must meet minimum standards for control of the collection, of and by themselves, they do little to improve access to the collection. As long as these routines are implemented manually and static shelflist card files are maintained as the control instrument, service will be no better than it was in 1895 when the first issue of the *Monthly Catalog of United States Government Publications* was published.

It has been nearly 25 years since the emergence of computer technology in libraries. While documents librarians have long been familiar with the use of

---

[1] Generally, the GPO considers that it is acceptable to process shipments within 10 days of receipt (Conversation with Joe Paskosky, GPO Inspector).

technology in online databases and information retrieval, they have been slower to move into the arena of applying technology to the routine tasks involved with technical processing.

PLANNING FOR AUTOMATION OF TECHNICAL PROCEDURES

The first and most important step in automating technical processing for documents is planning. Planning contains four components:

- *Determine goals and objectives.* It will be necessary to determine both short- and long-range goals for the project. The librarian must be specific about what is to be accomplished and be able to demonstrate the benefits of automation. For some libraries the immediate goal may be to acquire a microcomputer, but if the equipment will not help to achieve the end objectives, it is a wasted resource. Basically, the options are to automate single functions, such as the item file or the shelflist, or to have a completely integrated system with cataloging records, check-in capabilities, circulation, and report generation capabilities.
- *Establish priorities.* A clear set of priorities will help to plan each step in the automation process. Each stage must be planned so it contributes to the next, and so on down the line until the final objective is achieved. If the goal is to integrate the GPO/MARC records in the library's online catalog, the first step may be to convince the library administration of the worth of documents as a source of information. Since this usually requires evidence, the librarian should be prepared with statistics, arguments in favor drawn from the literature, and help from the user community.
- *Acquire the computer skills.* No documents librarian should use as an excuse that he or she does not know anything about microcomputers, about MARC records, or about integrated systems. It is not necessary to know programming, but it is essential to be able to operate a computer and its peripherals, search a database using Boolean logic, and interpret and work with the records in the local online catalog. For the past two years the American Library Association's Government Documents Round Table/ALA/GODORT has sponsored workshops on MARC records for documents librarians. These workshops have introduced documents librarians to AACRII cataloging and to MARC tags.
- *Keep abreast of current practices and future possibilities.* Today the possibilities for automating the various technical processing functions are too numerous to list. The librarian must find out what applications are available for automating the processing of documents and determine which of these are suitable for local applications. The professional journals and newsletters identify and review specific programs. The "Readers Exchange" column of

Administrative Notes frequently has articles by librarians who have automated all or some of their procedures. There are a variety of programs available with various strengths and weaknesses; the librarian should make comparisons among them to see if they are suitable for the goals he or she wishes to achieve. If there is a system already in place the documents librarian needs to learn as much about it as possible. Consultations with other librarians are helpful to determine how the system works and how it can be used for various applications related to documents processing.

AUTOMATION: PRACTICAL APPLICATIONS

A number of libraries have automated certain segments of the processing functions. Some have started with item files, others with shelflist check-in, and still others have combined item verification and check-in with an online catalog. Because of the diverse ways libraries manage their documents collections, no single method for automating the collection is appropriate for every library. Additionally, some functions are more suited for automation than others. The remainder of this chapter will examine those processing functions which most lend themselves to automation and discuss possibilities for implementation of automation.

Item Files

One of the files which the GPO requires in order to maintain a depository collection is an item file. The term *"item"* usually refers to a single entity in an enumeration; however, for documents librarians, "item" has a totally different connotation. The term designates a category of documents which are available from the Superintendent of Documents for distribution to depository libraries. The number of publications in a category under a single item number varies from one to many. When librarians at selective depositories choose publications available from the Superintendent of Documents, they select by item number. Each depository library receives a printout of active item numbers once a year which it uses to select or deselect items. Additionally, libraries may change item selection numbers at anytime during the year by filling out the drop/add cards received from GPO.

Maintenance of an item record file is essential to the management of a depository collection (*Instructions to Depository Libraries*, Chapter 8-2). To this end, the GPO provides each depository library with a complete set of 3x5 cards, one for each item (or group of publications) available for selection. Each card contains the item number, issuing agency, series title, Superintendent of Documents classification number, and a brief description of the series. As new items are added into the system the GPO sends new cards to the libraries. The item record files are used in conjunction with the item selection printout and the drop/add cards to indicate any changes in the selection profile; any changes made by the GPO to the item numbers must also be noted on the records. Depository libraries must distinguish in some way the selected items from those not selected; additionally the cards should indicate the dates items are added or dropped. As the GPO makes changes to the classes in an item and adds new classes the item files are updated.

The principal use of the item file is to match the receipts against the shipping list, or packing slips, which come with the shipments of materials to depository libraries. *The shipping list* is an itemized record of all the publications sent to depository libraries in a shipment. Only regional depository libraries receive all the documents listed on the shipping lists; other libraries receive only those publications which fall in the categories or items they have selected. The selective library must match its item file against the shipping list to see if all selected publications have been received. Any publications not received must be claimed as soon as possible.

The item records are also used for collection development. Items may be selected or deselected, depending on the changing needs of the user community and other management requirements, such as shelving and space. Some libraries have used item records in cooperative efforts with other depository libraries in a geographical region (Wilson, 1990, p. 2).

Finally, because the item files contain the history of a depository library's selections they can be used to construct a profile for purchase of retrospective GPO/MARC tapes from a vendor (Gillispie, 1989; Somers, 1989).

Automating the Item File. Probably the first example of an automated item file was that developed at Carleton College in the early 1980s by Morton (1981). The file was a mainframe-based system developed in-house by Morton and a computer programer. Data elements which could be accessed were item number, classification number, and status (active or inactive). In addition to functioning as a collection development tool, the automated file also served as an automated check-in file. It had the advantage over a card file by providing immediate and concurrent access in various locations of the library. According to Morton (Ibid, p. 185), the advantages of an automated item file are that it "permits the documents librarian to perceive the dynamics of addition, deletion, rejection, and documentation as a continuing and fluid process by which a depository collection develops and can be managed."

Mooney (1986, p. 2) of the University of California, Riverside, introduced a microcomputer-based item file using dBase in 1985. The file contains all of the depository item numbers available for selection in the depository library program. There is a separate record in the database for each classification number associated with an item number. Each record contains a number of fields including: title/series, Sudocs number, issuing agency, and item number. All of the fields are searchable so the file can be used as a reference tool. The records also have a field to indicate the selection status and a field which indicates location within the library. The Montgomery County (Maryland) Library developed a system called *Depository Helper*, which it is willing to make available to other depository libraries for a nominal fee. It offers the advantages of ease and speed of entry for new documents, as well as a reference tool for identifying government publications.

Check-in/shelflist Maintenance

Depository libraries are required to maintain a record of each separate publication received. These piece-level records are the final authority for determining the status of materials in the collection; they tell whether or not a document was ever received or withdrawn. Each depository library must establish procedures for checking in its receipts, either on a card file or on an automated file.

Card Files. Libraries which have maintained a card file have usually followed the procedures outlined in the *Federal Depository Library Manual* (1988). Written by practicing librarians, the manual contains detailed instructions showing typical check-in routines, including examples of the different 3"x5" cards used to process various types of materials. The records usually contain the Superintendent of Documents classification number, title, holdings, item number, format, and location. The cards also note cross references when there has been a call number change. For most libraries, the shelflist continues to be the only method of bibliographical control, but its limitations as an access tool are obvious. It must be used in conjunction with other finding tools such as the *Monthly Catalog* to verify whether or not the library has received a specific publication.

Automated Check-in

PC-based. A number of depository libraries have begun to automate documents check-in using a PC-based system. Most of these programs require hardware with sufficient internal memory and storage space to handle a large database. A number of computers on the market meet these specifications. Unless the systems are connected to a local area network (LAN) they are only accessible through one workstation. Libraries which use PC-based systems use software that can perform a number of functions—sorting, searching, and report generating. When a documents collection is automated, the shelflist information must be entered into the computer to ensure that each piece is checked in. The usual fields include item number, status (selected or non-selected), Sudocs number, title, issuing agency, and a note field for special instructions. Librarians using a PC-based program tailored for documents report that it takes less time to check-in documents since each piece is checked in and verified against the item status in the record, in one operation (Mooney, 1986, p. 2). At Appalachian State University, documents are being checked in using PC-File:dB (Wise, 1990, p. 3). A comprehensive database management file for documents check-in can provide a quick, up-to-date detailed index to the holdings in the collection. Such a check-in is recommended for small collections and for libraries which have not integrated documents check-in into their online systems.

Online Systems. A second alternative to manual check-in is in conjunction with an online catalog. Although machine-readable catalog records for U.S. government documents have been available through OCLC and other bibliographic utilities since 1976, they have not been widely included in library online catalogs. This has been due in part to the quality of the catalog records and also to the large number of records involved. Libraries acquire GPO created MARC (Machine-Readable Catalog) records for documents by downloading them from a cataloging utility such as OCLC or RLIN, or by purchasing the GPO/MARC tapes from the Library of Congress or from a vendor, such as MARCIVE or OCLC. Libraries using a bibliographic utility create a holdings record of each piece as it is entered into the catalog; that is, in effect, the check-in record, and no other record need be created.

Libraries have found that it is more cost effective to batch load tapes than it is to download records piece by piece (Bowerman and Cady, 1984, p. 340). The availability of enhanced GPO/MARC tapes from vendors has resulted in a greater number of depositories acquiring cataloging records for inclusion in their online catalogs. Not only does this improve access to government publications, it also provides the potential for eliminating some of the time-consuming routines associated with manual check-in. In the July 17, 1990, issue of *Administrative Notes*, the GPO sounded a warning lest libraries confuse the batch loading of GPO/MARC records with check-in. Libraries which batch load tapes must find a way to indicate that the library has actually received the publication. The tape containing the GPO records should be "tailored to the library's item number profile, checked against actual accessions and coupled with the library continuing to record individual issues of serials received" ("GPO Guidelines for Online Processing of Depository Documents," 1990, p. 2).

The problem is that distribution of the cataloging records is substantially later than receipt of the document. Except for existing serials and multivolume titles, bibliographic records will not be available in the database at the time of receipt. The GPO also requires that libraries complete initial processing within a week to ten days, although it does allow a library to maintain a temporary holdings record, such as a marked shipping list, for up to three months as a "bridge" until the bibliographic records are available for marking holdings.

These problems are not insurmountable. Librarians planning to automate check-in using catalog records which have been batch loaded will have to examine the capabilities of the online system in order to find a way to meet GPO requirements for shelflist accountability. A few options are listed below:

- Use a temporary record containing the following data elements: author, title, call number, report number, item number, and volume holdings. This record can be later replaced by the full bibliographic record, and the holdings information transferred to the new record.
- Create a brief cataloging record in a separate database that is searchable in several fields. This file may be maintained as a permanent file, such as an automated "shelflist," or the records may be deleted when a full bibliographic record is added to the main database.
- Use appropriate system records to serve as temporary records until the full bibliographic record is added to the database.

In addition to finding a way to check-in documents which arrive before a bibliographic record is available, the library must decide whether or not to close the shelflist, what to do about retrospective holdings information, and how to enter holdings information so that it conforms to standards and can be easily understood by the library user. Libraries planning to automate should draw upon the experiences of other libraries with similar systems for help and suggestions. Appendix A gives a brief overview of the automated check-in procedures at Louisiana State University (LSU) using NOTIS (Northwestern Online Totally Integrated System) software. Vendors will supply the names of other libraries which have purchased tapes for batch loading and identify the system which the libraries are using. Appendix B is a list of references pertaining to automation of technical processing. Finally, the GPO keeps a list of documents librarians who have indicated that they are willing to serve as resource persons for other librarians who are seeking help with automation.

CONCLUSION

The technology for improving access to government information is available on a variety of levels, ranging from single task procedures on a microcomputer to full-range processing in an integrated online system. It is now possible to acquire GPO/MARC records from a vendor which are tailored to the library's item selection and which can provide a quick, up-to-date, comprehensive index to the resources in the collection. Converting library records from printed cards to an electronic catalog requires detailed planning. To do this, documents librarians must research the various possibilities for incorporating check-in into the online system, and they must be educated in the use of the computer for processing applications. It has been shown that technology can eliminate a number of the more labor-intensive tasks associated with the check-in process and improves public access to U.S. government documents. Although significant progress has been made in the application of technology to technical processing, it is generally acknowledged that more needs to be accomplished. While it will take support from library administrators and from the GPO to automate the processing of documents, the impetus must come from documents librarians themselves. They must show that automating technical processing procedures for governments documents is not only feasible but also mandatory if the library is to serve its users to the full extent of its capabilities.

REFERENCES

Bolner, Myrtle Smith and Barbara Kile. "Documents to the People: Access through the Automated Catalog," *Government Publications Review,* 18 (1991): 51–64.

Bowerman, Roseann and Susan A. Cady. "Government Publications in an Online Catalog: A Feasibility Study," *Information Technology & Libraries,* 3 (December 1984): 331–342.

Federal Depository Library Manual (Washington, D.C.: GPO, 1988).

Getz, Malcolm. "Some Benefits of the Online Catalog," *College & Research Libraries,* 48 (1987): 224–240.

————. "More Benefits of Automation," *College & Research Libraries,* 49 (1988): 534–544.

Gillispie, Jim. "GPO Tape Load Profile." [Unpublished paper presented to the NOTIS Documents Cataloging Interest Group, ALA Annual Conference, Dallas, June 24, 1989].

"GPO Guidelines for Online Processing of Depository Documents," *Administrative Notes,* 11 (July 17, 1990): 2–3 *(GP3.16/3–2:11).*

Hernon, Peter, Charles R. McClure, and Gary R. Purcell. *GPO's Depository Library Program* (Norwood, NJ: Ablex, 1985).

Instructions to Depository Libraries (Washington, D.C.: GPO, 1984, 1988).

Jones, Beverly L. "Is a Microcomputer Really Necessary in Your Library Setting?," in *Microcomputers for Library Decision Making: Issues, Trends, and Applications,* Edited by Peter Hernon and Charles McClure (Norwood, NJ: Ablex, 1986), pp. 3–17.

Mooney, Margaret T. "Automating the U.S. Depository Item Number File," *Administrative Notes,* 7 (November 1986): 2–4 *(GP. 3.16/3–2:7).*

Morton, Bruce. "An Items Record Management System: First Step in the Automation of Collection Development in Selective Depository Libraries," *Government Publication Review,* 8A (1981): 185–196.

Smith, Diane H. "Depository Libraries in the 1990s: Whither, or Wither Depositories?," *Government Publications Review,* 17 (1990): 301–324.

Somers, Herb. "Developing a Tape Load Profile with MARCIVE" [Unpublished paper presented to the NOTIS Documents Cataloging Interest Group, ALA Annual Conference, Dallas, June 24, 1989].

Turner, Carol and Ann Latta. *Current Approaches to Improving Access to Government Documents* (Washington, D.C.: Association of Research Libraries, Office of Management Studies, 1987).

Walters, John. "Using Automated Item Files as the Basis for Effective Collection Management and Cooperative Collection Development: A Note," *Government Publications Review*, 17 (1990): 251–256.

Wilson, John S. "Readers Exchange," *Administrative Notes*. 11 (January 30, 1990): 2 *(GP3.16/3–2:11)*.

Wise, Suzanne. "Readers Exchange: Automated Documents Check-in Using PC-File:dB at Appalachian State University," *Administrative Notes*, 11 (October 31, 1990): 3–7 *(GP3.16/3–2:11)*.

APPENDIX A:

ONLINE CHECK-IN WITH BATCH TAPE LOADS

In Summer 1989, the Louisiana State University (LSU) Libraries loaded the GPO/MARC enhanced database acquired from Marcive, Inc., into its NOTIS system.[1] Since that time tapes acquired from Marcive are loaded monthly. Prior to loading the tapes, drafts of automated workflow were developed in an iterative process in which various options and their implications were considered. It was decided that documents processing would be handled entirely within the documents department and that a separate processing unit would be set up within the NOTIS system for handling documents records. The following assumptions were incorporated into the procedures:

- As a general rule, new shelflist cards would not be generated or filed once the online processing had begun (i.e., the shelflist was frozen from the day the online check-in began).
- Item records (NOTIS) will be used to record receipt of most materials (excluding individual bindable serial issues). When there is a bibliographic record in the database, a *linked item* record will be used to record item-level information. Copy holdings information will be entered on the appropriate copy holdings record. When there is not a bibliographic record, an *unlinked item* record will be used.
- Until a program is available that will automatically link unlinked item records to the correct bibliographic records, it will be necessary to link unlinked item records manually and to trigger the process through the use of action dates.
- The current year's issues of regular periodicals will be checked in on an order/pay receipt (OPR). When the complete volume of a periodical is received the completed volume information is transferred to the volume holdings record. Item records will be created at that time for the bound volume.
- Barcodes will be placed on most documents; the exceptions are individual issues of a serial which are to be bound together; transmittals, changes, and revisions which are to be filed into a manual or other looseleaf service; and publications which are to be retained for a limited time such as *Commerce Business Daily*.
- Holdings for new serial issues/volumes will be recorded online as they are received. Retrospective holdings will generally not be entered until later.

---

[1] The check-in system described does not discuss item verification, since LSU is a regional depository. When a selective library profiles with a vendor for its tapes loads, it should receive only the items it has selected. The library still has to match receipts against its item selections to make sure it has received all of the documents to which it is entitled.

- Special codes will be used to indicate locations, special loan periods, retention decisions, and routing instructions.
- Format for holdings will conform to the same standards as other areas of the library in order to avoid patron confusion and to improve access.
- Format for serial check-in will conform to the same level as the remainder of the collection.
- Updating of records will be the responsibility of the database manager in the documents department. Class changes, item number changes, and other corrections and updates, either from the GPO or from other sources, are to be kept up-to-date in the online database in the same manner as a manual shelflist.
- Appropriate staff training will be given for those persons actually working directly with the database as well as for public service staff who must be able to move around in the technical services mode and to interpret information for the public.

Figure 4-1 shows the relationship between NOTIS system records. An explanation of the records follows:

- *Bibliographic Record.* Machine-Readable Catalog (MARC) record with numbered fields containing full bibliographic description of a publication, namely title, author, publisher, date of publication, place of publication, call number, note(s), etc.
- *Copy Holdings Record.* Screen that displays brief bibliographic information, along with location and copy number (CN) lines. This record is used to reflect the status of each copy of a distinct title. Volume holdings, order/pay/ receipt (OPR), and linked item records are all essentially "attached" or linked to copy number (CN) lines. Unlinked item records are eventually "linked" to a particular copy number line located on a copy holdings record.
- *Item Record.* Item-level record that is either linked or unlinked to a line on the copy holdings statement. Each item record contains piece-level information, including the item ID (barcode), loan code, status and related information about the document.
- *Linked Item Record.* It is attached to a particular copy number (CN) line of a copy holdings record. *Unlinked Item Record* is a record that is not "attached" or linked to a bibliographic record, and can only be searched by the NOTIS record number, item ID, or copy number. Once a bibliographic record is available in the database for this "temporary" record, the unlinked item is "linked" or attached to the appropriate copy number (CN) line of the copy holdings record.
- *OPAC Record.* Screen which appears in the online public access catalog. Describes the publication and gives special locations.
- *OPR (Order/Pay/Receipt Record).* Record used to record receipt of the *current*

issues of regular serials. Once the volume for a particular period (e.g., year) is complete, the holdings information is transferred to a volume holdings record.

- *Provisional Record.* Temporary bibliographic record created for new serials without bibliographic records, and for monographic titles for which there is not a bibliographic record for an extended period of time.
- *Volume Holdings Record.* Record used to record the volume holdings of multipart monographs and irregular serials and noncurrent holdings for regular serials. The detailed or summary holdings statements are created and linked to each copy number (CN) line of a copy holdings record as appropriate for serials and multipart monographs.

The workflow patterns for checking in monographs and serials and for linking unlinked item records are shown in Figures 4-2-4-4. Documents are "checked in" on the item record which is linked to the copy holdings record. Documents which have no bibliographic record in the database at the time of receipt are checked in on an unlinked item record, containing the title, call number, location, and circulation codes. Current receipts of bindable periodicals are checked in on an order/pay/receipt (OPR) record. Volume holdings are entered on the volume holdings record.

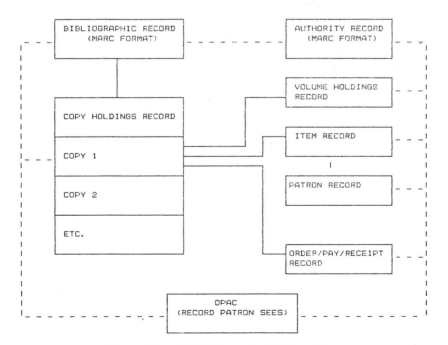

Figure 4-1. NOTIS Records Relationships.

MONOGRAPHS CHECK-IN

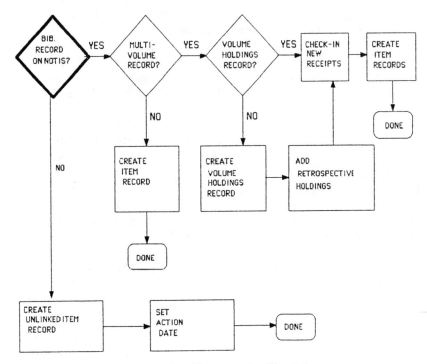

Figure 4-2.   Monographs Check-in.

SERIALS CHECK-IN

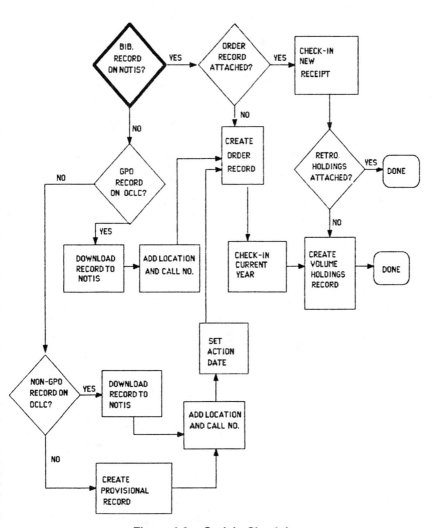

Figure 4-3.   Serials Check-in.

ACTION DATE REVIEW

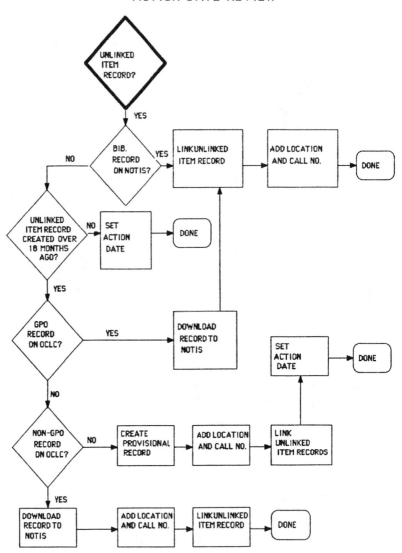

Figure 4-4.   Action Date Review.

APPENDIX B

AUTOMATED PROCESSING: WHAT OTHERS ARE DOING

"Automatic Bibliographic Control of Government Documents: Current Developments," *Documents to the People*, 15 (December 1987): 224–246.

Dobbs, Christopher C. "Quality Control in Implementing OCLC G0VD0C Current Cataloging Service," *Documents to the People*, 18 (September 1990): 166–167, 170.

Higdon, Mary Ann. "Federal Documents Processing with OCLC: The Texas Tech Experience—Planning, Utilization, and the Future," in *Government Documents and Microforms: Standards and Management Issues*. Proceedings of the Fourth Annual Government Documents and Information Conference and the Ninth Annual Microforms Conference, edited by Steven D. Zink and Nancy Jean Mellin (Westport, CT: Meckler Publishing, 1984), pp. 89–97.

Honeyman, Justine P. and A. Richard Starzyk. "Readers Exchange: Confluent Streams: The Production of an In-house Government Documents Catalog Using a Facilities Management System (Insite)," *Administrative Notes*, 8 (May 1987): 3–4 *(GP3.16/3–2:8)*.

Kirby, Diana G. "Readers Exchange: Helping to Preserve and Improve Access to Government Posters," *Administrative Notes* 10 (August, 7, 1989): 17–18 *(GP3.16/3–2:10)*.

Kiser, Chris and Clyde Grotophorst. "G0VDOX: A Government Documents Check-in System," *Library Software Review*, 7 (January/February 1988): 42–43.

Kiser, Christine B., "Automated Shelflist at George Mason University." *Administrative Notes*, 7 (March 8, 1986): 3–4 *(GP3.16/3–2:7)*.

Maclay, Veronica. "Automatic Bibliographic Control of Government Documents at Hastings Law Library," *Technical Services Quarterly*, 7 (1989): 53–64.

Mooney, Margaret T. "Automating the U.S. Depository Item Number File," *Administrative Notes*, 7 (November 1986): 2–4 *(GP3.16/3–2:7)*.

_____ "Matching Library Holdings against GPO Tapes: Issues, Concerns, and Solutions," *Government Publications Review*, 17 (1990): 421–428.

Morton, Bruce. "Implementing an Automated Shelflist for a Selective Depository Collection," *Government Publications Review*, 9 (1982): 323–344.

_____ . "An Items Record Management System: First Step in the Automation of Collection Development in Selective Depository Libraries," *Government Publications Review*, 8A (1981): 185–196.

Myers, Margaret and Janice G. Schuster. "Readers Exchange: Development of an Online Database for Bibliographic Control of Government Documents in a Selective Depository," *Administrative Notes*, 11 (July 31, 1990): 19–22 *(GP3.16/3–2:11)*.

Nergelovic, Paul. "Readers Exchange: An Automated Documents Shelflist and Current Awareness Checklist System at the United States Military Academy Library," *Administrative Notes*, 10 (July 14, 1989): 10–12 *(GP3.16/3–2:10)*.

Olivia, Victor T. and Michael K. Reimer. *Usinq INNOVACQ to Process G.P.O. Titles* (Garden City, NY: Adelphi University Libraries, 1989) (ED 316 195).

Palincsar, Stephen F. "Online-assisted Collection Development in a Government Depository Library Collection (U.S. General Accounting Office's Technical Library)," *Library Software Review*, 9 (March/April 1990): 94–96.

Powell, Margaret S., Deborah Smith Johnston, and Ellen P. Conrad. "The Use of OCLC for Cataloging U.S. Government Publications: A Feasibility Study," *Government Publications Review*, 14 (1987):61–73.

"Procedures for MARCIVE Monthly Printout of GPO Tape Loads." Documents Department, Sterling C. Evans Library, Texas A&M University, Spring 1991 [unpublished].

Prudden, Terry M. "Readers Exchange: Depository Helper Program Available to Libraries," *Administrative Notes*, 10 (August 21, 1989): 5–6 *(GP3.16/3–2:10)*.

Redmond, Mary. "From Backwater to Mainstream: Government Documents in the Online Catalog," *Bookmark*, 47 (Spring 1989): 161–165.

Stanfield, Karen. "Documents Online: Cataloging Federal Depository Materials at the University of Illinois," *Illinois Libraries*, 68 (May 1986): 325–329.

Stephenson, Mary Sue and Gary R. Purcell. "The Automation of Government Publications: Functional Requirements and Selected Software Systems for Serials Controls," *Government Information Quarterly*, 2 (1985): 57–76.

Thompson, Ronelle K. H. "Managing a Selective Government Documents Depository Using Microcomputer Technology (at Augustana College)," *College & Research Libraries News*, 4 (April 1989): 260–262.

Walbridge, Sharon. "OCLC and Improved Access to Government Documents," *Illinois Libraries*, 68 (May 1986): 329–332.

Walters, John. "Using Automated Item Files as the Basis for Effective Collection Management and Cooperative Collection Development: A Note," *Government Publications Review*, 17 (1990): 251–256.

Wilson, John S. "Readers Exchange," *Administrative Notes*. 11 (January 30, 1990): 2 *(GP3.16/3–2:11)*.

Wise, Suzanne. "Readers Exchange: Automated Documents Check–in Using PC-File:dB at Appalachian State University," *Administrative Notes*, 11 (October 31, 1990): 3–7 *(GP3.16/3-2:11)*.

Chapter Five

Checklist for Loading GPO Cataloging Records into the Online Catalog

Gary Cornwell
Thomas Kinney

Documents and systems support staffs at many libraries are currently facing the prospect of loading large files of Government Printing Office (GPO) produced cataloging records into their online catalogs. Due to the special characteristics and complex nature of these records, most libraries are unprepared for such an undertaking. The following discussion and resulting checklist are designed to familiarize libraries with the various steps that must be followed to integrate the GPO cataloging records successfully into the workflow of the library.

The load of GPO records into a library's online catalog is a complex undertaking which has far-reaching effects on both the documents unit and the library as whole. The success of the load depends on the amount and quality of thought and effort devoted to its planning. Planning for the GPO record load at the University of Florida started with the formulation of an extensive (35 pages) initial proposal. The proposal was developed by the authors of this chapter in consultation with UF library staff, colleagues at other libraries, GPO record vendor representatives, and staff at the Florida Center for Library Automation (FCLA), the library automation support agency which manages the online catalogs of Florida's nine state universities. Discussion and refinement of this document within the Libraries and FCLA led to the development of the final, detailed plans for loading GPO records into the Libraries' online catalog.

This approach combines the efficiency of planning by an individual or small group with the benefits of broader input. It also serves to alert the library staff as a whole that the GPO record load will have significant effects outside the documents department. We find it hard to overstate this last point. Given the revolutionary changes that a GPO record load can create in a library's documents unit, it is easy to neglect the effect of the load on the rest of the library. At UF, we placed great emphasis on preparing for this wider effect and believe that this effort paid off well in terms of interdepartmental harmony and service to the users.

MODEL FOR AN INITIAL PROPOSAL FOR GPO RECORD LOADING

The following is recommended as an outline of an "Initial Proposal" for loading GPO cataloging records. Whether or not your library follows the specific "Initial Proposal" approach suggested here, it is strongly recommended that all of the points listed below are addressed in some manner at an early stage, and that some way is found to ensure librarywide involvement in planning.

INTRODUCTION

Briefly describe the project and explain why it is important and worthwhile.

The Library's Documents Collection

Describe the library's documents collection(s), including: their size; what formats are included; where they are located; how and by what library unit(s) they are acquired, processed, circulated, and serviced; and types of bibliographic access currently provided.

Sources of GPO Catalog Records

Review options for obtaining GPO catalog records and present preliminary estimate of one-time and ongoing costs.

The Role of GPO Catalog Records in the Database

Discuss the role that the GPO catalog records will play in the library's database, which typically includes: (1) provide access to Federal documents through the online catalog; (2) automate the circulation of Federal documents; (3) automate check-in and recording of holdings for Federal depository and nondepository documents (including the display of check-in and volume holdings information in the public catalog); (4) support acquisitions functions; (5) bring together all copies of each Federal document held by the Main Library System on a single record; and (6) support and complement the existing authority structure of the database.

Impact on the Documents Department

Discuss the impact of the load on the documents department, including: anticipated increase in use of the collection; implementation of online processing of new receipts and online circulation; barcoding of the collection; conversion of retrospective serial and series holdings from manual to online records; and assumption of responsibilities for bibliographic record maintenance. Indicate additional resources that will be needed as a result of the load, such as additional staff, staff training, equipment, and barcode labels.

Impact on Public Services

Discuss the impact of the load on public service units outside the documents department. The following areas should be addressed: impact on the online catalog, including the number of records expected to be added to the database, new access points (e.g., Sudoc number), and new display elements (e.g., item number); anticipated increase in the use of previously uncataloged collections of documents located outside the documents department (e.g., ERIC microfiche); circulation support for documents serviced outside the documents department, including barcoding of documents; and the librarywide implications of an anticipated increase in user interest in government publications.

Impact on Technical Services

Discuss the impact of the load on technical service units outside the documents department. Areas to be addressed include: coordination of technical processing activities in documents with those of other units; division of authority control and record maintenance responsibilities between documents and cataloging; and use of GPO records to support acquisitions and serials control activities relating to documents located outside the documents department.

Appendix 1: Documents Terminology

Briefly define terminology peculiar to documents librarianship and/or GPO cataloging (e.g., Sudoc number, item number, depository library program, *Monthly Catalog*, availability record, and Marcive file).

Appendix 2: Suggested Reading

Provide a list of suggested readings giving background information on the GPO load, starting with Judy Myers's landmark article, "The Government Printing Office Cataloging Records: Opportunities and Problems" (Myers, 1985).

From "Initial Proposal" to Specific Plans

Assuming that librarywide discussion of the initial proposal leads to agreement that the GPO load should proceed, library managers should next begin to formulate detailed plans for carrying out the project. The remaining sections of this chapter discuss the various issues that will need to be addressed. These issues have been grouped together into six general areas: Special Characteristics of the GPO Cataloging Records; Vendor Evaluation and Selection; Profiling; Workflow Decisions; Record Processing Specifications; and Customization/ Modification of the Local Online System. The chapter concludes with a "GPO Record Loading Checklist" summarizing the points which must be addressed in planning a GPO record load.

SPECIAL CHARACTERISTICS OF THE GPO CATALOGING RECORDS

Once a library has decided to load machine-readable cataloging records for government publications into its online catalog and initiated the planning process, detailed plans must be developed in two areas. The first deals with the retrospective file—those records created since July 1976 and ending with the most recent records available at the time of purchase. The second deals with acquiring ongoing records for newly released publications. Together the two files should support all operations identified in the initial planning document (online check-in, circulation, etc). In order to ensure the records will support these functions, library staff must be familiar with the special characteristics of the GPO cataloging records and choose their vendor and profile their record selection accordingly.

The various problems associated with the GPO cataloging records have been well documented by Myers (1985), Swanbeck (1985), Jamison (1986), Tull (1989), Bolner and Kile (1991), and Kinney and Cornwell (1991). Equally important for planning purposes are the following special characteristics of the records which apply to both the retrospective file and to ongoing cataloging.

The tapes contain some records that libraries may not want to load. Of primary importance to any library is the fact that the tapes contain many records that the library may not want to load into its online public access catalog (OPAC).

The tapes contain records for all publications listed in the *Monthly Catalog*, therefore selective depository libraries will need to carefully profile which records they receive to reflect their holdings accurately. Since records for preprints, reprints, and advance reports are also included in the GPO file, even regional depositories will likely want to exclude some records from their profile.

All GPO cataloging is for paper versions of documents even if libraries receive them in microfiche. At the time of this writing, GPO does not catalog the microfiche format of a document even if that was the format distributed to depository libraries; rather they catalog all documents as if libraries received them in paper copy. As a result, the only way that the format of a document can be determined from the bibliographic record is by examining the item number. Since most libraries keep their microfiche and paper copies of Federal documents in different locations, it is important that they be able to assign accurate locations for this material in the online catalog. However, many item numbers are spilt between paper and microfiche, which makes assigning location based on item number alone extremely difficult. Some libraries have attempted to determine which format occurs most frequently and assign that location code to all publications distributed under a particular item number regardless of actual format. As one would expect, this leads to many incorrect locations in the online catalog. A more accurate method for identifying the format of an individual document is to look in the 074 field of each record for the word "microfiche" and assign location accordingly. (For a further discussion of using the item number for location decisions, see the section on "Record Processing Specifications.")

GPO cataloging records may contain multiple call numbers. For a variety of reasons, GPO cataloging records may contain multiple 086 fields giving the various call numbers that have been assigned to a title. Multiple call numbers may reflect changes in issuing agency or simply changes in philosophy or rule interpretation by the GPO. Whatever the cause, libraries must determine how they will display different call numbers for the same bibliographic record in the online catalog. The most current call number for a document is typically located in the last 086 field.

The same title may be cataloged as both a monograph and a serial. Many numbered series contain titles that are reissued every year. Each issue of a recurring title is listed in the *Monthly Catalog* and may be cataloged as a monograph one year and as a serial in others. The title *Fertility of American Women*, for example, is represented by some records in the retrospective file as a numbered monograph within the P-20 series and by other records as an open-ended annual report.

With an understanding of these special characteristics of the GPO cataloging records coupled with a familiarity of the problems inherent in the retrospective file and what has been done to correct them, libraries can proceed with planning for the load of retrospective GPO cataloging records into their online catalogs.

VENDOR EVALUATION AND SELECTION

Retrospective File

The Marcive Corporation is currently (and for the foreseeable future) the only vendor from which libraries should obtain retrospective GPO cataloging records. The retrospective files as available from any other vendor are filled with problems that would render them virtually useless in supporting even the most basic functions in the online catalog. An inhouse study at the University of Florida estimated that it would take nearly one year of programming and over 7,000 hours of labor to bring the records up to a usable level.

These estimates were substantiated when Marcive, through the efforts of the library staffs at Louisiana State University, Rice University, and Texas A&M University, enhanced the records contained in the retrospective file to a level that any library could load them with a high level of confidence. Tull (1989) and Bolner and Kile (1991) have done an excellent job of describing what was done to "clean-up" the GPO cataloging tapes.

While the heroic efforts of these institutions have immeasurably improved the GPO file, several characteristics of the enhanced file should be noted.

Marcive participants did no original cataloging. As pointed out previously, there may be instances where both monographic and serial cataloging exist for the same title. While participants in the Marcive project significantly enhanced various cataloging records by adding missing fields, moving data elements to appropriate fields, and adding beginning and closing dates for serials, they did not attempt to recatalog any documents. Consequently, it is possible for a recurring title to be represented by seven or eight monographic records and one serial record in the file.

Marcive participants also made no attempt to provide microfiche cataloging records for those microfiche documents cataloged as paper by the GPO. The content of the 074 (item number) field remains the only way to determine the actual format of a depository document.

Many item numbers were incorrectly added for nondepository publications. Many records lacking item numbers were identified as belonging to series that were distributed through the depository library program. As part of record enhancement item numbers were added to these records. However, since many depository series do contain nondepository titles, a significant number of nondepository documents have been coded as depository.

Serials within series. For recurring serial titles which were part of numbered series, each issue-specific cataloging record in the original GPO file contained the series number of the document. For example, the 1976 issue of the annual publication *Handbook of Agricultural Charts* was identified as Agricultural Handbook No. 504. When multiple serial records for the same title were collapsed into one record in the Marcive file, this issue-specific information was lost.

Mother–Daughter records. For many map series, the GPO uses a "mother" record as a template to create "daughter" records for all the individual maps in the series. For USGS topographic maps, for example, a single record exists for Florida with a unique OCLC number. In addition, there are hundreds of separate map records identifying different quadrangles in the series. Each of these individual map records have dummy OCLC numbers assigned to them by Marcive.

Authority Issues. There are a number of problems associated with authority control in the GPO cataloging records (Kinney and Cornwell, 1991). While problems with name and subject headings have, for the most part, been eliminated (Tull, 1989; Bolner and Kile, 1991), series headings from the earlier years of GPO cataloging still present problems. Since the automation of the GPO series files in September 1986 ("Automation of GPO Series Files," 1987), GPO series names have been consistent with the LC Name Authority File. However, prior to that time LC and GPO frequently established different headings for the same series.

Ongoing Records

Ongoing cataloging records for government publications are available from at least two vendors, which currently offer essentially the same product. Beginning in January 1990, GPO changed the way in which the GPO cataloging tapes were produced ("GPO to Produce Improved Cataloging Tapes," 1989, and "GPO Cataloging Tapes Ready for Production," 1990). The enhanced version of the tapes has four significant advantages over the earlier version. First, the GPO cataloging tapes are available more quickly. Second, "availability" records for serials and multipart monographs have been eliminated.[1] Third, collective records for these materials have been provided. Finally, the new tapes include all corrections or upgrades made on OCLC to earlier GPO cataloging records. Each of these improvements addresses a long-standing problem with the GPO cataloging tapes, which has at last developed into a product that can be used as produced by the GPO.

Both the University of Florida (UF) and Louisiana State University (LSU) are NOTIS libraries that use the GPO cataloging records to support online processing of government documents in essentially the same manner. LSU obtains ongoing cataloging records from Marcive while UF receives them through the OCLC GOVDOC service. Based on the experiences of these two

---

[1] For an explanation of "availability" records, see Myers (1985).

institutions, there seems to be no significant difference between the timeliness or content of the records as supplied by either vendor. There are, however, a couple of special characteristics that apply only to ongoing records with which the libraries should be familiar.

Expect a minimum of a four-month delay between the receipt of a depository document and the availability of a tape-supplied machine-readable cataloging record. Although the enhancement of the GPO cataloging tapes has resulted in a more timely availability of the records, informal studies at LSU and UF indicate that Margaret Mooney's estimate of a six-month delay until the availability of a tape-supplied cataloging record is still fairly accurate (Mooney, 1989). Additionally, recent delays in cataloging at GPO (particularly microfiche titles) have resulted in delays much longer than six months.

Updated/enhanced records. Ongoing GPO cataloging tapes contain up-dated versions of previously distributed GPO cataloging records, many of which may already have been loaded into the library's catalog during either the retrospective or ongoing load. According to Gil Baldwin, former Chief of Cataloging at GPO, these revised records will always be in some sense "better" than previous versions. They include updated or enhanced serial records, revised records for multipart monographs reflecting the availability of an additional part (such records frequently include additional subject headings and the subtitle of the new part), and a variety of corrections and enhancements to older GPO records. As discussed in the section on "Record Processing Specifications," the library must decide whether and how to incorporate these records into the database.

Since both Marcive and OCLC offer basically the same version of the records, libraries must consider other factors when choosing a vendor. Obviously, a major consideration will be the cost of the records. Other factors include the cost for setting holdings on OCLC, ability to load the records in other bibliographic utilities such as RLIN, and the flexibility that a library has in record selection— more commonly referred to as profiling.

PROFILING

With both the retrospective file and the ongoing records careful and precise profiling is essential if the library's online catalog is to reflect accurately the library's holdings of government publications. Marcive currently offers a number of variables which a library may use for profiling, while those currently offered by OCLC are somewhat more limited. Depending on the particular needs of the library, both services are viable options. A library should carefully compare the level of record selection that they need with the services offered by the two vendors. Areas to be considered in vendor selection and record profiling include:

Profiling options. Before libraries can make informed decisions about vendor selection, they should have a basic understanding of how the profiling process works. The following is offered as a summary of the key issues involved in record selection:

- The basic method used for record selection is for a library to assign 049 codes to item numbers which correspond to records that the library wants included in its customized GPO file. A set of 049 codes is established to reflect the various locations of documents in the library. For example, a record containing the 049 code *DOC* might load with the location *Main Library, Documents Department*, whereas, a record containing the 049 code *DOD* might load with the location *Main Library, Documents Department, Microfiche*. Those item numbers not assigned an 049 code are excluded from the profile. (For further discussion of 049 codes, see the section on "Record Processing Specifications.")
- Some item numbers represent more than one Sudoc class, so libraries must decide if record selection at the Sudoc class level is needed or if it is acceptable to select all the classes associated with a particular item number. Once this decision has been made they should determine which vendors offer the level of record selection required.
- Since the item numbers that a library receives from the GPO may vary significantly from one year to the next, it is important that a library be able to profile by year and update its profile as needed. Many libraries also find it useful to select records based on format—monograph, serial, or map. The ability of vendors to supply records based on these criteria should be determined.

Records to exclude from loading. Since the GPO cataloging records contain every item cataloged by GPO and listed in the *Monthly Catalog*, all libraries will want to exclude some records from their profile:

- Both the retrospective file and ongoing tapes contain records for a number of preprints and reprints (e.g., preprints from the *Minerals Yearbook* or *Preliminary Reports from the Census of Agriculture*). While the cataloging records for these publications offer a level of subject access not available in the bibliographic record for the final bound volume, they may tend to "clutter up" the database. For example, the title search "Census of Agriculture" in the retrospective file retrieves over 6,400 records, of which nearly 4,000 are for preliminary reports. Additionally, these records should not be loaded if (as is typically the case) the library regularly discards this material upon receipt of the bound volume, since they would represent items no longer owned by the library. Other publications falling into this category include

House and Senate documents and reports, Supreme Court slip decisions, and treaties.

- With map series, libraries must decide whether to load each individual "daughter" record or a single "mother" record for each state. Libraries may also select records by state level and receive records only for particular states.

Multiple locations. As discussed earlier, as part of the profiling process a library establishes a set of 049 codes to reflect various locations within the library. Assuming that the software available to the library for loading the GPO cataloging records into the local system supports the assignment of multiple locations based on 049 codes (which should be determined before the profiling process begins), the library may want to define codes which represent multiple locations. A number of factors must be considered when assigning these codes:

- Many large academic libraries are represented by two depositories, one for the main campus and another for the law school: In these instances, the institution must decide if it is going to try and profile the holdings for both libraries.
- Major series, such as ERIC microfiche, may be held in more than one library. The documents department, for example, might receive only those ERIC microfiche distributed through the depository library program, whereas the Education Library might maintain the entire collection. Libraries loading the GPO cataloging records for such series will want to load these records with both locations, if feasible.

Profiling decisions based on specific practices with the local library. Over the years, depository libraries make many local decisions on the most efficient way to handle government publications. Libraries should be aware that these decisions may impact the load of government documents cataloging records.

- A libraries may have historically cataloged certain depository receipts, such as periodicals or annual reports. Since the library may have depended on the Library of Congress (LC) or some other non-GPO institution for these records, they may not match the records contained in the GPO tapes. However, the library should be able to produce a list of these titles and their corresponding item numbers which can be used to exclude them from the profile.
- Similarly, selective depositories must be careful to exclude records for documents which have been weeded from their collections. For example, if all census material prior to 1985 has been withdrawn, they must be sure to profile by this date to exclude those records from their data tape.

Specific concerns for ongoing records. Most profiling concerns are relevant to both the retrospective file and to ongoing records. However, the following concern relates directly to ongoing GPO cataloging:

• For ongoing records, libraries using the GPO cataloging records to support online check-in must decide if they want to include serials in their profile. Given the fact that there is at least a four month wait between the receipt of a depository document and the availability of a cataloging record for tape loading, libraries wishing to begin online check-in of new serial titles must find alternative ways to get these records in the database. This may be done through downloading individual records from OCLC, original cataloging, or creation of provisional records.

Specific concerns for regionals. Regional depositories are not exempt from the profiling process. Even though they receive all publications distributed through the depository library program, all of the issues discussed above apply to them. Additionally, the following concerns relate specifically to regional depositories:

• Regional depository libraries should pay particular attention to dual distribution items. Publications from congressional committees, for example, are represented by two item numbers, one for the paper copy and one for the microfiche. A regional retaining both formats would want this reflected in the online catalog, although it would not want duplicate records for these series. Consequently, one item number should be defined with both locations, while the other item number is excluded from the profile.
• Regionals should also consult the "List of Superseded Documents for Regional Depository Libraries" ("List of Superseded Documents Now Annotated for Regionals," 1991) to identify any publications that they routinely withdraw and would not want included in their profile.

Concerns specific to the structure of the depository library program. Several other concerns that libraries must take into account when profiling are based on the nature and structure of the depository library program.

• Libraries must decide whether or not they wish to receive records for nondepository documents. Since these records do not contain item numbers libraries have an all or nothing option with these records (with the possible exception of profiling by format or date). Libraries with a substantial collection of nondepository material or that subscribe to the READEX nondepository collection might want to consider acquiring these records.

- Many item numbers undergo significant changes over the years. The item numbers for congressional hearings for example, underwent a major change when the GPO began to distribute them in dual format. Libraries relying solely on a list of currently selected item numbers could miss a significant number of historical records. In the case of congressional hearings, records for all documents distributed prior to 1980 might be missed.
- As discussed earlier, some libraries may depend solely on the item number for assigning microfiche locations to depository series rather than examining the 074 field in each individual record. Libraries using this system should carefully examine the history of the item number to determine which format was most frequently used. As the GPO converts more series to microfiche, libraries should be aware that they may need to make changes in the 049 code for particular item numbers to reflect changes in format.

Libraries involved in profiling should not hesitate to talk with other depositories that have already completed the process. Both OCLC and Marcive will gladly supply customers with the names of comparable institutions that have loaded the records. The profiling of over 7,000 item numbers is a tremendous undertaking that no library should attempt on its own. At this point enough libraries have loaded the GPO cataloging records so that we can begin to learn from one another's mistakes and accomplishments.

WORKFLOW DECISIONS

Depending upon the functions which the GPO records will support in the local system, a number of workflow decisions must be made. The library must determine which units will be responsible for using and maintaining the GPO records for online check-in, circulation, authority control, record maintenance, and public service.

Public Service

Following the load of the GPO cataloging records into the OPAC libraries can expect an immediate and potentially overwhelming increase in the demand for government publications (Kinney and Cornwell, 1991). Whatever unit in the library is responsible for servicing the documents collection must be prepared to handle the increase. At the University of Florida Libraries, where the documents department services the collection, staff were increased by three FTE and staff assignments to the reference desk were doubled to deal with increased demands on the collection.

If holdings are set on OCLC, RLIN, or some other bibliographic utility for this material, a significant increase in the number of ILL requests can also be expected. Decisions about which libraries to lend to (in-state vs. region vs. entire country) must be made. It must also be determined which unit will be responsible for providing photocopies, making fiche-to-fiche copies, pulling documents from the shelf, creating circulation records, etc.

Online Processing

Another area that will have a major impact on the library is the online processing of new receipts. The processing of government publications in most libraries has historically revolved around the card file. Conceptually, the move of processing from the card file to the online catalog is fairly straightforward. A large number of Federal documents are simply checked in as serials or numbered series and typically this procedure can be easily carried over to the online system.

Titles that require new bibliographic records for check-in pose a number of problems. As mentioned earlier, libraries can expect a minimum of a four-month delay between the receipt of a depository document and the availability of a cataloging record for tape loading. While the GPO has eased its guidelines for the processing of depository receipts ("GPO Guidelines for Online Processing of Depository Documents," 1990), most libraries will not want to wait four or more months to check-in new government publications. Libraries have adopted a number of methods for checking-in new depository items prior to the receipt of GPO cataloging records. Some libraries continue to check-in new titles into a card file, or use a microcomputer-based check-in system. Others create temporary bibliographic records that can be overlayed when the MARC records finally become available. Many NOTIS libraries create "unlinked item records" for new monographic receipts. While not tied to a specific bibliographic record, unlinked item records offer libraries shelflist access to the publications. Additionally, these records prepare the document for circulation and may be linked to a bibliographic record when it becomes available.

Another option that is expected to be available soon to depository libraries is the DNC (Documents Not Cataloged) MARC tape service developed by the InterArc Corporation. This product, already available in CD-ROM format, provides brief cataloging records for nearly 30,000 documents which have been distributed to depository libraries, but not yet cataloged by the GPO. Libraries using this service would have immediate bibliographic access to this material, but would need to develop a method for purging these records from the database when the GPO records become available.

Whichever of these options is chosen, a significant amount of staff time will be necessary to keep up with newly received publications. If retrospective holdings for serials or other recurring titles are to be recorded online, additional staff will need to be allocated. Due to the complex nature of government documents it would appear that the documents unit might be the logical place for these operations to take place. Unfortunately, while members of the cataloging and serials staff are not experts on government documents, most documents librarians are not experts in cataloging or online serials check-in. Consequently, whichever unit assumes responsibility for the online processing of Federal documents, it must be a team effort. That unit must have the authority as well as the support of other units in the library to carry out these operations efficiently.

Circulation

If GPO records are to support the circulation of government publications, it must be decided at what point the documents will be barcoded. The retrospective collection can be assigned "smart" barcodes as described in the "Record Processing Specifications" section, but some unit will need to take responsibility for the massive project of attaching the barcode labels. To the extent allowed by the online system, new items should be barcoded at the time of receipt allowing for their immediate circulation even if no GPO cataloging record has been tape loaded.

Libraries must determine if documents will circulate through the documents department as a separate circulation desk or through the main circulation desk. Decisions must also be made as to how documents without barcodes will be barcoded for online circulation. Presumably, most of these documents will have been received prior to the advent of GPO cataloging and consequently procedures must be established for loading bibliographic records into the database for these items. Libraries must also determine which unit will be responsible for overdues, recalls, fines, and credits for government publications.

Authority Control

While name and subject headings in the Marcive file have been changed to match those established by LC through either computer matching or manual review, some authority headings may still conflict with headings in the library's database. Bolner and Kile (1991) estimate that approximately 35,000 unrecognized personal names, uniform titles, and meetings in the retrospective file appeared to be valid and were not corrected. Some of these headings may nevertheless conflict with those already present in the library's database. Additionally, a number of subject headings for which no authority could be found were retagged as local headings. Libraries should be prepared to correct conflicts that emerge through either manual editing or, when feasible, using computer programs which allow "global" changes of headings.

Marcive project participants reviewed series headings for consistency and spelling, but made no attempt to bring these headings into conformity with series established by LC. As discussed above in the section on "Vendor Evaluation and Section," prior to September 1986, the LC and GPO frequently established different headings for the same series. As a result, libraries that cataloged government series using the LC Name Authority File should be prepared to deal with these conflicts.

Over the past 15 years, the GPO cataloging has improved to where it stands as the national cataloging authority for government publications ("Cataloging Branch Joins OCLC Enhance Project," 1990). The GPO now adheres to all national standards for authorities and libraries can expect relatively few authority problems with ongoing cataloging records. However, it should be noted that some problems with name headings in GPO abridged cataloging have been reported.[2]

Finally, a library which loads the GPO retrospective file must decide whether to obtain the related file of authority records from the vendor and must determine how to incorporate these records into the library's database. The library must also devise a mechanism for identifying new headings added to the file as the result of the ongoing load for which authority records will need to be loaded.

Due to the complex nature of authority headings, it is recommended that all operations associated with authority issues be handled by experienced catalogers rather than the documents staff.

Record Maintenance

No matter how meticulous a library is during the profiling process, a number of records must be edited, deleted, or added. Libraries will find that this holds true for both the retrospective file and for ongoing records.

More so than any other group of publications, government-produced serials have a tendency to change title, author (issuing agency), or even call number. As a result, it is not uncommon for a serial title to be represented by multiple bibliographic records throughout its lifetime. Since the GPO retrospective file only goes back to 1976, a library which wishes to record the entire holdings of a serial must acquire and edit records that represent pre-1976 versions of the title. Such editing typically includes adding beginning and ending dates, 780 and 785 fields ("continued by" and "continued from"), item numbers, and Sudoc numbers to non-GPO cataloging records.

Libraries may also want to consider restoring issue specific information back

---

[2] GPO currently produces abridged cataloging records for technical reports and nondepository documents.

to records for recurring titles when that information was lost as part of the Marcive record collapsing project. Records will also need to be edited to reflect the correct location for those titles that might have loaded as microfiche that are actually paper and vice versa. Also, information contained in the "Whatever Happened To" column of *Administrative Notes*, the "Newsletter of the Federal Depository Library Program," should be keyed into the records as appropriate.

Nondepository records that appear in the database as depository documents as a result of the Marcive project should be deleted from the database as they are discovered. In some cases, it is possible to delete large sets of documents as they are identified as nondepository. For a variety of other reasons, a significant number of documents appear in the tapes that were never actually distributed to depository libraries. Again, libraries should put in place a mechanism for deleting these records from their database.

Libraries will also find that they have thousands of publications in their documents collections that do not have GPO cataloging. While cataloging will eventually appear for some of these documents, it is doubtful that all of them will ever be cataloged by the GPO. Consequently, libraries must decide on a title-by-title or an agency-by-agency basis whether and at what level these documents should be cataloged.

The maintenance issues described here are peculiar to government publications. Documents librarians are in the best position to identify records for deletion and make judgment on editing and record creation. As a result, it is recommended that these functions be carried out by the documents staff.

RECORD PROCESSING SPECIFICATIONS

It is important to create detailed, written specifications which spell out how the GPO records are to be processed. Developing and refining these specifications provides an organized, coherent framework within which to make decisions, and ensures that these decisions are documented. During this process, "librarians" and "computer people" develop a mutual understanding of what is desired and what is feasible. The result is a set of unambiguous, detailed specifications which are agreed to by all involved.

The way a library does its profiling has a tremendous impact on the development of record processing specifications. Ideally, work on these two tasks should take place at the same time and be closely coordinated. Profiling determines what categories of records will be acquired by the library and what 049 codes they will contain. Decisions made during profiling will largely determine what type of processing will be feasible once the records are received by the library.

The content of these specifications will depend upon the characteristics of the library's local system and associated software, especially how bibliographic, authority, holdings, and item-level information is stored and retrieved, and how new and revised bibliographic records are loaded into the system. The following points need to be considered regardless of the specifics of a library's local system.

Authority Processing

As discussed above, the Marcive retrospective file has relatively few of the authority problems associated with the original GPO retrospective file. Any heading inconsistencies which do arise from the GPO load will probably just have to be resolved as they are discovered after the load.

The library may decide to acquire authority records along with the GPO retrospective file, in which case specifications for loading these authority records into the local system need to be developed. If feasible, the library will want to "deblind" these authority records at the time of loading so that public catalog users are not referred to headings which have not actually been used by the library. Authority records which duplicate those already in the local database may either not be loaded or they may replace the existing records. This decision depends on factors such as whether the library has made modifications to existing authority records (such as adding local cross-references) and which authority records are most current. The library may want to produce a printout and/or datafile listing any existing authority records which are replaced during the load.

Bibliographic Record Duplication between the GPO File and the Existing Database

Many of the duplicate records which made the original GPO retrospective file virtually unusable have been eliminated from the Marcive file, so that duplicate records *within* the file should not be a problem. However, even if the library's documents collection is essentially uncataloged it is likely that at least some Federal documents listed in the *Monthly Catalog* have been acquired and cataloged for other collections. While it may be possible to exclude many duplicate records through careful profiling, there will likely be some duplication between the GPO retrospective file and the existing online catalog database. GPO records which match records already in the database should be identified based on OCLC number matching (although this may fail to identify duplicates in cases in which the record in the local database is derived from non-GPO cataloging). The library may choose not to load these records, or may have them replace the existing catalog records, in which case a printout and/or datafile of replaced records may be produced.

As discussed in the section on "Workflow," the library may decide to create temporary records at the time that new documents are received. These records will need to be eliminated from the database once ongoing GPO cataloging records have been loaded. Ideally, each new GPO record would be matched with and then replace its corresponding temporary record. In practice this may not be feasible, since standard OCLC number matching cannot be used.[3] An alternative approach that can be explored is matching on Sudoc number.

Some of the records contained in ongoing GPO cataloging tapes will have the same OCLC number as records already in the local database: updated versions of previously created GPO records. As described in the section on "Vendor Evaluation and Selection," these updated records will be included for serials (if included in the library's profile), for multipart monographs, and for various older records which have been enhanced in some way. Since, for ongoing GPO cataloging, a new record is by definition an improved one, the library will probably want to replace the existing records and produce a printout or datafile listing the replaced records.

Assignment of Holding Location(s)

Each GPO record loaded into a local online catalog must be assigned one or more holding locations, which identify where copies of the document are shelved (e.g., "Main Library" or "Documents Department"). For both retrospective and ongoing GPO cataloging, codes which identify these local holding locations are typically added by the vendor in an 049 field in each GPO record based on profiling information provided by the library. Under the profiling systems used by most vendors, the library specifies which 049 code is to be added to each record based on the item number contained in the 074 field. When the record is processed by the library for loading into the local system, the 049 code is used— possibly in conjunction with other information contained in the record—to assign one or more locations to the record. (The exact way such locations are coded and stored in the local system varies from system to system.)

As discussed above, libraries typically set up separate and distinct locations within the documents collection (and other collections, for that matter) for print and microformat materials. At the University of Florida, for example, separate locations have been established (and displayed in the online catalog) for "Library West, Documents" (for print) and "Library West, Documents (microfiche)" (for microfiche). This means that it is important to determine for each GPO catalog record whether the document described has been distributed in print or microfiche. However, since *every* GPO catalog record describes the print version of the document, the only clue as to the actual format that has been

---

[3] The temporary record will not typically contain an appropriate OCLC number for matching, since it will have been created before GPO created the cataloging record on OCLC.

Figure 5-1. Holding Locations Table
Production of "Smart Barcodes" and/or Creation of Item-Level Records

049 Code	"Microfiche" in 074 field?	Number of locations	Online catalog location(s) to be assigned
DOCA	No	1	Documents Department
DOCA	Yes	1	Documents Department, Microfiche
DOCB	No	2	Documents Department Education Library
DOCB	Yes	2	Documents Department, Microfiche Education Library, Microfiche

distributed is the presence or absence of the word "microfiche" following the item number in the 074 field. For this reason, it is highly recommended that the assignment of local holding locations be based on the 049 code together with a check for the word "microfiche" in the 074 field.

The easiest way to specify how local holding locations are to be assigned is by using a table such as that shown in Figure 5-1 (based loosely on specifications developed by the UF Libraries and the Florida Center for Library Automation). This example illustrates how the 049 code together with the presence of the word "microfiche" in the 074 (Item Number) field may be used to assign locations. It also illustrates the use of a single 049 code to assign multiple holding locations, which may not be feasible with some local systems.

The record processing specifications should address whether "smart" barcode labels and/or online item-level circulation records should be generated from the GPO records. A "smart" barcode label contains not only a barcode number but also the call number (and usually part of the title) of the item to which it is to be attached. A tape is created containing the information necessary for a vendor to create the smart barcodes, and typically at the same time item-level information (including the barcode number assigned to each item) is added to records in the local database. This process may be carried out either before or after the GPO tapes are loaded into the local online system—the library's programming staff should be consulted as to which is the more feasible approach.

CUSTOMIZATION/MODIFICATION OF THE LOCAL ONLINE SYSTEM

In addition to developing new software (or adapting existing record-loading programs) for GPO record processing, some type of customization or modification of the local online system will probably also be needed. While such changes are likely to be fairly minor (e.g., setting up new valid locations in the local system), it is important that they be identified early so that they will be in place when needed. This is an area—like development of record processing specifica-tions—in which librarians will have to work closely with the programming staff to determine what is feasible. Given the range of different library systems in use, it is not possible to provide a comprehensive list all of the possible ways in which a given library's system may need to be customized or modified. However, based on the experience of the University of Florida Libraries, it is recommended that the following areas be considered:

- *Establishment of new locations.* New locations will almost certainly be identified during profiling and the development of record processing specifi-cations, since there will have been no reason to set up locations for uncataloged documents collections prior to the GPO load. These new locations need to defined in the local system.
- *Support for new documents department online processing capabilities.* It is likely that some customization of the local system will be needed in order to allow documents department staff to carry out new online processing activities. Such modifications might include (and did, at the University of Florida) establishing new sign ons and reconfiguring the capabilities of documents department terminals.
- *Support for new online access points.* If no online Sudoc number index existed before the GPO load, the library will want to establish one afterwards. It may also be feasible to set up online indexes to other data elements which are unique to GPO cataloging (such as item number and *Monthly Catalog* entry number), or which are of particular use in working with such records (such as stock number and report number).
- *Online catalog display modification.* Online catalog display is another area in which modifications should be considered in order to enhance the usefulness of GPO cataloging records. For example, the Florida Center for Library Automation was able to adapt the NOTIS Library Management System to allow display of the item number and *Monthly Catalog* Entry Number.

GPO RECORD LOADING CHECKLIST

The following checklist summarizes the steps that a library should follow when planning a load of the GPO cataloging records:

I. *Develop an initial proposal for loading the GPO cataloging records and distribute it to library staff/systems support staff for comment and refinement. The proposal should include:*
A) Introduction
B) Description of the library's documents collection
C) Sources for obtaining GPO cataloging records
D) Proposed role of the GPO cataloging records in the database
E) Impact of the load on the documents department

      F)   Impact of the load on public services
      G)   Impact of the load on technical services
      H)   Appendix containing documents related terminology
      I)   Appendix containing suggested readings

II.   *Special characteristics of the GPO cataloging records*
      A)   How to handle nonformat specific GPO cataloging
      B)   Multiple call numbers
      C)   Item numbers incorrectly added to nondepository documents
      D)   Issue-specific information missing from serials within series
      E)   Mother–daughter records for maps
      F)   Authority issues
      G)   Filling in gap between receipt of a depository document and the availability of a tape supplied GPO cataloging record
      H)   Processing of updated/enhanced records

III. *Vendor evaluation and selection*
      A)   Ability of vendor to deal with special characteristics of the records
      B)   Cost of records
      C)   Cost to set holding and ability to load records into various bibliographic utilities
      D)   Profiling capabilities

IV. *Profiling considerations*
      A)   Records to exclude from the load
          i)   Reprints, preprints, treaties, House and Senate reports and documents
          ii)   Map records
          iii) Serial records
      B)   Planning for multiple locations of specific documents
      C)   Impact of local decisions
          i)   Documents previously cataloged
          ii)   Weeding
      D)   Profiling considerations for Regionals
          i)   Dual distribution items
          ii)   List of superseded documents for Regionals
      E)   Considerations based on the structure of the depository library program
          i)   Nondepository records
          ii)   Changes in item numbers
          iii) Changes in format

V.   *Impact of loading the GPO cataloging records on library workflow*
      A)   Public service
      B)   Online processing
      C)   Circulation
      D)   Authority control
      E)   Record maintenance

VI.   Develop detailed, written record processing specifications reflecting a mutual understanding of what is desired and what is feasible as a result of loading the GPO cataloging records. Areas to consider include:
A)   Authority processing
B)   Duplication of records between the GPO file and the existing database
C)   Assignment of holdings locations
D)   Barcodes

VII. Customization/modification of the local database
A)   Establish new locations
B)   Support for new documents department online processing capabilities
C)   Support for new online access points
D)   Modification of online catalog display

REFERENCES

"Automation of GPO Series Files," *Administrative Notes*, 8 (February, 1987): 4 *(GP3.16/3–2:8/4)*.

Bolner, Myrtle Smith and Barbara Kile. "Documents to the People: Access through the Automated Catalog," *Government Publications Review*, 18 (1991): 51–64.

"Cataloging Branch Joins OCLC Enhance Project," *Administrative Notes*, 11 (July 31, 1990): 1 *(GP3.16/3–2:11/16)*.

"GPO Cataloging Tapes Ready for Production," *Administrative Notes*, 11 (January 30, 1990): 1 *(GP3.16/3–2:11/3)*.

"GPO Guidelines for Online Processing of Depository Documents," *Administrative Notes*, 11 (July, 15, 1990): 2–3 *(GP3.16/3–2:11/15)*.

"GPO to Produce Improved Cataloging Tapes," *Administrative Notes*, 10 (August 21, 1989): 1 *(GP3.16/3–2:10/17)*.

Jamison, Carolyn C. "Loading the GPO Tapes—What Does It Really Mean?," *Government Publications Review*, 13 (1986): 549–559.

Kinney, Thomas and Gary Cornwell. "GPO Cataloging Records in the Online Catalog: Implications for the Reference Librarian," *The Reference Librarian*, 32 (1991): 259–275.

"List of Superseded Documents Now Annotated for Regionals," *Administrative Notes*, 12 (March 30, 1991): 7–30 *(GP3.16/3–2:12/8)*.

Mooney, Margaret T. "GPO Cataloging: Is It a Viable Current Access Tool for U.S. Documents?" *Government Publications Review*, 16 (1989): 259–270.

Myers, Judy E. "The Government Printing Office Cataloging Records: Opportunities and Problems," *Government Information Quarterly*, 2 (1985): 27–56.

Swanbeck, Jan. "Federal Documents in the Online Catalog: Problems, Options, and the Future," *Government Information Quarterly*, 2 (1985): 187–192.

Tull, Laura. "Retrospective Conversion of Government Documents: Marcive GPO Tape Clean–up Project," *Technicalities*, 9 (August 1989): 4–7.

Chapter Six

Maps/Cartographic Materials

David A. Cobb

This chapter discusses the use of technology and its relationship to maps and other cartographic materials in depository libraries. The discussion will focus on current systems, the integration of electronic map information into libraries, management issues, electronic mail, bibliographic control, future issues, and suggestions for responses to this increase of Federal government information.

The impact of electronic information in the map collection is a very recent phenomena. This author recently compiled the second edition of the *Guide to U.S. Map Resources* (Cobb, 1990), and there was little discussion of CD-ROM's or geographical information software (GIS) at that time. In fact, during the compilation of this work (1988-1989) we thought we were "up-to-date" by including FAX numbers and e-mail addresses which then were few and far between.

Since that time the government has published hundreds of CD-ROMs, numerous commercial products have appeared on the market, and GIS software and products are available from a variety of government and commercial sources.

The mid-1980s probably represents the time period when map librarians became familiar with automated mapping through various discussions and presentations by U.S. Geological Survey (USGS) officials on the TIGER mapping system. This system was being developed between the U.S. Geological Survey and the Bureau of the Census and its objective was to create a seamless map (a map with no boundaries or edges) of the entire United States. This daunting task was difficult to relate to for the individual depository library which was used to receiving its usual topographic map shipments from USGS on a monthly basis. This TIGER system was to be finished in the late 1980s so that it might be used with data from the 1990 census. No librarian ever could have imagined then the impact that this one system might have on the average depository library nor the products of the 1990 census. This highlights, very briefly, how quickly librarians have had to learn this technology, be impacted by it, manage a reaction to it, and prepare their staffs with training and updates.

Similarly, it has become increasingly obvious that large amounts of cartographic information in every imaginable Federal agency was being digitized and maintained in files that were not available to the general public at large. This continues to be true and this information will never be printed as we had expected in the past.

OTHER MAPPING PRODUCTS

The current and future mapping systems that will be available to libraries in the future represent a technology that will challenge the very structure of our libraries in the future. Many of our libraries are divided to serve a particular clientele, a department, college, or business. Social science librarians are very used to dealing with Federal government statistics, while map librarians have usually waited for these statistics, for example, to be converted to map form and published by the Geological Survey or the Bureau of the Census. Today they can now share these data and the map via geographical information system software and a myriad of potential outputs. Have we reached a true parallax or convergence of information based on technology (McGlamery, 1990)? Will our libraries continue to maintain these artificial walls, or will we be able to take advantage of this technology, share the information, and bring these layers together for the overall benefit of library users? This may indeed be the challenge for structuring this electronic information in the library of the 21st century.

One of the first systems to be used in some research libraries was SUPERMAP, a commercial product distributed by Chadwyck-Healey. It is important to mention because it, like so many other products, is carefully packaged and reformatted and is a simple derivative of government information statistics. SUPERMAP is a CD-ROM product consisting of the 1980 Census Summary Tape Files 1A, 1C, and 3. It also contains data from the *County and City Data Book* and the old GBF/Dime boundary files. As a first generation product it was difficult to use, expensive, and not acquired by very many libraries. Its importance was its ability to provide library users with a combination of datasets and customized cartographic illustration heretofore unavailable at the library level.

Two additional commercial products appeared almost simultaneously which also made use of government statistics. The first to appear was PC-Globe, a simple floppy disc system. It was soon followed by PC-USA. These two products, unlike SUPERMAP, were "read-only" information with no ability to analyze or choose information or outputs for specific questions. Nevertheless, their map clarity and screen output quality far exceeded SUPERMAP. PC-Globe and PC-USA allow for regional or state/country maps and comparative data graphs, i.e., age/sex ratio's for foreign countries. We have installed these two systems onto our public catalog in the University of Illinois Map & Geography Library and use them often to illustrate answers to questions for our patrons. One of the more common queries we receive relates to "distance" questions—how far is it from here to there? PC-Globe allows you to select major cities to construct such distance tabulations and also allows you to customize your city location using latitude and longitude coordinates if they are not available in the tables. We have found this to be far more accurate, efficient, and quicker to use than the many distance tables that we currently have in print. While both of these systems have essentially reformatted government information they are offering it at bargain prices.

Another CD-ROM product was also introduced for the world mapping market called Mundo-Cart by Chadwyck-Healey. This is a detailed world mapping system consisting of maps derived from the Defense Mapping Agency 1:1,000,000 series (approximately 1 inch = 16 miles). This system, when combined with PC paint software, has various applications, and its mapping is detailed but its price tag of $14,000 has all but a few libraries shying away from this product.

JUST WHAT IS THIS GIS ANYWAY

Maps have been with us for many centuries and have been drawn since the dawn of mankind. Maps have witnessed the similar advancements that have followed the printed word: from manuscripts through copperplate engraving to a variety of computer applications today. We now have another tool, albeit a very powerful one. Essentially, the combination of reduced hardware costs and software developments have provided us with this technology called a geographic information system (GIS). "A geographic information system is an integrated package for the input, storage, analysis, and output of spatial information" (Chrisman et al., 1989, p. 776). The geographer will probably be most interested in the analysis aspect, while the librarian may be most interested in the output. For the librarian, it is important to realize that GIS is a tool to manipulate information as we know it today. GIS software will allow us to view information as if it were in layers (e.g., transportation, rivers, topography, population, census tracts, and economic values) and then integrate these parts as we wish. This analysis of our information makes GIS the powerful tool that it is and also such an interdisciplinary tool. Viewing information in this fashion will be of interest to social and physical scientists and researchers in all fields. For the librarian to have this option will indeed provide us with a powerful analytical component to study information and, in reality, to provide information upon demand.

To be sure, there are informational ingredients that are required to make this "soup" cook. I believe that we will be using information that is already digitized (e.g., the TIGER files, and the economic and population censuses), and few libraries will be involved with digitizing information for these databases. Nevertheless, so much government information is currently digitized that libraries will be able to integrate large amounts of information that will be readily available.

While the technology is spreading rapidly, the relation between GIS as a technology and the discipline of geography remains unclear (Chrisman et al., 1989, p. 794). As this technology and expertise spread into libraries, this technology will become a true public service utility. Libraries will bring this software and its applications from the engineering and drafting offices to a public service atmosphere. The success of this atmosphere may indeed depend upon the resources that libraries devote to it and if administrators envision the cross-disciplinary applications, be they academic or public. According to Chrisman et al. (1989, p. 794),

> In essence, a GIS database is a formal model of spatial information, and as such plays a fundamental role in geographical analysis. Whether this role will be recognized, and GIS regarded as fundamental . . . , or whether GIS will be relegated to the level of another techical fad, remains to be seen.

Geographers think with and through maps, and GIS technology will soon become indispensable to our thinking, teaching, and practice (Abler, 1987, p. 515).

TIGER—WHO HAS THE TAIL?

As mentioned earlier, the TIGER mapping system was developed during the 1980s by the Geological Survey and the Bureau of the Census. TIGER, or Topologically Integrated Geographic Encoding and Referencing System, is a complete and borderless map of the United States at the scale of 1:100,000. As its name implies, it allows for the integration of additional data, such as statistical information from the Bureau of the Census, to create thematic or subject maps on an accurate geographic base. The 1990 Census is the first graphic census because it collected a wealth of information electronically that can be manipulated with computer software to create endless maps and other graphics. The software allows the individual library user, for the first time, to query a statistical database, create a set of customized parameters, and ask for a graphic and/or tabular output.

The potential user satisfaction and impact on library service will be significant. Unfortunately, nothing in life is free. The issues surrounding this system and the entire area of geographical information systems are three:

- Training,
- Hardware, and
- Software.

While librarians are becoming increasingly more familiar with various application softwares, there remains a lack of coordinated training workshops, and library schools are just beginning to consider such information in their curricula. It is no longer sufficient to be able to use a word-processing system today as future librarians will surely be expected to have mastered database software (e.g., dBase), and spreadsheets (e.g., Lotus 1-2-3), and document librarians will continue to face too many dissimilar softwares from various agencies.

GIS software requires large amounts of computer space, and graphic analysis requires high-speed computers. One commercial vendor offering GIS software suggested, as minimum requirements, a 386 PC, 125MB hard disk, and 2-4MB of random access memory. These guidelines are similar to those recommended by the Depository Library Council to the Public Printer in 1990, although GIS applications will require larger hard disk memories. The platforms required to run increasingly sophisticated data and software will surely improve in speed and size. Researching computer hardware is often tedious, always confusing, and one of the most important decisions librarians make. Libraries are unable to update hardware regularly, and since staff will probably be working with the hardware acquired for several years, librarians must carefully plan the hardware acquisitions.

It is now becoming apparent that the Government Printing Office (GPO) will offer very little software to the depository library program to run the many CD-ROMs currently distributed or planned for distribution. At the same time, other electronic information will be distributed through the depository program. The government software that has been initially offered (MARPLOT) with the TIGER discs was cumbersome and very slow, and did not allow the user to import or export files from other statistical packages. There is a large amount of software available and, again, it is best to review and plan as much as possible. It is expected soon that a core group of libraries will have become familiar with this technology and become a source for others.

It is interesting to note the TIGER Project, which became an outgrowth of the initial distribution of pre-Census TIGER files, was a cooperative initiative among the Cartographic User's Advisory Council, the Government Printing Office, and the Bureau of the Census. It was initially centered at the University of Kansas. Geographers and librarians at the University of Kansas diplomatically arranged with several vendors to allow for a testing of their software with the TIGER files. Only 27 libraries initially chose to participate in this project, and it was only after the initial distribution of software and discs that libraries realized their individual deficiencies for training, hardware, and software. It is only now, nearly one year after this project began, that these project libraries, as well as others in the depository library program, have come to realize the significance of the TIGER CD-ROMs now in their libraries.

Who has the "tail" of this TIGER in library land? I do not believe anyone has, but there is light at the end of the tunnel as will be addressed later in the chapter. What should be communicated here is that TIGER is not insurmountable, but that in order for any library to take complete advantage of the 1990 Census, the staff will have to become familiar with TIGER and provide the necessary resources to operate it. Two publications that libraries should be familiar with are the Bureau of the Census's *Tiger Questions and Answers* (1991) and the special issue of *Cartography and Geographic Information Systems* on "The Census Bureau's TIGER System" edited by Robert W. Marx (1990).

The ultimate question may become "Who needs the tail of the TIGER?" As this system becomes the standard for boundary files, commercial vendors are building software around it. Numerous offerings from these vendors will provide segments of the TIGER system. The DeLorme Mapping Company has already issued one of the first such derivatives: Streetatlas, which provides all of the streets of the United States on one CD-ROM for $99 and includes software imbedded on the disk. While many librarians are daunted by the size of the TIGER files, with their 37 CD-ROMs and no software, enterprising software vendors will solve many of the problems by developing software such as Streetatlas. Will we pay for it? Yes. Can we expect the government to provide us with software soon because of some demand from the public? No. This is a pure case of the government believing that it is the purveyor of data which it will distribute. Since the government used commercial software to develop a dataset as a product, it does not believe that it can distribute that software. This issue of proprietary software has caused the Federal government some consternation. The government uses such software to distribute data relatively freely, but also refuses to work for the public good in arranging for site licenses at the front end of contracts.

CARTOGRAPHIC MATERIALS SYSTEMS

In addition to providing the Bureau of the Census with the TIGER database at the scale of 1:100,000 (ca. 1 inch = 1.75 miles), the Geological Survey has published and digitized these maps. These digital maps are "simply" the automated version of the printed map, but the digital information obviously allows parts of the map to be used in a variety of different ways and, again, with different datasets using census data, for instance. The USGS expects to begin distributing these 1:100K maps on CD-ROM during the 1991–1992 fiscal year and to include them in the depository library program. Because these maps include far greater information than the similar maps produced for the Bureau of the Census (contour lines to show altitudes, vegetation, etc.), there will be many more CD-ROMs than those comprising the TIGER files. It is questionable whether we should even refer to these digital discs as maps since the software used creates the map. Bytes are bytes (McGlammery, 1990, p. 89), and these disks simply contain the bytes from which maps can be made. Similarly, the Census CD-ROM's are not the *County and City Data Book* although they contain the same data; however, you must use software to "arrange" the data to create recognizable output. In conclusion, many more "CD-maps" will appear in depository libraries, and TIGER is just the beginning.

The Defense Mapping Agency, which initiated a large digital program several years ago, is converting many of its maps to this format. These include popular series: the Joint Operations Graphics (1:250,000 and classified); the Tactical Pilotage Charts (TPC) (1:500,000); and the Operational Navigation Charts (ONC) (1:1,000,000). The latter two are currently distributed in paper format to depositories, and experimental CD-ROMs of the TPCs have been shared with some libraries. There are plans currently to begin sharing the ONCs as a World Map to be distributed by the Geological Survey in the near future.

It is important that we not restrict ourselves in this discussion solely to maps with which everyone may be familiar. Enormous amounts of remotely sensed (e.g., satellite imagery) data have been accumulating, and much of these data are stored at the EROS Data Center in Sioux Falls, South Dakota, only in digital form. This collection represents several million images, and systems to view this vast storehouse of information are improving all of the time. The newest of these is the Global Land Information System (GLIS) which allows researchers to evaluate data, to determine availability, order material online, and to browse individual scenes covering their area of geographical interest. It is significant that GLIS is available through the INTERNET as well as through commercial telephone communications (Geological Survey, 1991).

Closer to the earth, Federal, state, and local governments have been flying airplane aerial photography since the late 1930s. These collections also number in the millions, and the largest collection is at the National Archives (Cobb, 1990, p. xiii) with several research libraries holding several hundred thousand. This imagery is a far more accurate "map" than those we are familiar with as it is literally a picture of a portion of the surface of the earth at a particular point in time. These photographs are usually black and white, and detailed, and provide excellent images for studying transportation, urban development, vegetation, etc. What is most important is that there is a guide to this photography, a CD-ROM called the Aerial Photography Summary Record System (APSRS), which lists on one CD-ROM aerial photography for the entire United States. Unfortunately, APSRS is not distributed by the Geological Survey because of proprietary software problems. Another product in the development stages (as of late 1991) is the Geological Survey's Geographical Names Information System. This is an automated listing for geographical names in the United States and is the database from which the National Gazetteer (Professional Paper 1200 series) is derived and distributed in print form. It too should be distributed to depository libraries as geographical names are one of the most common questions asked of library staff.

ELECTRONIC MAIL

Technological advances in computer technology have not only influenced our means of accessing and distributing information, but, in parallel, has also changed our methods of communication. One of these is the advent of electronic mail through the INTERNET or, for many research libraries, BITNET.

This ability, to access communication electronically versus waiting for the usual postal delivery, enables libraries and librarians to communicate more regularly and more efficiently. It is a better substitute for the telephone, since you need not call back or leave messages for persons; you simply send the message electronically and the recipient reads it at his or her convenience.

Map libraries, or those interested in cartographic information, have developed a network similar to GovDoc-L, which is called MAPS-L. This network is centered at the University of Georgia. Like other list servers, its major advantage is that one message can be sent to the Georgia computer and then rerouted to all the subscribers. In November 1991 there were 347 subscribers to MAPS-L, and at that time the network was barely 6 months old. Although it is somewhat difficult to determine an individual's location by an e-mail address, I was able to approximate that there were at least 35 foreign subscribers to MAPS-L. MAPS-L has become valuable for philosophical discussions on the impact of "e-info" and for answering reference questions and providing interlibrary loan services. For example, I recently had a discussion with a librarian in Hong Kong who wanted an early edition of an Army Map Service map. We must have corresponded three or four times, over a two-day period, on electronic mail. Similarly, a few subscribers to MAPS-L from the United Kingdom and Ireland regularly contribute their expertise to answering questions regarding Europe.

The value of electronic mail is only beginning to become appreciated and will increase for libraries seeking answers to questions on software, answering reference questions, and filling interlibrary loan requests, to name only a few applications. "In essence communications on a greatly enlarged scale is truly shaping the way we think and behave as individuals, members of communities and organizations" (Brunn and Leinbach, 1991, p. xv). The ability to communicate quickly and efficiently with our colleagues will allow isolated libraries to be informed sooner, conference updates can be transmitted on a more timely basis, and critical news items can be sent across the network immediately. Advances in communications and information processing are changing our perceptions of cores and peripheries as they existed earlier when transportation of information was slow and sent by mail via rail, road, or ship (Ibid., p. xvii). All of this means that librarians will be more informed and up-to-date than ever before, and this will only result in improved service for our library users.

BIBLIOGRAPHIC CONTROL

Although many institutions take cataloging utilities, such as OCLC, for granted, too few use these for map cataloging or for installing maps onto their online systems. Of 974 libraries listed in the recent *Guide to U.S. Map Resources*, only an average of 23% either used OCLC or RLIN for their map collections (Cobb, 1990, p. xiii), although 60% said they cataloged their maps and 64% said they classified their maps. Interestingly, there are still libraries that classify their maps using the Sudocs system (18%), which is far inferior to any other for cartographic retrieval. Comparatively, 64% of the libraries use the most popular and geographically accurate Library of Congress G classification. Nevertheless, only 22% of the collections included maps in their online catalogs while 58% were still using a card catalog as the major inventory control and retrieval system.

One of the remaining hindrances to better use of cartographic materials in libraries is the archaic practice of maintaining two separate collections. Some documents collections maintain the "GPO map collection," while the map library in the same institution has the "other" maps. This is usually made worse by the use of the Sudocs classification in the documents collection which almost prevents any type of geographical retrieval whatsoever. It is time that we bring down these artificial barriers, cooperate together as professionals, and share our expertise as information specialists for the good of the library and its users.

Despite these problematic issues, there is improvement. The first edition of the *Guide to U.S. Map Resources* (Cobb, 1986, p. xiv) revealed that only 18% of the libraries used either OCLC or RLIN. Future editions of the guide will probably continue to show improvements in this area. Similarly, map libraries have been reluctant to cooperate in collection development and interlibrary loan in the past. Price increases affecting libraries everywhere inhibit the purchasing power for maps and make libraries aware of the need to cooperate and share resources. Using OCLC and other utilities for holdings information will increase our knowledge of other libraries and, hopefully, encourage more cooperation.

OCLC holdings included 278,115 map records in the third quarter of 1991. Total LC records numbered 129,132 and total member input was 144,589. GPO catalogers contribute significantly to this growth, thereby allowing depository libraries to catalog their depository government maps and include them in their online catalogs.

FUTURE ISSUES AND IMPACTS

A recent discussion on the INTERNET (McGlamery, Bartlett, Cobb and Koepp, 1991) focused on issues related to e-info's impact on cartographic information. Could it be that e-info is a new format just as microfilm or the card catalog were, and that reactions are similar? E-info requires additional equipment and staff training, but will, it is hoped, improve service to the library user. Similar to introductions of previous "advancements," the initial period, in which we find ourselves, is mostly spent reacting to the technology rather than preparing for or learning it. As that stage comes to a close, we are beginning to realize the impact of this "new" technology, to prepare for the lack of software, and to plan for staff training. We have reached the proverbial bottom line from which we must move forward and stop looking at all of the obstacles we can find to either interrupt or hinder progress.

User Demand

The demand for e-info will grow dramatically as users are introduced to vast amounts of easily accessible information and given the choice of color outputs in textual or graphic form. Additionally, another group of users may wish to visit the library, download numerous data files, return to their offices, and manipulate this information for their own individualized outputs. E-info will create an increased demand on library services already stretched to their limits. Although libraries have suffered economically and reduced hours and staff, they are still being asked to absorb additional information and services.

Collection Development, Archiving, and Preservation

Libraries have stored vast amounts of information for centuries. Will libraries be able to continue to collect these vast amounts in electronic form? A second question, which is no less important, is "whom will be responsible for archiving this e-info?" These data are so easily updated that old data are simply superseded, but, unlike the paper analog form, there is no other copy of these "old" data. At this very moment, as Federal agencies debate this problem, data are disappearing. We do not know which libraries currently collect these data currently or which institutions actively use e-info. Many libraries are just beginning to realize that if half of the floor at the ALA exhibits are covered with CD-ROM distributors, then maybe these products are really coming. However, these "backward" libraries may not be any further behind those of us who know they are coming and even have them.

The issue of preservation for CD-ROM and hard-disk data still has many question marks and is a serious issue around which library organizations should form alliances and lobby for standards and adequate testing. It has been stated that CD-ROMs should have an expected life of 10–25 years (McFaul, 1991). When Census and USGS maps begin to "peel" off of our CD-ROMs in the year 2006, whom do I contact for replacement copies—the GPO, the Census Bureau, or the Geological Survey? Is anybody maintaining an archival copy of such data that should be of vital interest to writing the social history of the United States? Does anybody care? I am reminded of Mark Twain's words at this point: "That's the difference between governments and individuals. Governments don't care, individuals do" (Ayres, 1989).

Bibliographic Control

The sheer volume of e-info may require a whole new set of descriptive cataloging techniques in order to catalog more on the file and perhaps even individual fields (McGlamery, 1991; Lai and Gillies, 1991). While MARC (Machine Readable Cataloging) has a format for computer files it does not provide for layered, or item, cataloging. Will it be enough to know that a disc contains the TIGER boundary file for Montana, or should we catalog the disc to say that it includes street files, place names, tracts, etc.? How much more complicated is the possibility of a file that includes TIGER, STF 1A population data, sections of the agriculture census and the economic census, as well as land use data from a USGS data file? Complicating matters, the data might be layered in a GIS software? Information and data are, indeed, becoming holistic and not the purview of "walled libraries." This issue of providing access will have to be addressed as e-info changes dramatically and quickly. Nevertheless, this information and data are too dynamic to produce long, drawn-out indexes to them.

Data Sharing

We are entering the stage of technology where we can use digital information, once thought to be the arena of mainframe computers, on more powerful personal computers. The result is a democratic effort to share more information across more levels of an educated society. Libraries will create datasets that may be of use to others, just as our bibliographic information and library catalogs are now. How do we share these data? How will we announce that we even have them? Although the INTERNET currently exists and is useful for networking, it is becoming overloaded and is not a satisfactory medium for graphic communication. Will the National Research and Education Network (NREN) provide us with such a network? Libraries have a history of sharing information, and e-info should be no exception in the future, although the addition of graphic imagery will present additional challenges to improved communication. Any possible reorganization of the depository library program will place further emphasis upon improved communications and the sharing of e-info among libraries, regardless of size. The future may dictate that certain libraries not collect certain information, but that they will always have the ability to access the collection of another library, as in the current regional library concept. While document delivery and faxing will continue, there will a new emphasis on electronic delivery of files and documents which will become much more cost-efficient.

With GIS technology spreading rapidly among municipalities and engineering firms, libraries will receive additional data of interest. These municipalites and firms create information having cartographic implications. The information relates to zoning, planning, tax assessing, etc. Unfortunately, there bodies remain less than open in sharing their information and as large files of data will now only be stored digitally, another challenge to access emerge.

Education

Currently, the knowledge of geographical information systems and their applications to integration with other data resides in the academic geography community. This presents the greatest hurdle to the effective use of GIS. Librarians have the opportunity to join this community, share the information, and bring GIS to a new level in a true public service role in the nation's libraries. The challenge is not small and will not be resolved overnight.

Several vendors with GIS software are willing to cooperate with the library community to meet the challenge. No longer will libraries think of information in its current static state, but they must realize that GIS allows for different analysis and outputs and a choice of many layers of information. The map will only be one choice and may, in many cases, not be the most appropriate method of displaying information.

Currently, few in the library community are familiar with GIS, its applications, or its potential impact upon library service. With the assistance of these few we will begin to crawl with this technology. Soon we will walk, and, it is hoped that we can run in the next few years. Much of the early generations of GIS are cumbersome, complicated, and slow. However, the more recent versions and developments in GIS technology hold much promise for its role in libraries in the near future.

Perhaps the greatest challenge will be introducing this technology into the library school curriculum which will provide the profession with its next generation of librarians. This is not a subject that should be restricted to the geography curricula and, until library science embraces GIS, we will all be limited to just statistical tables or general maps. Will our profession be prepared to knock down those walls we find in today's libraries? Dangermond (1989) notes that:

> GIS technology can help us overcome the technical problems of making our organizations function more effectively. Will we be willing to share our information? Will we then be able to think about problems holistically? How we meet these personal challenges may determine how well our institutions are allowed to function.

Is it possible that we have reached a parallax or convergence where information is no longer recognizable, and will we use information as we have in the past? Regardless, it is still information, and e-info has many advantages. We have an opportunity to take information, divide it into various layers, and customize how we use it as never before. To put it another way, we will have the opportunity to determine the outline and index of our books and not be subservient to the interests of the author or publisher. We must learn to use other aids (software) to enhance, massage, or realign this e-info. We have the capability to provide better information by using e-info, and we owe it to ourselves and our clients to pursue this path.

REFERENCES

Abler, R.F. "What Shall We Say? To Whom Shall We Speak?," *Annals of the Association of American Geographers*, 77 (1987): 511–524.

Ayres, Alex. *The Wit and Wisdom of Mark Twain*. New York: Penguin, 1989.

Brunn, Stanley D. and Thomas R. Leinbach. *Collapsing Space & Time: Geographic Aspects of Communication & Information*. London: Harper Collins, 1991.

Bureau of the Census. *Tiger Questions and Answers*. Washington, D.C., 1991 *(C 3.279:T 62)*.

Chrisman, Nicholas R., David J. Cowen, Peter F. Fischer, Michael F. Goodchild, and David M. Mark. "Geographic Information Systems," *Geography in America*. Columbus, OH: Merrill, 1989, pp. 776–796.

Cobb, David A. *Guide to U.S. Map Resources*. Chicago, IL: American Library Association, 1986, 1990.

Dangermond, Jack. "The Organizational Impact of GIS Technology," *ARC News*, 11 (Summer 1989): 4.

Geological Survey. *Global Land Information System*. Reston, VA, 1991.

Lai, Pohchin and Charles F. Gillies. "The Impact of Geographical Information Systems on the Role of Spatial Data Libraries," *International Journal of Geographical Information Systems*, 5 (1991): 241–251.

Marx, Robert W., ed. "The Census Bureau's TIGER System," *Cartography and Geographic Information Systems*, 17 (January 1990), special issue.

McFaul, Jerry. Presentation given to the National Meeting of the USGS Earth Science Information Center's, Reston, VA, April 1991.

McGlamery, Patrick, Jane Bartlett, David Cobb, and Donna Koepp. BITNET Correspondence, November 1991.

McGlamery, Patrick. "Parallax: Cartographic Information in Transition," *Reference Services Review*, 18 (Summer 1990) : 89–92.

CASE STUDIES

Chapter Seven

Wellesley College

Claire T. Loranz

Wellesley College has applied new technologies in its documents collection, especially in the areas of office automation and reference service. While a great deal more remains to be done, a firm foundation for the use of new media has been laid.

Wellesley College Library, a depository since 1943, serves a college community of 2,400 undergraduate students, plus faculty and staff. Our extended community includes: students, faculty and staff from many nearby colleges and universities, such as Babson College, Brandeis University, Boston College, and the Massachusetts Institute of Technology (with whom we share an academic cross-registration program); an active and highly educated citizenry; and a business community in the Route 128/495 areas which consists mostly of service and high-tech industries. The needs of our various patrons are quite congruent; they require access to the same types of resources, although to satisfy a diversity of needs.

The Wellesley College Library is comprised of the Margaret Clapp Library (humanities and social sciences), and separate art, astronomy, music, and science libraries. The core documents collection is housed in the Clapp Library building, but depository materials are found at all library sites. Depository maps are housed in the Geology Department, in the same facility as the science library. The depository selects 42 percent of the available items offered by the Government Printing Office.

Adjacency of the Documents Collection at Clapp to the Reference Area and the Microtext Area—all located on the main floor of the building—facilitates much of our service. However, a long-standing policy of cooperative reference service among the professional staff makes it possible to offer 62 hours of coverage of the reference and documents desks with a small staff. Serving at these desks are the readers services team (two readers services librarians and the documents librarian who administer the Readers Services Division of the Clapp Library), the reference librarian, collection management officer, acquisitions librarian, special collections librarian, systems librarian, bibliographic services librarian, catalog librarian, and the senior library assistant in the Acquisitions Department. Occasionally documents and readers services assistants augment the services of the reference staff.

STAFF TRAINING

At the heart of the documents reference program is staff training, increasingly vital as new technologies arise, requiring not just subject expertise, but ability to use a variety of equipment successfully to facilitate access to government information. We can no longer rely wholly on an occasional in-house brush-up session on census or legal research, plus a written documents reference notebook to accomplish all training. Instead, at each monthly reference staff meeting, some time is given to training in one or more documents subject areas. Often, a demonstration of a new CD-ROM tool is given, accompanied by an explanation of its likely use. Other information is passed on via e-mail to a reference staff distribution list.

The documents librarian tries to take advantage of as many extramural opportunities for training as possible to augment professional reading. These include Census Bureau and other agency training in use of specific tools, attending conferences, such as the one recently given by EDUCOM on use of the INTERNET, and studying any materials which may become available. For example, the Census Bureau often shares the scripts and visuals used by its trainers, such as the materials produced by Robert Marske and Paul Zeisset for use in demonstrating *Extract* software. The GPO provides helpful tips regularly in the "Electronic Corner" of *Administrative Notes*. The Government Publications Librarians of New England, a regional documents group sponsored by NELINET, often brings in speakers to demonstrate new tools and sponsors an annual conference. Other forms of collegial learning range from discussing the current state of each library's technology at the Boston Library Consortium's Government Documents Interest Group meetings to getting together with a colleague to pool our knowledge of sources and software. Use of INTERNET and other bulletin board opportunities informs the reference process as well, as will be discussed below. Clearly, making time for education is a necessary survival skill in the electronic era.

OFFICE AUTOMATION

Initially, access to word processing in support of administrative and bibliographic instruction activities was made available to the library staff at a terminal room on the third floor of the Clapp Library which served students, faculty, and staff. There, dumb terminals connected to the College's VAX computer offered Emacs as a text editor. Later, terminals and personal computers connected to the campus network became available in staff work areas. The readers services team had access to a special storage space on the VAX for files which facilitated sharing of jointly used texts. Thus, an annotation used in one bibliography could easily be moved into another without retyping, or a person could work on a staff manual equally well while sitting at a service desk or in an office. In recent years, more and more of the documents office work has migrated from the mainframe to PC-based wordprocessing and other software packages, making compatibility of equipment very important. At this time, documents staff and student workers use three personal computers. Each computer has a hard drive; one a 5.25" drive, another a 3.5" drive, and a third has a 3.5" drive and an external 5.25" drive. PC Tools is run on all three machines for backup, data compression, and file restoration. PC Tools version 7 offers virus protection which we are now working into our routines.

The current campus standard for word processing, Word Perfect 5.1, is used for correspondence, bibliography production, manual maintenance, report and script writing, etc. Draw Perfect has been added for desktop publishing. The ability to print locally on a dot matrix printer is expanded by the network to allow printing on an HP Laserjet in the readers services office nearby, or at other sites. This can be done by using "kermit print" within Word Perfect or by kermitting files up to the network level before issuing the print command.

Statistical work is done in the readers services office using Lotus. Graphic presentations for annual reports will probably be done via Draw Perfect now that that is available.

The documents collection has, since 1989, relied most heavily on dBase (first dBase III Plus, then dBase IV), the relational database, for its record maintenance. All depository documents which are not recorded in the online catalog are controlled in a dBase file which contains the following elements:

- Sudoc number;
- Item number;
- Title;
- Alternate [i.e., non-Sudoc] location;
- Receipt date;
- Format (paper, microfiche, CD-ROM, floppy disk, etc.);
- Discard in 1 (supersession indicator) or 5 years; and
- Note.

The file is sorted by Sudoc number, and occasionally selected fields are printed out for public consultation, in conjunction with the *Monthly Catalog*. We are just about to use the automatic supersession indicator to print a list of documents presumed superseded for verification and pulling. Our first automatically produced discard request lists will be run in 1994. Other databases are maintained as dBase files. Map receipts are recorded separately by type. Discard lists of older materials are produced in dBase format. An effort is being made to enter (after weeding) all items from the 1984-1988 manual shelflist retrospectively in a separate dBase file so that the old shelflist can be withdrawn, reducing the kinds of files to be consulted to locate older uncataloged holdings. A list of microfilm census holdings highlighting various geographic areas is another early finding aid produced in dBase. More recently, we have begun a separate listing of CIA maps on file, coded to their storage folders. The University of California/Riverside item file is being customized to indicate Wellesley holdings and decisions; it will serve as a basis for documents collection management activities. We have been working with this for some time, but an intensive effort to complete the work is necessary before we can really reap the benefits of its use for collections decision making.

dBase is mounted on two of the three documents microcomputers. Files are built largely by student workers, with maintenance and revision done by Documents staff members. The template-style of entry with field tags listed makes it possible to train workers to use dBase readily.

Also available on at least one PC are various simple graphics programs used for signage production, although much of this will now be accomplished by the pairing of Word Perfect and Draw Perfect. Recent acquisition of a scaleable fonts package augments these capabilities for signage; previously SAS-Graph was used via the network for making extra large letters.

ONLINE CATALOG

Selection of a vendor for an online catalog system was a very beneficial process for the documents collection. While some documents (those classified in Dewey or LC) had previously been represented in the card catalog, the majority of receipts were recorded only in the *Monthly Catalog* by the documents staff. Selection of Innovative as the system vendor made possible building on an initial agreement for Technical Services to process many more government publications by the same means as any commercially procured library materials.

The system planning process addressed the needs of the documents collection in many ways: fitting documents into standard acquisitions procedures, specifying a Sudoc index among the search keys, testing the capacity to build complex documents serials records and generate reports isolating depository receipts, and so forth. The result was a great leap forward in access to documents when the system came up in 1987, marrying a policy change to the right technology.

Today, more and more depository items are appearing in the public access catalog. Records are downloaded from OCLC, moved into the Innovative system, and made available on a timely basis due to GPO's enhanced cataloging authority. The Sudoc number is always indexed, whether or not it is the call number location, allowing browse searching of all documents by those aware of the Sudocs scheme. GPO materials can be isolated in a regular search by limiting by publisher. Serials records are still being built, but we are enjoying having full access to the check-in records, something which had previously caused us to keep serials check-in in documents long after it should have been transferred to bibliographic services. Claims reports are turned over to the documents staff for checking against rainchecks and taking action. Binding notice production has regularized a process previously carried out in a haphazard, time-available manner by the documents staff.

Circulating documents has always been a chore, because the small documents staff (1 FTE professional and .75 FTE support staff) seldom had the time for follow-up and proper record keeping. Using the Innovative system, the Circulation staff now tracks the circulations of documents and gives these works the appropriate followup. Cataloged documents are bar coded and have full records, obviating the need to figure out how to record transactions with proper bibliographic identification. For uncataloged documents, a simple "on-the-fly" circulation template simplifies the requirements of an old manual form. Circulation statistics by collection are available at any time.

The create-a-list feature in the Public Access Catalog (PAC) and in the Acquisitions/Serials module (VACQ) makes statistics derivation for government reports or in-house requirements viable. Monographic acquisitions records are coded to indicate depository status, and this makes it possible to report the number of documents cataloged in a year, or the desired time period. Serials records also bear this coding, so that they may be isolated during the serials budget projection process. Many other things can be done with the create-a-list feature, as we shall investigate as time allows.

SEARCHING REMOTE DATABASES

The readers services team has long used Dialog for mediated searching and ready reference. Searching can be done while at service desks or in offices, dialing out via the campus network or using a PC with an internal modem and dedicated line. For depository needs, the *MONTHLY CATALOG* (file 66) was searched online prior to subscribing to the *MARCIVE GPO CAT/PAC* on CD-ROM. NTIS's file (file 6) is consulted from time to time, and *FEDERAL*

REGISTER ABSTRACTS (file 136) is a tool regularly used to facilitate *FEDERAL REGISTER* access. *CENDATA* (menu-driven version), formerly consulted at regular intervals for press release information and other news, is now even more significant as a means to get the latest 1990 census data prior to its release in CD-ROM or paper form. Patrons inquire as soon as word of new data releases appears in the media; once faculty are informed that data they have been awaiting for research and/or publication purposes is now available, downloading begins. We have purchased and hope to mount soon the new Dialog front-end for *CENDATA* to enable reference staff who are not regular Dialog searchers to access this resource with ease.

FirstSearch, the newest OCLC reference product, was tested for end-user searching in late 1991. This service now provides easy searching for a variety of databases, including the OCLC Online Union Catalog, the ERIC database, and the GPO's *Monthly Catalog*. End-user searching is a direction we look forward to pursuing.

CD-ROM

Wellesley College's entry into the world of CD-ROM indexes and databases coincided nicely with the initiation of the depository CD-ROM program. Some of the best start-up information we found came from the GPO, in fact. Our first CD-ROM station was located in the reference room, directly adjacent to documents. The second station, added not long afterward, is a portable teaching station (CPU, monitor, overhead projector, and liquid crystal display unit on a cart) for use in the library lecture room, classrooms in the library, or wherever needed. The portable system is sometimes wheeled to documents for patron use when not being used for bibliographic instruction, computer training, product demonstration, or testing new software and CD-ROMs. Because campus network drops are widely available, this station can be used to demonstrate dialing into remote databases, use of bulletin boards, INTERNET access, or the library catalog. A third CD-ROM station in documents has just become operational. Each station has a single CD-ROM drive, an IBM-compatible PC with a hard drive, and a printer (except the teaching station). A MAC-based CD-ROM station is in use at the science library.

In 1990, a CD-ROM Task Force was convened to identify issues surrounding the library's entry into this new area and to set policy for selection, acquisition, processing, cataloging, patron access, and so forth. Processing rules for depository CD-ROMs are identical to those for commercially procured titles, with the exception of the additional depository identification. Staff and user training, preparation of user aids, and publicity are handled by the readers services team for the Clapp Library. The systems librarian mounts the software at each station and makes sure that there is an Automenu interface to aid users.

At present, the Automenu is divided into two parts: Government Databases and Non-Government Databases. A bridge has been built between the two menus, and Marcive's *GPO CAT/PAC* is listed in both sections. The luxury of using a given CD-ROM at any station is not one we will be able to sustain forever unless disk storage is continuously added. The multiplicity of software loaded on these machines will be difficult to manage before long as we have no two commercial CD-ROMs running on the same software. Certainly, the Census Bureau's new approach of bundling the software with the data on the CD-ROM disk is very helpful, even though the approach locks them into the type of software issued on the CD-ROM.

What do we currently offer to documents users at the CD-ROM stations? All Census Bureau titles have been selected—decennial census, export and import data, *County and City Data Book*, *County Business Patterns*, and economic censuses. These are joined by *National Trade Data Bank*, *Congressional Record*, CIS's *Statistical Masterfile*, and Marcive's *GPO CAT/PAC* (*Monthly Catalog*, 1976).

The *TIGER Line Files* have been selected for loan to interested patrons. Each title, government or commercial, is fully cataloged in our Innopac online catalog, with associated serials check-in records as appropriate. Software is backed up (if on a floppy) and stored in bibliographic services; manuals are cataloged and placed at the reference or documents CD-ROM workstation.

Technical documentation for government titles is cataloged and kept in the documents stacks. A special notebook, labeled "Census Bureau CD-ROMs," gives hints on use of the various census titles. User-support phone numbers are retained here as well. We have not had time to create a lot of user documentation at this point, and appreciate it when others share information via *Administrative Notes* or the INTERNET. A small amount of signage has been created for the workstation describing use of the equipment. One especially helpful Word Perfect list posted on a tent above the *PL 94-171* census disks is a list of states telling which disk has the data for that state.

Physical access is very direct and easy. Patrons—faculty, students, staff, and community members—have free access to the reference and documents workstations as well as to the teaching station when it is in a public area. CD-ROMs are transferred from their jewel cases to caddies which are used in the players we have purchased. The caddies are labeled on their edge with the title of the publication, then stored in open plastic racks (10 CD-ROMs per rack) with the labels showing at the workstation. Brief instructions regarding loading/unloading and printing are posted. The patron is free to proceed at will, loading the desired product, accessing it via the Automenu, downloading, printing, etc. Staff at the nearby reference desk can intervene if problems are observed or if assistance is requested. So far, it has not been necessary to make appointments or limit time for CD-ROM use, although some queueing does occur. An addition of the new workstation in documents should eliminate this problem for a while, and ultimately we may consider mounting some heavily used items on the network.

DIAL-IN BULLETIN BOARDS

The documents librarian accesses the GPO and census bulletin boards as time allows, and has experimented with the use of the Commerce Department's Economic Bulletin Board as well as the Federal Reserve Bank of Boston's *New England Economic Indicators* board. The systems librarian creates scripts automating dial access which are stored via Telpac software for use on a nonpublic PC. We are not presently equipped to make appropriate dial-in bulletin boards available to end users, nor to perform downloading in all formats. More equipment and practice will be required before that is feasible. However, if public need for this service builds, we will investigate a more automated user interface and the costs associated with offering such an opportunity to end users. It is hoped that the government will shift to the INTERNET as a means for bulletin board delivery to reduce costs to depositories and simplify access routines.

INTERNET ACCESS, E-MAIL, AND BLC INFO SOURCE

The availability of the INTERNET and fast, low-cost, widely accessible e-mail and access service has revolutionized librarianship in so many ways. Monitoring GOVDOC-L, INT-LAW, and MAPS-L on a daily basis brings current news, opportunities for "remote" collegiality, information on equipment and new publications, the chance to share reference problems and resources, and so much more. Recently, for example, several messages have brought news of miscollated or faulty depository items, flaws which might have been overlooked in normal depository mail processing. Instead, one librarian's discovery was communicated to others in a timely and useful fashion, enabling claims to be made. E-mail communication to colleagues also reduces the frustration of trying to reach an individual by phone—difficult in today's busy library world.

Beyond the bulletin boards which are delivered to a network "mailbox" or are available for shared access on the public structure, there are other possibilities to take advantage of on the INTERNET. Use of the file transfer protocol makes downloading from remote hosts easy. Downloaded information can then be printed via our networked printers or kermitted down to the disk storage on a personal computer for manipulation with word processing software.

Use of the telnet protocol to connect to other library catalogs and campus-wide information systems is also a possibility which we now exploit. Recently, Wellesley has mounted *INTERNET Access Software, v.0.9a*, the front-end designed by Mark Resmer at Sonoma State University. This provides easy, menued access to the INTERNET-accessible library catalogs and databases. By typing "irg" at the network prompt, the user is stepped through the process of selecting within the following categories:

- United States Library Catalogs,
- Foreign Library Catalogs,
- Campus-wide Information Systems,
- Miscellaneous Databases, and
- Information for First-Time Users of This Program.

After making this initial selection, the next levels of choices are presented, for example, the states, then the individual library catalogs available within those states. The most critical step is taken just before making the connection to the system chosen: The user must record the unique instructions for the use of that system, especially the disconnect string.

Why is this telnet feature so useful to documents librarians? Many online catalogs which are INTERNET-accessible have documents represented in them, enhancing referral possibilities. Some stand-alone government documents catalogs are available as well. It is possible to use this interface to reach OCLC services such as EPIC.[1] In addition, a few government databases are already available via the INTERNET. Some campus-wide information systems post local weather information from the National Oceanic and Atmospheric Administration on their systems. The National Bureau of Standards Time Service is directly accessible via the INTERNET interface, and the Merit Geographic Name Server makes use of place identification data from the Postal Service and other government agencies. There are probably many other such resources available as well.

Wellesley College and the other Boston Library Consortium libraries have begun to share access to CARL's Uncover[2] service and their own database of serials holdings via the INTERNET. Later, this "BLC Info Source" will include access to the member libraries' online catalogs. This service will be a choice on Wellesley's public-access catalog screens, providing a smooth interface for users. Now, patrons must use one of two terminals in the reference room to consult other library catalogs. One has an Automenu which offers scripted dialing after the initial library selection is made. The other terminal is intended for network

---

[1] EPIC is OCLC's service which offers enhanced access to the OCLC Online Union Catalog and other databases via use of the NISO standard command language. It is primarily aimed at reference and research, rather than cataloging, data needs.

[2] Uncover is a table of contents service of the Colorado Area Research Libraries. It offers timely keyword, name, and browse searching of article titles from over 10,000 journals and magazines. Coverage is for the period from 1988 to the present.

access. An adjacent desk holds the various INTERNET guides by Art St. George, Billy Barron, and the NSF Network Service Center. Patrons can consult the guides to make preliminary choices, then log in to their network accounts, and telnet to an address given in the guides. Alternatively, they can type "irg" for the menu access version. At the end of a session, users may fill in an electronic interlibrary loan request form at the same terminal, by typing "ill" at the network prompt.

TECHNICAL SUPPORT

The Library has an excellent working relationship with the Academic Computing staff, who have been supportive throughout all of our technological progress. Recently, at the request of the systems librarian, several Academic Computing staff members joined her and the documents librarian in discussing new and anticipated government products as well as responsibilities for CD-ROM-related activities. At present, the systems librarian coordinates activities between the Library and Academic Computing, including equipment budgeting and recommendations for procurement, policy formulation, mounting software, and constructing the Automenu files. Academic Computing procures, installs and maintains CD-ROM and computer equipment, and provides general support services and training for the college community. Academic Computing will do any data extractions required for student/faculty/staff research using *Extract* or other appropriate software. The data might be used by an individual with Lotus or mounted on a public structure for group access. The documents librarian will assist non-Wellesley patrons in downloading via *Extract* if that assistance is required. No research support for dBase is available on campus, although that software is used in the documents office. So far, supporting this area has not been a problem since so few users have required data extraction, and those patrons have known how to use *Extract*.

CONCLUSION

We feel that we have come a long way in a short time, but that we shall always be on this technology highway, pursuing the next goal. What is on our current "wish list"? We have been so busy inaugurating new services that we seldom take the time to publicize them effectively. The library is now concluding a strategic planning process, which has focused our thoughts on publicity. What is the sense of making new services available if they are not utilized because they are unknown? Clearly, as a depository library, we need to renew our custom of inviting in the librarians from public and other nondepository libraries in the area to demonstrate our new capabilities. Other means of reaching all of our audiences will be explored, as well.

The final report of the strategic planning team will allow us to manage change more effectively by giving us a touchstone by which to live. We, as an entire staff, shall more clearly understand our goals for technological innovation because all have participated in this process. It is likely that we shall consider mounting databases on the College network. This might easily include some government resources. Inevitably, we shall press our desire to have CD-ROM and other technologies accessible via smooth interfaces to aid the end user. If Congress favorably treats WINDO legislation (see Chapter 1), we will eagerly investigate its place at Wellesley. More cannot be said with certainty at this time, but we are sure many challenges await us.

Chapter Eight

Information Technology Development and the Documents, Maps, and Microforms Department at Colgate University*

John A. Shuler

INTRODUCTION

In March 1988, when I arrived at Colgate University, the department and collections for which I assumed responsibility were on the threshold of explosive possibilities. From the vantage point of hindsight, I believe the tensions I felt those first few weeks were generated from the inevitable conflict between two formats of information storage. On the one side, the department enjoyed a rich 150-year tradition of collecting paper government publications. And on the other, there was the first tentative generation of government information products distributed in electronic formats. At times, it seemed that the only thing the two formats had in common was the U.S. Government Printing Office (GPO). All the bibliographic skills and library techniques gained from the experience with paper proved to be of little value in this new age of electronic information.

If this was the only electronic revolution at Colgate University, I would have

* The opinions and observations expressed here are solely those of the author. They do not represent the official policies or positions of either the library or the university.

been challenged enough. The library was also well into its own transition from a tradition of paper catalogs to a complex electronic, bibliographic record system. These parallel technological revolutions would share many common concerns, but would also clash over critical differences.

This case study will examine these two library automation experiences, explaining how one revolution had both obvious and unknown affects on the other. Together they capture the essence of a small academic institution in search of its proper role in the brave new information order.

DESCRIPTION OF COLGATE UNIVERSITY AND ITS COMPUTING FACILITIES

Colgate University is a highly selective, independent, coeducational liberal arts institution with approximately 2,700 undergraduate students, and a small graduate program which offers a general Masters of Arts and a Master of Arts in Teaching. The university was established in 1819 as the Baptist Education Society of the State of New York's central school, and in a few years, through further consolidation, became the Hamilton Literary and Theological Institution. For the next 20 years, the Institute served as the state's principal seminaries for Baptist clergy. This religious affiliation continued until the late 1830s, when male students who did not intend to go into the ministry were admitted into its programs.

Through a new state education charter, issued in 1846, the Institute became Madison University. It was also given the right to grant degrees. The University became Colgate in 1890, in recognition of the Colgate family's support throughout the institution's history. In the 1920s, the remaining Baptist seminary programs were transferred to a new Theological Institution in Rochester, New York. Colgate became an independent nondenominational university for men. In 1970, the University admitted its first coeducational class.

According to the *Colgate University Catalogue* (1991, p.1), Colgate "offers 42 concentrations (majors) including several interdisciplinary programs." These concentrations are administered through a curriculum based on five academic divisions: Humanities, Natural Sciences and Mathematics, Social Sciences, and University Studies. All students must take courses in areas of General Education, their chosen fields of concentration, and an additional two courses from three areas: the social sciences, natural sciences/mathematics, and the humanities. Students must demonstrate a minimal competency in a foreign or classical language and English composition. All first-year students participate in a coordinated program of First-Year Seminars during their first Fall term. Colgate has approximately 200 faculty members, and 450 support staff in administrative, secretarial, and maintenance operations.

Colgate's investment in computing resources began in 1967. Based on a self-study report issued 10 years later (Colgate Self-Study Report, 1977, p. VI. 37),

> ... the National Science Foundation established a group to deal with proposals to develop research and education with computers ... Colgate was one of four universities in the country—the only liberal arts institution—to receive major support of such a program in computers and education from the NSF. Previously (the university) had received a $50,000 dollar grant from IBM covering a five year period for similar exploration ... and became the main enabling force for development of a computer center at Colgate.

Building on this governmental and corporate support, the University conducted a comprehensive survey for the next three years. The results of the study suggested several significant critical roles that a campus computer facility could play in a liberal arts curriculum. The University also explored several alternative arrangements to meet these goals: remote batch processing with Cornell University's computer center; remote time-sharing at the computers maintained by the Griffis Air Force Base in Rome, New York; and local batch processing through Colgate's own IBM 1130 computer. In the end, the University committed itself to establishing a time-shared central facility on campus.

Today, the Academic Computer Center operates as the University's primary service point for all its computer hardware and software needs. With its two mainframe Digital Equipment Corporation VAX 4000 machines, the center provides systems management and advice. The center also houses the VAX unit which operates the library's automated bibliographic system. The center's VAX system also serves the University community as a major node within a growing campus-wide fiber optic network. Access to the center's computers (including the library's online system) can be made from 200 remote terminals in other offices and buildings on campus. Off-campus users can dial in through the center's modems. Other computing facilities, which are also included through the network, exist in the astronomy, mathematics, and computer science departments. The University's administrative offices operate a separate IBM AS400 system.

DESCRIPTION OF COLGATE UNIVERSITY LIBRARIES

The University's library system consists of two major collections: the Everett Needham Case Library, which serves the needs of the humanities and social science programs; and the George R. Cooley Science Library, which serves the curricular needs of the natural science and mathematics programs. Both libraries offer a traditional array of public and technical services to the campus community. These include reference, bibliographic instruction, interlibrary loan, online database searching, circulation and reserves functions. Bibliographic access services, such as acquisitions, serials processing, and cataloging are handled through central offices located in the Case library. Both libraries have extensive microformat holdings. The Case library houses the University's Archives and Special Collections/Rare Books department, which administers an expanding preservation and conservation program designed to protect the library's paper collections.

Together, the two libraries hold nearly 480,000 volumes and subscribe to approximately 2,600 periodical titles. Twelve full-time library faculty members manage the public and technical service departments and are supported by about 25 FTE staff members. The library also maintains a cooperative relationship with several small reading rooms, libraries, and other department collections scattered throughout the University's buildings.

DESCRIPTION OF DOCUMENTS, MAPS, MICROFORMS DEPARTMENT

The library has always recognized government publications as a crucial source of information. The current department is but the latest administrative arrangement used by the library over the years to acquire, collect, and manage this material effectively. Departmental responsibilities extend to six unique collections. Four of these contain documents from state, national, and international governments, one houses the University's principal map collection, and the sixth is Case library's microformats collection.

The department manages the daily routines for proper identification, acquisition, processing, cataloging, organizing/shelving, and public services for these collections. The Department head reports to the Head of Public Services, and the Case library's central reference desk serves as the collections' principal public service point. Since the department acquires and catalogs this material for other collections in the library, it works closely with the central technical services departments. In addition, the department processes selected material for the Cooley collections. This includes periodical titles, items cataloged for Cooley's reference and main book collections, as well as a small, but growing, collection of U.S. Federal publications organized under the Superintendent of Classification (Sudoc) system.

The collections bestow the department with several difficult management and bibliographic problems:

- As a matter of tradition, very few government documents were cataloged and included in the central catalog;
- Material housed in the Case collections are scattered among four different floors and organized by at least four different classification schemes; and

- Some collections have not be classified or cataloged; others are shelved according to title, date, or some other informal method.

A brief description of the major Case collections illustrates these management and bibliographic access problems. Each collection will be described, outlining its relative strengths and weaknesses. Afterward, a short overview of the Case floors, and the kind of material located on each level.

Publications Published and Distributed by the U.S. Government Printing Office and Other Federal Agencies

Colgate has been a Federal depository since 1902. However, the University acquired government publications since the early 19th century through earlier depository agreements and major gifts. Currently, the depository collection has about 100,000 items in paper and microfiche. It serves the citizens of the 27th Congressional District. Its size and age makes it the third largest, and oldest, depository collection among higher education institutions in the Central New York region, with Cornell and Syracuse universities topping the list. The current GPO item number selection percentage is 50. The majority of the collection remains uncataloged.

New York State Executive and Legislative Publications Distributed by the State Library

Colgate was designated as a depository for state documents in the 1950s. However, as with the Federal publications, it has received publications from state offices since the first half of the 19th century. Through the years, the library acquired a significant collection of legislative and executive documentation, which currently contains about 10,000 volumes. In 1989, the state library restructured the depository system, and the University assumed a reduced depository status, receiving approximately 25 titles per year. The majority of the older volumes publications remain uncataloged.

Maps Received through the Two Depository Agreements and Purchased through the Library's Budget

This collection contains about 15,000 map sheets. Specific map series include the topographical maps of the Northeastern United States, as well as large-scale maps of the United States, Canada, and the world. The library has also purchased specialized maps from several Federal agencies, state offices, research organizations, and private publishers. The department obtained map cases in 1989 and has made slow progress in organizing the collection for public use. There are also small map collections in the Cooley library and the geography and geology departments. The Case collection remains uncataloged.

The United Nations and Affiliated Organizations

Colgate established a standing order with the United Nations sales publications office in the late 1940s. Currently, this 3,000 volume collection is shelved according the UN sales number, which presents several challenging obstacles to easy bibliographic access. However, over the years the library has cataloged selected series and periodical titles for its main collections. The collection also has the official records of the UN General Assembly and its several commissions and committees.

International Labour Organisation

As with the UN publications, Colgate has acquired the ILO's major publication series for decades. The library cataloged what it considered the more important titles for its main collections. The remaining 500 volumes were left in an unorganized, uncataloged collection.

League of Nations

The department has been given responsibility for a nearly complete collection of the public reports, documents, and records from the League of Nations. Some serial and periodical titles have been cataloged, but the great majority of the collection (about 2,000 volumes) remains uncataloged, and much of it appears to be wrapped in the original shipping papers.

Microforms Collections

The department has responsibility for the daily management of the Case library's microforms room. Collections in this area include the GPO depository microfiche, microfilmed runs of periodicals, major research sets purchased on microfilm or microfiche, and a modest number of Readex microprint cards. Some of the research collections are cataloged, all of the periodical titles appear in the library's online catalog, part of the microprints are cataloged, and none of the GPO microfiche are cataloged. The department also maintains the room's reader/printers, and supervises the student workers who staff the room's public service desk during the evenings and weekends.

These collections are distributed among four different floors:

- *"B" Stacks. Basement Level.* The department shares this space with several other Library units (special collections, acquisitions, and serials.) It is a floor closed off from the public. The department's material occupies the greatest part of the "B" stacks shelf space. Nearly all of this material is uncataloged, unorganized, and in serious need of preservation and conservation care.
- *Federal Documents:* (1) miscellaneous looseleaf publications, (2) miscellaneous publications that are either duplicates or uncataloged, (3) oversized cataloged and uncataloged titles, (4) early volumes of the U.S. congressional *Serial Set*, and (5) early volumes of the U.S. *Congressional Record.*
- *New York Documents:* (1) New York legislative documents series, (2) Senate and Assembly *Journals*, (3) New York State laws, and (4) executive department documents (covering about 80 years).
- *International Labour Organisation:* this collection remains unorganized and uncataloged. A quick inventory indicates monographs, series, and serial titles.
- *League of Nations:* a preliminary inventory of this material indicates a nearly complete collection of documents distributed by the League's sales publications office. Many of the titles remain stored in their original shipping packages and boxes.

The department finds its resources stretched to the limit as it tries to maintain rational management and bibliographic control over these dispersed collections:

"A" Stacks. First Level. This floor is the Case library's main location for collections classified according to the Dewey and Library of Congress systems. All volumes are supposed to be in the central catalog. This includes several major documents series from all governments, such as the volumes of the decennial census, *Foreign Relations of the United States, U.S. Reports, Statistical Abstract, U.N. Demographic Yearbook,* and *New York Legislative Annual.* Some of these titles are divided between the Dewey and LC classification systems, and others have been continued in the Sudoc and UN collections on the main level. In some cases, the bibliographic records in the catalog do not reflect this change in location or classification.

Main Level. This level contains the department's office, the Sudoc and UN documents, and map collections, as well as the microforms room. Other collections housed on this level include the music room, reserve collection, reference collection, index/abstract room, and the current periodicals. The reference desk, the circulation desk, and main offices for reference, interlibrary loan, technical services, and library administration offices are also on this floor.

Second Floor. This level houses the collection of serials kept in paper, the special collections and archives department, and the Langworthy Computer Room, which contains a dozen terminals connected the computer center's main computer on the other side of campus.

GENERAL OVERVIEW OF LIBRARY AUTOMATION
DEVELOPMENTS AT COLGATE

To place impact of automation on the department into its proper context, one must first understand Colgate's development of library automation in general. A great deal of the library's management assumptions about government information technology were forged in the larger crucible of selecting an integrated online library system over 20 years. The perspective that grew from these two decades of experience judged information retrieval as a *bibliographic* problem. The intellectual principles of a card catalog were still sound. In an automated form, these bibliographic connections between the catalog record and items in the library's collections would only become faster and more efficient. The catalog's primary purpose was to point to the material. How the individual used the information contained in the volumes was of little concern to the catalog's creators.

The first government produced electronic formats challenged this traditional library perspective in a significant way: shifting the library's involvement from the creation and management of bibliographic records to the direct manipulation of numerical and text data. The government data disks created an information environment where it was no longer enough to know just where the information was located. It was also important to know how the information could be retrieved, read, and manipulated. The medium and the message had became one.

An analysis of Colgate's library automation evolution is grounded on four institutional assumptions about information technology and its applications:

- The financial obligations of any new technology;
- The desire to avoid unnecessary technological "obsolescence";
- The University's traditional desire to encourage interlibrary cooperative relationships with Hamilton College, Colgate's sister institution in Clinton, New York; and
- The development of interlibrary cooperation with Colgate's "peer" institutions in general.

One cannot underestimate the impact of Colgate's decision in the late 1960s to become a co-educational academic program. The University's enrollment in 1965–1966 was 1,610 male students. In 1975–1976, it was 2,576, split between

1,702 males and 874 females. By 1990–1991, the enrollment had grown to 2,716, with 1,464 males and 1,252 females. This expansion created demands on the University's resources, including the library, and radically altered the academic community's perception of research and study on campus.

Faculty members gradually shifted their professional focus from teaching to research, placing greater expectations on the library to fulfill a larger role beyond its traditional undergraduate collection. Students took their bibliographic cues from the faculty and adapted similar expectations, often demanding comparable services and collections offered by larger universities and their research libraries. Throughout the 20 years outlined, the University's perception of library automation was sometimes painfully focused on particular library technical and public service shortcomings. Through the mid-1970s, several library campus committees investigated library operations, and automation was consistently identified as a critical solution for many of these problems. This perception would continue to color the University's perspective for many years.

Finally, the long sought-after cooperation with Hamilton College would slip away once more in the late 1980s, as Hamilton chose a different automation solution for its bibliographic challenge.

The First Stage, 1970–1980

As with many academic libraries, Colgate's introduction to the problems and opportunities of automated bibliographic systems came through the services of OCLC, Inc. In 1973, the library considered using OCLC's growing national bibliographical services. However, after much study, financial constraints caused the library not to act on the opportunity. A year and half later, with growing pressures on the library's resources, the decision was reevaluated. A consultant's report (Becker and Hayes, 1975, p. 26) offered several significant recommendations that would provide "the University Administration with a general appraisal of ongoing library services, comments on certain specific library problems, and recommendations concerning the library's future growth." Among other points, the consultants strongly supported the library's acceptance of OCLC's services.

Over the next two years, through direct experience of the benefits gained from OCLC's partial automation of its cataloging routines, the library launched its first tentative explorations into other automation applications. In 1979, the interlibrary loan services began to share the cataloging OCLC department's terminal. A year later, the reference department began to offer online database searches to the university community. However, additional automation enhancements remained unrealized as the library invested its time and resources in other pressing problems: space expansion planning for the Case library and the establishment of the Cooley library. In addition to these demands, the cataloging department dealt with several bibliographic problems created by the mid-1970s decision to convert the library's collections from the Dewey classification system to the Library of Congress scheme. Further energies were diverted into planning for the 1980/1981 revisions of the Anglo-American cataloging rules.

The Second Stage, 1981–1983

Although most of the library's administrative efforts focused on the completion of the Case and Cooley building projects, the OCLC terminal in the cataloging department served as the library's window on the rapidly developing library automation landscape. The serials department began to convert its records into a machine-readable database by using the resources of the University's computing center. In 1982, the interlibrary loan unit received its own OCLC terminal. The library's first personal computers were also purchased during this period. Plans were proposed for a retrospective conversion of the library's pre-OCLC catalog records. By 1983, these automation pressures led to the creation of a Library Automation Evaluation Committee (LAEC).

Automation cooperation from outside the University emerged as the library became involved in the regional OCLC system's development of a union serials list. The public service departments in the Case and Cooley libraries expanded their respective online searching resources and skills. The next generation of OCLC workstations were announced during this time.

The Third Stage, 1984–1988

These four years were the first of two intensive periods of self-examination for the library. These years represent the library's comprehensive investment in expanding its professional knowledge of automation applications. What was researched, studied, debated, and eventually applied would create the intellectual foundations about library automation for the rest the decade and quite possibly into the next century.

Earlier automation plans and developments began to bear fruit. Using an Apple computer, the library completed its retrospective conversion of older non-OCLC records. During this time, the next generation of OCLC workstations, which served as microcomputers, arrived. Building on the experiences gained from the earlier listing project, the serials staff improved its machine-readable holdings list, forging closer ties with the academic computing center. The computing center also established the Case Langworthy Computer Room. Users obtained the appropriate software from the library's circulation desk.

However, LAEC served as the library's principal forum for its shaping automation future. Its highest priority focused on the conversion of the card catalog (and its supporting paper-based bibliographic, acquisition, and circulation processes) into a comprehensive online system. The committee organized its efforts around a systemwide framework. During the 1984/1985 fiscal year, its members defined the proposed integrated system's functional requirements. The committee requested, and studied, other library automation proposals, read the available literature, and applied what was useful to Colgate's unique situation. After this research, it drafted a document listing the system's minimum requirements.

Using the document's guidelines, LAEC members visited installations at other libraries and asked vendors to come to Colgate for onsite demonstrations. In the end, the committee and library faculty recommended, with the University administration's concurrence, the acquisition of the Carlyle, Inc. online catalog system. After a brief test period, the library accepted the system.

The choice of Carlyle established the next threshold for library automation at Colgate by forcing the library and University to reconcile automation's limitations with its promised opportunities. Carlyle's system was a partial package: only offering an online public-access catalog subsystem. Modules for acquisitions/serials, cataloging, and circulation were still in the development stage, and their future implementation dates uncertain. However, the Carlyle system provided an excellent opportunity for the library to acquire the necessary professional knowledge about automation, with only a modest financial investment and acquisition of hardware. Carlyle was a shared system among a consortium of academic institutions. One could search Colgate's collections or with a menu selection from the system's public screen search the other system members holdings. The consortium's central computer facilities were maintained by the regional OCLC office in Albany, New York. System access was provided through telecommunication/phone lines.

For the next two years, the library quickly discovered the advantages of automation, as well as the powerful expectations generated by a community of users encouraged to use these improved resources. While the cooperative nature and limited capital investment provided the library with certain advantages, it also created greater expectations of an automated library among Colgate's community of scholars and students. There was a growing demand for an online system that was dependable, complete, and user friendly. Carlyle only met the last of these conditions. Its telecommunication lines between Albany and Hamilton suffered from persistent interruptions, and the proposed implementation dates for the system's other modules kept slipping further and further back. Meanwhile, the library's users grew to expect similar electronic advantages from the library's nonautomated services. They also learned to rely on the Carlyle's ability to search other collections from the same terminal. Unfortunately, this did not include Hamilton College's library holdings. During Colgate's search for a system, Hamilton chose a different and slower path to automation.

By the end of 1988, the library and University realized that they would have to decide on whether to stay with Carlyle or invest in a completely new automation solution to these growing bibliographic access demands.

In other automation applications, the library acquired several new microcomputers and appropriate software for its administrative operations. The acquisition department converted its financial information into a commercial spreadsheet package, and nearly all the Library's offices agreed on a common word-processing program for their individual computers. The next generation of OCLC terminals enabled the library to place OCLC terminals in other departments and at the Case reference desk. Also, the first bibliographic CD-ROM workstations were made available to the community. At the University level, the computing center expanded its services through more sophisticated hardware and software resources, and the University established new connections in a network that would eventually link its scattered computer resources.

The Fourth Stage, 1989–1990

With the University administration's blessing, the library began its second major effort to acquire a serviceable and complete library automation package. Using LAEC as the core group, several subcommittees identified the critical system elements. These recommendations were incorporated into a draft request for proposal (RFP).

For the last part of 1989, the committees examined several vendor proposals and systems. After careful consideration, the library narrowed the field down to three systems. In January 1990, the Case and Cooley collections were smart barcoded from tapes generated through the OCLC database. By early Spring 1990, the library recommended, and the University administration approved, the selection of the Innovative Interfaces, Inc. system. Over the next few months, the library planned for a rapid implementation of the new system. The target date for implementation was the beginning of the Spring 1991 term. The new system's computer would be housed and serviced in cooperation with the computing center, solidifying the cooperative relationship between the two information organizations.

Meanwhile, the library received the initial reports on OCLC's future systems and telecommunication enhancements. The first generation of OCLC terminals, acquired in the early 1980s, were placed on a replacement schedule. OCLC also launched EPIC, its new public interface, offering the first opportunity for its database to be searched by subject. The library's first generation of non-OCLC microcomputers also began to show their age and slowness as new and more powerful hardware/software applications were purchased. The library obtained its first laser printer, and a microcomputer with the capability to perform online database searches was placed at the Case reference desk. The Cooley library acquired a Meridian CD-ROM tower to search the multidisk MEDLINE. LAEC continued to serve as the library's principal forum for addressing systemwide automation issues.

The Fifth Stage, 1991–2001

The Library's online system, dubbed MONDO by a winning entry from a University naming contest, came online in January 1991. Through the hardware in the Computing Center, MONDO became available to any computer connected to the network and accessible via modem from other computers with the proper telecommunication applications. After the expected initial frustrations, the Colgate community embraced the new system.

However, the choice and successful application of the system created new demands on the library's professional resources. By mid-1991, the library faculty recognized a critical need to maintain and expand the automation expertise acquired over the last few years. After much discussion, the faculty recommended the creation of a new professional position for a systems librarian. The search was conducted, and the position filled by the end of the November 1991.

During this same period, OCLC implemented its enhanced operating and telecommunication protocols, forcing the library to deal with not only the staff training for MONDO, but further training for the new OCLC systems. The computing center expanded its networking capabilities, and plans were announced to become part of INTERNET by the end of the year. The library began to consider the opportunities and problems created by searching other library holdings through INTERNET. Meanwhile, OCLC, building on the initial acceptance of EPIC, implemented FirstSearch, a more sophisticated public search system.

The library continued to upgrade and replace its older microcomputers, and explored the possibilities of implementing local area networks (LANs) within Case library. The microcomputer at the Case reference desk is "hardwired" to the computer centers facilities, and provides access to the MEDLINE CD-ROMs in the Cooley library. There are plans to network other parts of Case library in late 1992.

AUTOMATION IN THE DOCUMENTS, MAPS, MICROFORMS DEPARTMENT: RIDING THE WAVES OF INFORMATION TECHNOLOGY

The previous discussion outlines the critical organizational context within which automation plans and management of information technologies were developed in the department. More to the point, however, is that this management environment plunged the department into not one, but two technological revolutions. The first was the librarywide implementation of an integrated library package, which reflected an internal struggle. The second revolution was the rapidly evolving electronic government information products, which reflected an external struggle. The department had to propose reasonable responses to both challenges while faced with limited personnel, reduced financial resources, and technological support. It must also be pointed out that the total organizational energy funneled into the department's automation operations reflects but a fraction of the library's total investment in automation resources for the last two decades. Indeed, the greatest portion of that smaller effort has only occurred since 1989.

To understand how these challenges were met, Colgate's historical assumptions about government documents and about library services have to be explained. The library's administrative paradigm for government documents had been fairly consistent from the early 19th century through the early 1960s. Although there has always been a core group of material processed and housed separately from the library's regular collections (primarily the U.S. congressional *Serial Set*, other selected state and Federal executive and legislative volumes, as well as documents from the international organizations), government documents were processed and cataloged as any other kind of library material. They were given little special consideration or treatment by the staff in the acquisition, cataloging, or public services departments.

By the late 1960s and early 1970s this approach was challenged by a new set of perspectives. Part of this transformation came from the increased publishing activity of all levels of governments, part of it was determined by the reorganization of the Federal depository laws in the early 1960s, and part of it developed as more faculty members and students used government publications as primary sources for their research and studies. During this time, as Hernon and McClure (1988) pointed out, many libraries viewed government publications acquisition and collection development as both a curse and blessing. What had begun as a simple acquisitions problem mushroomed into several bibliographic access and service problems. Many libraries consigned their document collections into a separate physical or administrative existence. Integration, once of little concern, became more of a dream than a reality (Ibid., p. 255):

> For too long, government publications have been seen as information resources that are "cheap" (thus, not valuable); pamphlet, ephemeral, and loose materials inappropriate for library collections; or "popular" materials that have limited utility for scholarly collections. Such beliefs simply misrepresent the value of the information content contained in government publications, and exacerbate the difficulty of integrating documents successfully into library and information services.
>
> The term "integrate" suggests a combining of parts to form a whole. General systems theory, when applied to the concept, would add that the whole is more than the sum of its parts. Furthermore, each part has an interdependent effect on all other parts of the system as well as the total "essence" of the whole.

Colgate's search for this bibliographic unity and administrative consolidation took place over a 20-year period: from 1967 to 1987. Since the early 1970s, several library committee recommendations and consultant reports offered numerous suggestions on how the library's documents could be integrated in the library's services and catalog. Some of this advice was acted upon and some remained unfulfilled because of heavy administrative or technological costs.

By late 1987 and early 1988 the library made some significant organizational commitments to the provision of government publication services. As a result of the Case library expansion, and a professional staff reorganization after several retirements, the library provided the department with the minimum level of administrative stability, financial support, and personnel resources to reestablish bibliographic integration. By the end of 1988, the department had a new Department Head; a recently funded full-time staff member; its own student worker budget; its own equipment and supply budgets; a new and larger office space; the latest model (a M310) OCLC workstation that doubled as the Department's microcomputer; a new and expanded Microforms Room; and an end to five years of fairly constant relocation and shifting of its collections.

The Internal Revolution: The Struggle for Automation Applications

The successful transformation of the department's paper records to automated data systems was driven by two conditions: first, the need for a logical approach to gain administrative control over the department's collections, and second, the successful inclusion of the government documents bibliographic records in the library's central catalog database. Some of the department's responses to these demands were crafted through rational planning and some resulted from unhappy accident.

The demands of proper librarywide administrative control required the department to develop its office automation capabilities in a fashion which was consistent with other library units. These needs included common word processing and statistical software packages, and the capability to network with other offices in the library and on the campus and with documents departments in other institutions. The imperatives of providing bibliographic access to the department's collections demanded the identification of efficient (and economical) methods for retrospectively converting the department's vast number of uncataloged volumes housed in its various collections. At the same time, an equally efficient method had to be found to include the bibliographic records for current material processed by the department.

In the case of office technology, the department followed a similar growth curve as most other library units. The staff's knowledge of various commercial and library software packages grew considerably. They made greater gains in word processing and document production, and slower progress in the applications of statistical/financial packages.

For the last two years, 1989 through 1991, the department worked on expanding its office automation applications. The monthly statistical records have begun to be converted to a Lotus 1-2-3 spreadsheet loaded onto the department's OCLC workstation. In late 1990, a half-time staff member was added to the department. The person assigned to this position brought to the department a knowledge of more sophisticated WordPerfect applications. This skill enabled the department to produce better documentation. And, the department began to build a database management system of U.S. Federal documents based on their depository item numbers, titles, and Sudoc classification numbers. A new microcomputer was purchased in early 1991. With the necessary memory and configuration the department could meet these expanding numerical and text database needs, run the computer disks being distributed by government agencies, and provide a telecommunication capability to search remote government and other electronic bulletin boards and information services. As a result of these efforts, the department has established a combined capability of human and technical resources able to further exploit existing and future software/hardware applications.

The Internal Revolution: The Struggle for Bibliographic Control

The department's greater automation effort, and one which involves other library operations, developed from the goal to include bibliographic records for government publications in the library's central database. When the department acquired its OCLC terminal in 1988, a limited plan was put into place to catalog a certain percentage of the currently received U.S. congressional publications. Further consideration concerning the retrospective conversion of the department's older collections was held off until the library settled on a integrated library system. In the meantime, the department continued to inventory and weed its collections.

From the beginning, there was little debate about the most economical method of converting the U.S. Federal documents collection into a machine-readable database. Production of the Government Printing Office's cataloging tapes provided the best opportunity, at least for post-1976 publications. However, before proceeding, the library needed to consider several critical factors.

As has been reported in the professional literature, several commercial companies have produced versions of the GPO tapes that enable libraries to specify the bibliographic records of the documents they selected through their depository agreements. This degree of specificity was possible, because the companies would customize the GPO tapes according to a collection profile submitted by their customers, a profile based on the depository library's selection of item number classes offered by GPO. A further variation was provided by modifying the selection of item numbers by the Sudoc class stem assigned to each document.

However, as Margaret T. Mooney (1990) pointed out, many documents librarians viewed these cataloging tools as a mixed blessing, because:

- Libraries do not always receive what they are supposed to from the GPO according to their depository selection profiles. *Claims* for titles missing from depository shipments and *rain checks* for titles not received due to shortage of copies are often not filled by the GPO within a short period of time. In the case of the University of California-Riverside (UCR) library, for example, there are currently over 300 claims and rain checks that have not been filled. Over one-third of these claims and rain checks have been outstanding for more than a year. If cataloging records for these titles were matched against the item numbers or Sudoc class numbers selected by UCR, it would result in erroneous tagging of records and misrepresentation of library holdings;
- Sudoc numbers assigned to individual titles are provided to depository libraries at the time of depository distribution. While this is definitely a convenience for libraries that use Sudoc numbers for shelving their U.S. documents, GPO's practice of making corrections to these numbers at a later date could result in variation between the Sudoc numbers in the GPO tapes and the Sudoc numbers used by libraries as call numbers for their depository titles received;
- Many depository items contain more than one Sudoc class and libraries may assign different locations for various classes with a given item number. Since matching library holdings against GPO tapes by item numbers would necessarily limit the assignment of housing location to only one per item number, libraries will not have the flexibility to assign correct location information for individual titles housed in a branch library; and
- For certain categories of materials (e.g., soil surveys published by the U.S. Soil Conservation Service), the GPO has the practice of assigning a single Sudoc number to various item numbers. Since libraries do not always select all item numbers belonging to a single Sudoc class, matching library holdings by Sudoc classes could result in erroneous tagging of records not selected and, therefore, not received by the library.

A critical factor in selecting a tape service to resolve these bibliographic access problems was the idea that the "chain of evidence," which binds a single bibliographic item to its proper bibliographic record is broken when the acquisition function is severed from the cataloging function. Simply dumping the GPO tapes into the library's central database, without any special treatment, would be similar to dumping bibliographic records generated through a publisher's approval plan (e.g., university press titles) generated from a tape of a database containing the Library of Congress' cataloging in publication (CIP) records. A library would exercise little control over the quality of the records and have limited ability to correct the CIP records and to match them to the individual titles before they were added to the library's catalog. Most catalog librarians would strongly object to such CIP tapes and would find little reason to replace their traditional cataloging routines for such "valuable material." Yet, some of them are quick to recommend such an approach for material received through the GPO.

Even if tape loading was considered, a library would first need an adequate online bibliographic system to receive and process the tapes. From 1986 to late 1990, this system was in the process of implementation at Colgate. In addition, the department was only partially through its inventory to update its GPO item record files in order to create an appropriate profile for a tape service. With the installation of MONDO in early 1991, both the library and the department can now give serious consideration to the GPO tape solution. The department is implementing a plan to convert the item numbers into a dBase IV format. This project will not be completed until the end of 1992. The library plans to begin some kind of monthly tape service by 1993.

The rest of the collections present a greater challenge if the department and library are to bring them under bibliographic control. There are no GPO tape solutions for this material. If the library decides to keep the collections, or even parts of them, then the department faces some basic library inventory, weeding, organization, preservation, and binding decisions. The department would have to catalog and classify titles individually on OCLC and find room somewhere in the library's main collections. There is no quick and easy alternative.

The External Revolution: The Struggle with Electronic Formats

Over the last four years, the department has had to deal with several technological developments from government publishing and distribution centers. Many of these innovations exploited the power of transferring text and data into electronic formats for more effective and economic storage, rapid retrieval, and sophisticated manipulation. The U.S. Federal government is the largest producer of this kind of information. However, other levels of government realize the political and economic benefits of electronic formats.

An increasing amount of Federal statistical data have migrated from paper to electronic format, including publications from the Department of Commerce, Congress, Department of Defense, and the Department of the Interior. Although CD-ROM is the predominant format of choice for depository distribution of large datasets, there remains a growing number of government supported electronic bulletin boards, online databases, and floppy disks for depository collection and use. For instance, the GPO was chosen as one of the dozen institutional sites to receive the U.S. Supreme Court's opinions electronically. The GPO then makes these records immediately available to depository libraries through Project Hermes, an electronic bulletin board operated, in part, out of its main offices.

This migration from paper to electronic media presents the library and the department with some difficult choices. Though some of the information sources will continue to enjoy a dual status (paper and electronic), it is clear that government agencies are committed to electronic access and dissemination. The agencies find electronic formats cheaper to develop, produce, and distribute. However, this economy carries a certain price. The U.S. government produces CD-ROM, but has not engaged in software development on any significant scale. For example, some representatives from the Commerce Department have firmly stated that they have fulfilled their information development/distribution obligations by distributing agency statistical data in electronic formats, with no or very primitive public domain or shareware software. If users want more sophistication in their data manipulation, many Federal officials maintain that libraries and others will have to purchase value-added enhancements from the private sector.

Implications for the library and the department focus on the need to make substantial investments in computer resources in order to use large full-text or numerical databases effectively. Furthermore, the wide distribution and use of these formats will affect our ability to manage the department in several critical areas. In the area of collection development, the department must somehow join together about 150 years of paper documentation with three years of electronic data. Currently, there is little bibliographic connection between paper and electronic formats. This means, for the time being, that documents librarian must make the necessary connections through an active public service or outreach program. Such a program will inform and instruct the library's community on where, when, and how to obtain a particular format.

The department must also be able to select the proper electronic products. For paper formats, this problem was relatively simple. If the government produced a publication with information important to the library's community, there were several options to acquire, catalog, and make it available. Problems with using and understanding the publication's information could be partially solved through an organized plan of bibliographic instruction.

With the introduction of information in the electronic formats, new considerations emerged. First, the electronic product must be evaluated according to how the public will use it. Second, what kind of equipment will be needed to use the format effectively? And, third, how much staff training will be needed before the library's public services staff can effectively help the University community understand and use the data?

The department was unable to purchase a CD-ROM workstation configured with the minimum GPO recommended features until April 1991. The department then lost another four months when it experienced trouble in getting the computer and CD-ROM player to work together. It appeared that the problem involved the software, so we ordered a new release. That did not work. When there appeared to be problems with the computer's hardware, the Computer

Center staff replaced some boards, but the CD-ROM player and computer still would not work together. Finally, a Computer Center staff member went through the operating system command programs and discovered that a single digit had been loaded incorrectly during the initial CD-ROM set-up program. It was supposed to be a 1 and not a 0. The department finally had a viable workstation *nearly four years* after it started receiving electronic formats from the GPO.

Even when the staff got the workstation operational, it was faced with a new set of problems. Upon examining the collection of data disks, it became clear that the department would have to deal with a small legion of software applications and operating systems. There was little consistency in how Federal agencies applied software solutions to retrieve the data on the disk. In addition, some of the larger numerical databases came on several disks, and the department had only one disk player. It also became apparent that the staff would have to learn how to use several new commercial software applications if they were going to be able to help the library's community effectively manipulate the data on the disks. Issues of networking and multiple access have also developed as important considerations. The department is searching for the most effective and economical method of distributing electronic data. It is readily apparent that one workstation will not serve everyone's research needs.

CONCLUSION

Can there be a place for the traditional documents librarian perspective in the information and electronic age? Some librarians have watched the technological waves crashing against the walls of the GPO, while others have spoken of *information highways* carved out of a data wilderness and using supercomputers. Still others have outlined the benefits and disadvantages of lesser technologies: CD-ROMs, local area networks, and other localized information products/ services. Very few have tried to shift all these electronic formats into a new paradigm of government information delivery through libraries. Where do documents collections have a role in all this? If their banner carries the credo of "documents to the people," how do they stake a claim in a universe where paper is not necessarily the format of choice?

When viewed through the perspective of the internal automation revolution, these development and application questions for a documents department must be studied, planned, and implemented within the larger administrative context of the library organization. This environmental factor remains unchanged from the paper traditions of collecting and organizing documents. The electronic formats are certainly more efficient, complex, faster, and expensive than their paper counterparts. But, the basic decision stays the same: Does this material meet the goals of the library and the university community it serves? If yes, then the library must invest in the necessary technological, financial, and professional support to service the material. If no, then the library should reevaluate its historic commitment to collecting government information, especially when it has been acquired through depository agreements. Perhaps the library should find cheaper, albeit more limited, ways of providing its users with the government information they need.

When examined through the lens of the external revolution, the last 25 years have radically altered the paper universe well known to documents librarians. Up until a few years ago, they considered themselves as agents of information distribution or mediators for those who wish to explore the murky world of government information and data. Our bibliographic skills were honed to a fine edge on the hard stone of bureaucratic paperwork and serviceable 19th-century traditions of depository libraries. Document librarians valued, organized, and promoted the utility of the limited and obscure bibliographic by-products produced from government processes that most people chose to forget after their high school civics courses.

Herbert Schiller is the author of several critical works on governments, culture, and information policies. He characterized these pre-1960 years of government information production, collection, and dissemination as comparatively peaceful times (1989, p. 68):

> In sum, a good part of the information field a half century ago was an orderly, routinized, and largely governmental sphere of activity. It was not particularly exciting. All the same, it constituted a vital component of the public sector. Individuals could access great masses of information if they had such an interest. Depending on the locale and character of the specific library, more or less of the information would be available. With few exceptions, little money was to be made in the information field. Government materials could not be copyrighted. Accordingly, commercial publishers, for the most part, were not interested in issuing books or manuals that were originally published as government documents. These were available for the asking a modest price.

If documents librarians are to thrive in this electronic universe, they must redefine their professional roles, levels of expertise, and other professional commitments for the distribution of government information. It will no longer be enough just to be responsible for a collection of "difficult library material," or to demonstrate professional expertise as masters of volumes with which other library professionals do not want to deal. Future government information professionals must locate, identify, and distribute all types of government information. In addition, they must acquire the information management skills that will help their institution's community retrieve, understand, and effectively manipulate information and data regardless of format. Ultimately, we have nothing to lose but our own bibliographic paper chains that bind us to the past.

REFERENCES

Becker, J. and R.M. Hayes. *A Survey of Colgate University Library.* Los Angeles, CA: Becker and Hayes Division, John Wiley & Son, 1975.

Colgate Self-Study Report. Hamilton, NY: Colgate University, 1977.

Colgate University Catalogue, 1991. Hamilton, NY: Colgate University, 1991.

Hernon, Peter and Charles R. McClure. *Public Access to Government Information: Issues, Trends, and Strategies.* Norwood, NJ: Ablex, 1988.

Mooney, Margaret T. "Matching Library Holdings against the GPO Tapes: Issues, Concerns, and Solutions," *Government Publications Review*, 17 (1990): 412–428.

Schiller, Herbert. *Culture, Inc.: The Corporate Takeover of American Expression.* New York: Oxford University Press, 1989.

Chapter Nine

Ball State University Libraries and Cataloging of Government Publications

Diane Calvin

The Ball State University Libraries undertook a two-year project to add retrospective and current government publications records to its online catalog. A committee studied the options, recommending vendors and a procedure that allows customized profiling to fit the records to Ball State University's collection. Loading government publications records into the online catalog has greatly increased collection use and altered the Government Publications Services' workflow.

LIBRARY PROFILE

The Ball State University Libraries are comprised of the main library, the Alexander M. Bracken Library, and the Architecture and Science/Health Science branch libraries. The Libraries first used the Carlyle online catalog, but later moved to the NOTIS system.

As of 1991, the University Libraries hold 1.4 million volumes or volume equivalents of books, periodicals, microforms, and other media. Bracken Library has held U.S. depository status since 1960. The percentage of items selected has varied from a high of 65% to the current level of 45%. From 1960 to 1970, many depository serials and monographs were cataloged, assigned

Library of Congress classification numbers, and shelved in the library's general collection.

Since 1970, virtually all new paper documents were left uncataloged and arranged by the Superintendent of Documents Classification System in the library's Government Publications Service area. Microfiche documents were filed in Sudoc number order in the library's microforms collection. In 1977, Bracken Library became a U.S. Geological Survey map depository, and in 1984, a Defense Mapping Agency depository. These items were shelved in the library's map collection.

FORMATION OF A COMMITTEE

In July 1988, at the request of the Dean of University Libraries, the Assistant Dean for Library Technical Services appointed a committee to explore the possibility of adding government publications records to the online catalog. As government publications librarian, the author was a member of the committee, as were the Head of Cataloging Services, a Serials Cataloger, and the Director of Library Automated Systems.

The committee was charged to:

- Compare the options for adding document records to the online catalog. We were to include cost estimates of records and labor and to determine the compatibility of computer tapes with our automated system.
- Recommend one of the options. We were to address the issues of adding current and/or retrospective (post-1976) holdings, of adding both paper and microfiche formats or only selected formats, and of adding records for serials and maps, noting potential problems with these.

PRELIMINARY RESEARCH

The cataloging committee began its work by searching library literature for articles about Government Printing Office (GPO) cataloging and catalog records available from private vendors. Because MARC cataloging for documents became widely available after July 1976, we chose to focus on post-1976 catalog records.

We also read articles about other libraries that had undertaken a cataloging project. This was worth the time spent, as it familiarized us with the terminology, current trends, and problems of documents cataloging. Judy Myers, University of Houston, for instance, has outlined the basics of cataloging preparation (see Chapter 1).

CALCULATING THE SIZE OF OUR COLLECTION

In order to calculate the cost of options, we estimated the number of documents records likely to be included in any post-1976 load, as well as the number of records for current documents. In its 30-year history, Government Publications Service had never made an inventory of its collection, but had kept statistics on additions and withdrawals for both paper and microfiche documents. Statistics for depository maps received and withdrawn were kept, in part, by Government Publications Service and, in part, by the map collection.

We estimated our post-1976 collection to be roughly 65,000 titles. Based on those statistics, we could expect to receive about 4,800 current records annually.

OPTIONS FOR ADDING RECORDS

After much reading and discussion, the committee identified three options for adding post-1976 documents to the online catalog. First, the library could purchase the GPO catalog tapes from the Library of Congress (LC), load them in the online catalog, and then review and correct the records to reflect our depository holdings.

The advantage of this option is that the GPO and LC offers both GPO and LC retrospective as well as current GPO-cataloged records. There are several disadvantages:

- A tape load could include records of thousands of documents not in our collection;
- There are numerous discrepancies and inadequacies in GPO cataloging procedures;
- GPO catalog tapes are "dirty," with many duplicate serial records, records for title pages and ephemera, and other errors requiring local correction;
- Delays of as much as six months occur between the receipt of a document and the receipt of the document's record on a GPO tape; and
- GPO tapes could be incompatible with our local system.

Second, the library could purchase customized tapes from a vendor. Such tapes would reflect our depository holdings as we specify using a collection profile. There are advantages to this option:

- Vendors offer both retrospective and current GPO-cataloged records;
- Vendors offer "cleaned-up" GPO catalog records with numerous duplicates eliminated and errors corrected;
- Vendors offer flexible profiling options. We could edit a list of item numbers,

specify a range of years, and note any additional Sudoc stems to add or delete from the profile;
- We could receive customized records as specified in the collection profile; and
- Vendors could produce tapes compatible with our local system.

There are disadvantages:

- Despite the best profiling, we would still receive some records for documents not in our collection: For example, records for lost and withdrawn documents, as well as for titles claimed but never received; and
- If we chose to receive records for current documents, we might experience an additional delay in receiving these records as the vendor cleaned up GPO cataloging before forwarding the records to us.

Third, the University Libraries' technical cataloging assistants could search OCLC for each title in our documents collection and add its record to the online catalog. There are several advantages to this option:

- The OCLC database offers both retrospective records (back to and prior to 1976) and current GPO-cataloged records;
- Any records added would match our exact holdings;
- No special programming would be needed because we already load OCLC tapes into our system; and
- If we chose to receive records for current documents, OCLC offers the records sooner than most alternate sources.

But several disadvantages remained:

- Searching and adding individual records would be a time-consuming and labor-intensive process;
- The documents themselves would need to be removed from the stacks during the OCLC searching process, making them unavailable to library users;
- Many early GPO records found on OCLC contain errors and omissions which would have be corrected locally; and
- In order to have document records in the online catalog within a reasonable amount of time, the library would have to consider adding more OCLC terminals and/or adding staff on more cost-effective schedules.

The cataloging committee calculated the labor and automation costs for each option. Option three was the most expensive in terms of record price, online time, and employee hours. Neither Government Publications Service nor Cataloging Services could spare the personnel for this. Option one meant cleaning up record errors in the GPO tape and deleting thousands of records, again requiring much staff time. Option two seemed the most suitable: It would be less expensive in the long run to pay vendor charges for extracting and "cleaning up" records to produce a customized tape.

LIBRARIES SURVEYED

In mid-1988, Marcive, Inc. and Brodart were two leading vendors of retrospective and current document catalog records in magnetic tape format. At our request, both vendors provided a list of customer libraries similar to the Ball State University Libraries in size and collection characteristics.

The cataloging committee created a detailed survey to send these customers, asking about the library's documents collection, automation circumstances, and recent experience with the vendor (see chapter appendix). In October and November 1988, we sent copies of this survey to six libraries, addressed to the heads of the documents collections and of technical services or cataloging. We telephoned the librarians for their answers.

Although conducting the survey was a time-consuming task, the findings proved useful. The librarians were cooperative and helpful, and they often provided answers to questions we had not thought to ask. Some librarians complimented us on the idea of a survey, wishing they had done the same before beginning their cataloging projects.

VENDORS CHOSEN

After completion of the survey and several follow-up phone calls to Marcive and Brodart, the cataloging committee made a preliminary recommendation in Spring 1989 to purchase Marcive records. Our plans were delayed several months while the University Libraries made its transition to the NOTIS system.

In the meantime, OCLC announced its GOVDOC service to provide current document records to depository libraries. GOVDOC seemed to combine the best features of a vendor without the drawbacks of individual OCLC record searching. After much discussion in-house and with Marcive and OCLC, in the Spring of 1990, the cataloging committee recommended purchasing retrospective records from Marcive and ongoing records from OCLC. We recommended that all formats (paper, microfiche, and maps) be included and that we purchase records for both monographs and serials. We also recommended buying a printed product for both the retrospective and current tape loads, that we might verify and track receipt of catalog records.

As a member of the cataloging committee, the Director of Library Automated Systems wrote the specifications for the Marcive purchase. The specifications required the vendor to provide a processing profile for selection of records, to provide bibliographic and authority records, and to produce a sample tape conforming to NOTIS requirements. In April 1990, the sample tape was received and loaded. Committee members reviewed the records and found them satisfactory.

MARCIVE PROFILING PROCESS

In May 1990, Marcive sent us a profile diskette holding hundreds of item numbers. The author added, deleted, or amended almost 1,900 item numbers, matching the diskette files with our item card files.

The author spent about 150 hours (spread over seven weeks) reviewing these item numbers. Fortunately, the documents staff had done a thorough job of annotating the item cards over the years. The staff had noted on each card when the number was surveyed and when the number was added or dropped.

Government Publications Service's Kardex file shelflist was used to check dates when documents issued under an item number were withdrawn, and to verify paper and microfiche holdings for each Sudoc number received.

Item numbers that had never been selected by our library were deleted from the diskette files. For item numbers that we had once selected and then dropped, the number was amended on the diskette to show the years of holdings. The same procedure was followed for item numbers selected since 1976. Easiest of all were item numbers always selected since 1976: These were simply left as they appeared on the diskette files.

Marcive permitted one location designation for each item number. Bracken Library houses documents in three locations: Government Publications Service, the microforms collection, and the map collection. This one-location limit was a problem for item numbers with multiple titles kept in different locations. In these cases, we chose the location that held the most titles; the location for any individual record could be changed later.

We made a printout of the amended diskette for further reference. We copied the amended diskette for our files and returned the diskette to Marcive. Within a week, Marcive called to say they were ready to run our tape.

MARCIVE RECORDS RECEIVED

The tapes arrived within two weeks of Marcive's call. The tapes, with 112,731 records, were loaded on July 26, 1990. We received many more records than anticipated. These included records for multiple editions of monographs that could not be eliminated in the profiling process without losing records for other documents. There were also records for individual map sheets; we were unaware that the GPO cataloged its maps to produce so many seemingly duplicate records.

After learning that we would receive more Marcive records than expected, we decided not to purchase shelflist cards. Rather, the University Libraries' automation staff produced a 3,838-page printout with the Sudoc number, location, and short title of every record loaded. We have used this list to note records to be deleted or corrected.

OCLC PROFILE AND RECORDS

While waiting for the Marcive records to arrive, the author reviewed the OCLC profile to select current records from the GOVDOC service. GOVDOC provided a 63-page profile with the item numbers selected by our library; OCLC had extracted the numbers for our collection using GPO's *Depository Union List of Item Subscribers* (September 1989). The profile required only a location code to be typed next to each item number. GOVDOC also allowed us to add or delete any item numbers. Our first GOVDOC tape arrived on August 15, 1990 and was loaded into NOTIS on August 20th. We chose to receive shelflist cards from the GOVDOC service.

THE OUTCOME

Adding document records to our online catalog has brought both benefits and difficulties to the library and to Government Publications Service. Most notable is that every librarian we surveyed and every periodical article we read predicted an increase in collection use. This was true in Ball State University Libraries. Government publications had received steady use over the years, but business boomed after document records appeared in the online catalog. The number of patrons using the Government Publications Service area increased 35% over the previous fiscal year: in-room use of documents increased 14% and circulation increased 154% for the same time period. Personnel in the library's microforms area also reported an increase in the use of documents on microfiche.

Because document records were now in the online catalog, Government Publications Service could move to automated circulation with the rest of the library when this was implemented at the end of 1990.

Government Publications Service clerks have always been responsible for the collection's physical processing and record keeping. The clerks experienced changes in their routines: Typed Kardex shelflist cards for monographs have been replaced by OCLC shelflist cards, and barcodes (for circulation purposes) are attached to documents and their shelflist cards.

It had been our hope that the timing of the Marcive and GOVDOC projects would leave no gap between retrospective and current records. Despite our efforts, the documents received during a four-month period in mid-1990 have no online records. We are identifying these documents as time permits and requesting Cataloging Services to search OCLC and to add these records to the online catalog.

Despite the amount of time spent on the Marcive profiling process, many documents represented in the online catalog are not in our collection. We are identifying and deleting these records as time permits, often when a patron finds the record in the online catalog and requests the missing document.

Location errors are an ongoing problem. Due to the fact that Marcive and GOVDOC allowed only one location per item number, we had to specify one location even if the item number included both paper and microfiche series. Therefore, a record may identify a document as housed in Government Publications Service when actually it is in the microforms area. The problem persists when the GPO distributes on microfiche a title usually issued in paper. We are correcting location errors in retrospective records as time permits. For the maintenance of ongoing GOVDOC records, we identify and correct the discrepancies when the monthly shelflist cards arrive.

There was a massive problem with the map records resulting from GPO's cataloging practices for certain large map sets, such as the topographical maps. Rather than creating new OCLC master records each time a particular item in the set is cataloged, the GPO reuses the record for the set. This generates numerous bibliographic records containing the same OCLC control number. This situation interfered with Cataloging Services' ability to identify duplicate records in the local database. It also resulted in numerous identical or nearly identical online catalog displays, which confused library patrons. In late 1991, we decided to drop map item numbers from the GOVDOC profile; current depository maps will be cataloged individually in a future project. (In September 1991, the GPO announced it would change this practice by creating separate map cataloging records, each with its own OCLC control number.)

Finally, we chose to purchase authority records from Marcive. However, after receiving them, we learned that it would be necessary to write a program to separate subject, name, and series records on the tapes, prior to loading them into the NOTIS system. Had we known beforehand that this was necessary, we could have asked Marcive to process the tapes differently.

Overall, adding document records to the online catalog has been a positive experience and a worthwhile expenditure of time and money. Our documents collection is better used, and almost daily, we hear grateful patrons say that they did not realize all this information was available until now.

REFERENCES

Depository Union List of Item Subscribers (Washington, D.C.: GPO, 1989).

APPENDIX. GOVERNMENT DOCUMENTS COMMITTEE QUESTIONNAIRE

Evaluator ————————————   Vendor ————————————

Date ——————————   Library Name & Address ——————————————

Contact Person: ————————————————————————

Title: ——————————————   Telephone: ————————————

Library Data:

Size of total collection: Titles ——————— ;   Volumes —————
Size of gov. doc. collection: Titles ——————— ;   Volumes —————
Depository library: No ——————— ;   Yes —————————
  If yes, selective ————   full ————————
  If selective, what percentage selected? ————————————————
Percent of document collection that is serial (including periodicals): ————
microform: ———————————————— maps: ————————————

What is your cataloging utility? ————————————————————

What is your online system? ————————————————————————

Vendor/Record Selection

1. Why did your library decide to purchase cataloging records for government documents through a vendor?

2. What vendors were considered? Which vendor did you select and why?

3a. What tapes did you purchase?
    Retrospective only: ———————————— Date of purchase: ————
    Current only: ———————————————— Date of purchase: ————
    Both: ———————————————————— Date of purchase: ————

  b. What was the total number of records loaded? Was this done all at once or in phases? Please elaborate.

   c. What percentage of your entire government documents collection appears in
      your online catalog?

4. If you did not purchase records for your entire post-1976 document
   collection, how did you select the materials for which records would be
   obtained from the vendor? For example, did you limit your selection to
   certain years? Were there certain categories of government documents that
   you decided not to include (such as congressional reports, ephemeral
   documents)? Please elaborate.

5. Did you purchase cataloging records for government publications in special
   formats (microforms, serials, maps) or were these handled differently? If
   so, how? Did you make any distinction between current and retrospective
   holdings in making this decision?

6. Did you catalog pre-1976 documents? If so, how?

7. Had any of your library's documents been cataloged and classified previously—that is, integrated into the regular collection with LC or Dewey
   call numbers? If so, did this create any problems?

8.a. How was your library's profile set up? How successful was it in matching
     your holdings? (i.e., were records omitted that you wanted, or were records
     included that you didn't want?)

   b. Approximately how long did the initial profiling process take?

9. If your library subscribes to the current tapes, how often do you change your profile to add or delete selections? Is it difficult to make profile changes? If so, please explain.

Content of Tapes/Record Quality

1. Did you encounter any problems in loading the tapes?

2. Did the tapes meet the specifications of your online system, or were some adjustments required? If so, please elaborate.

3. Who processed and loaded the tapes into your system? Was it the library or the vendor of your online system? Was it different for retrospective than for current tapes?

4. After loading the tapes, did you check the cataloging of any of the records? If so, to what extent?

5. Were the records generally of good quality?

6. Had the vendor made any attempt to correct errors in the records or to provide authorized headings? If so, please elaborate. [For Marcive customers: Had the tapes you loaded been "cleaned up" in the cooperative project with Rice, LSU, and Texas A&M?]

7. Was much work (corrections, verification, etc.) required of your staff after the tapes had been loaded? If so, please elaborate.

8. Please comment on any problems that you may have encountered with records for serials, microforms, or maps.

9. Does the catalog record indicate that a document is in microform? If so, how does it appear?

10.a. If you receive the current tapes, how do you know when a document has been cataloged? Must you check your online catalog after the tape has been loaded, or does the vendor notify you? Or is it in conjunction with the *Monthly Catalog*?

   b. How long does it take to get a record after the item has been received in-house?

   c. How does the vendor handle GPO corrections of Sudocs numbers or item numbers?

11. Do the tapes contain records for nondepository documents?

Vendor/Performance

1. Do you feel the vendor represented the product and services accurately?

2. Did the vendor provide you with a sample of the records?

3. Did you ask the vendor to provide an estimate of costs? Was the actual cost consistent with this initial estimate?

4.   Did your library receive adequate help/support from the vendor?

5.   Who in your library contacts the vendor/supplier regarding profile changes, etc.?

General

1.   What has been the impact of cataloging on the usage/circulation of government documents? Do you have any statistics readily available?

2.   Rate your overall satisfaction of the following on a scale of 1 to 10, with 10 as the highest satisfaction:

        Record selection _____
        Record quality _____
        Vendor performance _____

3.   If you had to go through the process again, is there anything you would do differently?

Additional questions for documents librarians:

1.   Do you mark or stamp cataloged documents to distinguish them from uncataloged ones?

2.   Where do you place documents received but not yet cataloged? (For example, are documents kept on special shelves? Do you retain the shipping lists?)

3.   How do you check out new documents that have been received but not yet cataloged?

4.   How do you check out materials which were excluded from the tapes? Are they cataloged on a title-by-title basis, or do you simply create item records in the system?

5.   By what classification number do you retrieve government documents from your online system? Sudocs? LC? Dewey?

Chapter Ten

Government CD-ROM Information in the University of Notre Dame Libraries

Stephen M. Hayes and Laura Bayard

The Standing Committee on Electronic Media at the University of Notre Dame was established by the Director of the University Libraries in 1990 in an attempt to resolve increasing problems surrounding electronic media. The interdepartmental Committee published a report of findings after convening for one year. The following chapter describes the climate and issues resulting in the Committee appointment, the Committee's procedures and findings; and its ensuing policy recommendations.

Four compelling reasons to establish the Standing Committee on Electronic Media are:

- Availability, use, and demand for electronic based information is increasing within the University environment;
- Expansion of electronic media from index and abstracting resources to nonbibliographic, numeric and full-text datafiles;
- Distribution of government produced information, especially in CD-ROM, through the Federal depository program; and
- The terrifying rumor that data from the 1990 Census of Population and Housing would be issued on as many as 300 CD-ROMs.

ENVIRONMENT AND ISSUES

Collection development and acquisitions responsibilities at the University of Notre Dame are decentralized. The teaching and research faculty in conjunction with the Library Faculty are charged with these activities. Library funds are allocated for academic disciplines with the materials acquired housed in the library. There is no requirement that information resources purchased with nonlibrary University funding reside within the University Libraries. For example, videotapes, full-text datafiles, and films are purchased and housed in an independent Educational Media department. In addition, computer-tape datafiles are maintained by the Social Science Training and Research Lab (SSTRL), within the College of Arts and Letters. Finally, business-oriented datafiles are housed on the University computer, accessible only through a lab located in the Business School.

Technically, the *bibliographic control* of campus information resources, regardless of format, resides with the University Libraries; however, all materials are not represented within the Libraries online card catalog—UNLOC. Cooperative projects have incorporated various collections into UNLOC, but a systematic inventory undertaken several years ago of campus resources was unsuccessful due to lack of cooperation by various campus entities.

Physical access to electronic media is the responsibility of the University Libraries for material housed with the Libraries. Other resources, once known, are made available on an informal basis through referrals to and personal contacts with the involved departments.

Within the Libraries, the quality of physical access varies due to the continual evolution of technology. A Local Area Network has been established within the Reference Department. The Hesburgh Library has been "wired" for UNLOC; however, the Libraries are not "wired" for other electronic resources, the campus-wide network or Ethernet. The Libraries are scheduled for networking and should have access to the Ethernet by 1993 as campus computing services are a major priority within the University.

Reference services to the resources of the University Libraries do not discriminate based on medium. Reference services are centralized within the University Libraries, with science branches performing reference services within the respective branch libraries. Reference services for electronic indexes, full-text CD-ROMs, and documents are all provided from the main reference desk. Technical support services, i.e., use of microfilm readers, are provided in the respective departments. The level of services is perceived to be of high quality and extremely user-supportive. Instruction and education in the use of resources are as important as "providing the answer." Services are provided by a variety of staff from professional librarians to student assistants. The levels of reference services to electronic products would be an integral part of the Committee's initial charge.

A new area of concern to reference service is the downloading, movement, and manipulation of electronic-based information. The full responsibility for downloading and partial responsibility for movement of information reside with the Reference Department and University Libraries. However, within the University, the unit responsible for facilitating the use and manipulation of electronic information is the SSTRL. Recently, the College of Business and the College of Arts and Letters have also added similar staff to support personal computer use within those Departments. Further, the Department of Economics is presently seeking grant funding for both electronic data *and* staff to support and facilitate faculty use of such data.

The role of University Computing tends to support technical access. The use of PCs, various software, word processing, and mainframe activities tend to be its purview. However, actual data manipulation and detailed user support for faculty, students and staff do not reside with University Computing. Thus, decentralization of user support in the area of access and manipulation of electronic data is increasingly becoming a problem on campus.

MEMBERSHIP

As indicated above, the University environment is decentralized with the individual academic college or department assuming a great deal of independence; therefore, the shareholders involved with the issue of electronic data is equally decentralized. In order to address this decentralization and to reflect many areas of expertise, individuals from the following campus units were appointed to the Committee:

- University Computing provides detailed expert technical support on the various aspects of computer, networking, and user support;
- Law Library is a separate depository library and has extensive experience in providing reference and end-user training to such full-text databases as Westlaw and Lexis/Nexis;
- University Libraries' expertise is bibliographic control, physical access, reference service support to a variety of media, and various "coordinating" responsibilities and experience;
- SSTRL's proficiencies are data manipulation, statistical software, and end-user support; and
- Representatives from the College of Arts and Letters and the Business College provide experience and information concerning faculty needs and the PC environment.

Bringing representatives from as many units on campus as possible is critical. In addition to providing needed information and technical expertise, participation on the Committee sensitized the various shareholders to the issues and needs of the entire University community. By facilitating communication, the potential to influence resource allocation was greatly increased; thus, the University Libraries gain more than just recommendations concerning electronic media.

CHARGE

The initial charge to the Standing Committee was limited to providing recommendations concerning

> government-produced CD-ROM received on the University Libraries' depository program. Recommendations should address physical housing of the materials; accessibility of appropriate workstations for users; responsibility for technical assistance to users in downloading information to PCs/uploading to a campus mainframe; and academic support in the use of statistical packages, both PC and mainframe-based, to manipulate such data. Related issues include the extent of responsibility to non-Notre Dame users in light of requirements of the depository program, group training opportunities, and the relationship of and proper referral to print and electronic versions of government produced data.

OPERATING PRINCIPLES

The chairperson either explicitly or implicitly assumed the following operating principles:

- This was new, uncomfortable territory for most participants because areas of expertise were not held in common among members. Each individual had expertise upon which the Committee could draw. No individual attempted to develop or duplicate the expertise of another committee member. In combination, the Committee had the expertise needed to function efficiently.
- This was an opportunity to educate and sensitize important members of the University Community to issues, needs, and limitations.
- Resources, programs, and agencies that were already existing within the University were depended upon (the committee did not recommend the creation of new ones).
- A static budget was assumed. An extensive infusion of money was not to be expected.
- A progressive process was recommended, from modest beginnings to ideal "blue sky" scenario, paralleling present day to future development timetable.
- While the charge addressed government produced CD-ROMs, the rec-

ommendations are to be generic and to apply to all CD-ROM-based information and to electronic information in general.

- Universitywide cooperation cannot be required; therefore, implicit incentives for cooperation can be incorporated into recommendations.

RECOMMENDATIONS AND ANALYSES

The recommendations listed in the Committee's report relate to government produced CD-ROMs, but many of the findings can be applied to other electronic formats.

The primary areas of concern to the Committee were: location of the CD-ROM information; moving data on and off the mainframe computer or other target platforms, such as PCs and workstations; the role of the University Libraries in accessing the CD-based information; and the role of other campus shareholders, such as the Social Science Training and Research Lab (SSTRL) and the Teaching & Research Faculty (T & R).

Location of CD-ROM Information

There are three separate issues: (1) coordination of information about CD-based information on campus, (2) the bibliographic control of this information, and (3) the physical location of the compact disks.

Administration, Bibliographic Control, and Housing. Traditionally, bibliographic control and access are the responsibility of the University Libraries. When purchased or when discovered on campus, bibliographic records for information are entered into UNLOC. This is consistent with the aim of UNLOC as a gateway to the information resources of the University. However, given the complex and dispersed nature of this new area of information, the Committee felt that the appointment of an individual to oversee all aspects would be beneficial. Therefore, the Committee recommended the following:

(1) Coordination of CD-based information, available on campus and elsewhere, is the responsibility of the University Libraries. A librarian should be appointed to: coordinate communication between various shareholders concerning CD-based and potentially other electronic media; be knowledgeable in various electronic data resources and support services available to campus users; and supervise a support staff familiar with file transfer, subsetting, partitioning, and other technical procedures. An appropriate staff and budget should be made available to facilitate such coordination.

(2) Bibliographic access to and control over CD-ROMs will be the respon-

sibility of the University Libraries. Records will be entered into UNLOC, with any usage or access restrictions noted on the record.

The Libraries consistently house materials which have been purchased with Library funds. Since the Libraries have the greatest public service hours and staff, this is the location of choice for materials. Therefore, the physical access and housing of the CD-ROMs should continue to be provided within the Libraries. Circulation of this material was not recommended since CD-ROMs should not be touched, exposed to dust, or scratched; are expensive to replace; require special readers; and are difficult to administer.

The "carrot" to encourage departments with electronic products to house or deposit the products in the University Libraries is the availability of equipment and support staff and the ability to add any usage and/or access restrictions to the UNLOC records, such as "usage restricted to law students," or "access available M-F, 8 a.m.–5 p.m."

Additionally, departments often encourage or request that electronic products be purchased, even though equipment to access the product is not available. The Libraries do not purchase media which it cannot access and make available. In order to allow departments some flexibility and to get the Libraries needed equipment, electronic media would be purchased if departments buy the equipment and transfer the ownership to the libraries for use with that and other products. The committee recommended:

(3)   The Libraries will provide physical access to the CD-ROMs. The location of the access point for CD-based information should be near user assistance (i.e., the Reference Department). Where usage is particularly high, academic departments are encouraged to provide the Libraries with workstations to insure maximum access.

Moving Information from PC to Mainframe. The issue of movement of information is one which is dependent on the configuration of CD-ROM equipment and workstations. The movement issues will be discussed first followed by various options of CD-ROM configurations.

A basic assumption by the Committee was that the Libraries was not the place for data manipulation to take place. Rather, data or information would be retrieved, downloaded, or moved to another computer by the user. The following discussion centers on those methods of movement. "Mainframe" here is synonymous with any computer powerful enough to manipulate the data to meet the needs of the users. In some of the options for arranging CD-ROMs, this movement will be an issue, while in other options, the discussion is moot.

There are several options for connecting the PC workstations to the mainframe. One possibility is to establish a mainframe connection through telephone lines and a modem using the existing dial-in ports. Transfer protocol would be a

Kermit-like suite. This is considered a less viable option, since the transmission speed is slow.

Another option connects the PC workstations to peripheral devices, such as tape drives. The datasets can be extracted from CD-ROMs and physically transported by tape to the mainframe for processing. Other than regular tape transport, the mainframe has limited peripheral choices. In light of today's modern technology, this is not a useful option.

The most desirable method connects the PC to an Ethernet connection and uses the TCP/IP protocol (such as the NCSA's TCP/IP package). With the use of the TCP/IP file transport protocol (FTP), the files can be quickly transmitted to the mainframe. Although FTP is less than user-friendly, interfaces can be programmed to ease this burden.

The arrangement of equipment to read and manipulate CD-based information is a complex issue. Technically, the ability to arrange CD-ROM in such a way as to access them from a variety of terminals via the campus computer network is possible. Unfortunately, it is expensive and financially risky. Equipment purchased today may soon be obsolete because of rapidly changing CD-ROM technology. Therefore, the Committee assumed a multistage process to accomplish its objectives.

To facilitate movement of information to more powerful computers the Committee next recommended methods for accessing CD-ROM data in both numerical and textual formats. The following options provide guidance for addressing the CD-ROM data handling issues. These recommendations cover the spectrum from accessing CD-ROMs using a single user workstation to a networked CD-ROM system for many users. Various software packages are available to transfer numerical and textual data. Unfortunately, additional programming is needed for each option and software. The main thrust of these recommendations is for the generic retrieval of information from CD-ROM media.

The campus computer clusters have low- to high-end workstations. The low-end clusters include Macintosh SEs and DOS 286 equipment. The high-end clusters use Sun Sparc-stations and IBM PS/2-55s, Macintosh IIcis and Next machines. The common denominators for all clusters are the ability to communicate using TCP/IP protocols and their connections to the campus backbone. None of these clusters contains CD-ROM readers.

Presently, the University is not close to completing the campuswide network. However, the future design of the system should take into consideration a functioning campus network. Consequently, the Committee should standardize on the NeXT computer as the front end target platform because of its computing and multimedia capabilities, its secondary storage designs, and its ease of use. However, this creates a problem with interfaces to the Macintosh and DOS machines on campus unless primitive forms of access can be arranged by a TCP/IP interface.

Technical Arrangement of CD-ROM The following six options were considered by the Committee; however, only three were viable alternatives.

OPTION 1: This option addresses a single-user using a PC with a disk reader, a printer, and primitive software. The reader can be single disk, multiple disk, or a daisy chain of either or both. A high-end DOS machine with Ashton-Tate's dBase statistical package is the simplest configuration. Additional software packages can include SAS, SPSS, or Lotus for manipulation.

Hardware at least → $8,000   Single user, accessing from one tò a maximum of six CD-ROMs without manually changing the compact disks.

ADVANTAGES: This configuration can use dBase software which is available today and the primitive page turning software already on many CD-ROM products. Implementation is fast with a minimal start up cost. With minimal risk, there is immediate access to CD-ROM datasets.

DISADVANTAGES: One workstation required for each user. Unless multiple CD-ROM copies of the same datasets are purchased, there may be only one user per CD-ROM product. CD-ROM can be used only where these special workstations are placed. Programming is necessary to make the use, extraction, and downloading of the information as user friendly as possible. Some files on the CD-ROM will, however, remain unavailable for downloading due to the size of the file and the limited capacity of floppy disks.

While this is the first of six options, the Committee immediately recognized this as a minimum requirement; therefore, it made the following recommendation concerning CD-ROM configuration:

(4)   At a minimum, the University Libraries should develop, as soon as possible, a stand-alone workstation consisting of a high end DOS machine attached to a multiple disk CD-ROM reader, such as a Pioneer. This workstation would have a modem for transfer of information to the mainframe, but, ideally, it would have an Ethernet connection.

OPTION 2: This option configures the stand alone workstations of Option 1 into a local area Novell network of DOS machines. Several readers can be connected to different DOS machines for a larger CD-ROM selection. The reader station costs begin at the Option 1 cost of $8,000.00. Additional workstations cost approximately $3,000.00 per workstation.

Hardware at least → $8,000   Multiple users able to select from multiple disks.

ADVANTAGES: The advantages are similar to those discussed in Option 1. An additional advantage is that users can access the CD-ROMs from different workstations simultaneously. Remote access to the CD-ROMs is possible through the Novell network.

DISADVANTAGES: A limited number of CD-ROMs may be available depending on the number and arrangement of CD readers. Again, programming will be needed to make the use, extraction, and downloading of the information as user friendly as possible. Some files will, however, remain unavailable for downloading due to their size and the limited capacity of floppy disks or lack of FTP to the mainframe.

Again, building on the previous recommendation and assuming that more individual workstations would be established, the Committee recommended:

(5)   The Libraries should develop, by the summer of 1992, a local area Novell network of DOS machines, based on the above workstation. CD-ROM readers, holding upwards of six CDs, should be part of a Novell network used to access the mounted CDs.

With the above arrangement, two issues still remain. First, the preceding provides a temporary arrangement of CD-based information while the limitations of moving information to a more powerful computer for manipulation and analysis remains. Second, if the Libraries is to provide access and move information, there must be an infrastructure to support this. Therefore, assuming that the Novell network might be the only configuration for a while and that the library would support data transfer to the mainframe, the Committee recommended:

(6)   The University Libraries must develop, after the building is wired for the campus network (see recommendation 14), an Ethernet connection for the above Novell PC network. Using the TCP/IP protocol and the file transport protocol, files can be transmitted to the mainframe.

Again, the Committee viewed this recommendation as an interim solution that did not address the issue of either multiple users or non-university users requiring information for manipulation.

Caution must be expressed here. Cost, estimated to be in excess of $250,000, is significant. The potential loss of investment is significant if CD-ROM technology changes from whatever Notre Dame selects.

OPTION 3: This option (see Figure 10-1 which illustrates a generic view of a campus networked CD-ROM server) proposes that a V-Server/CD Net, marketed by Virtual Microsystems, Inc., be incorporated into the campus network. A user would access the system using terminals or terminal emulators via Decent protocols. An interface, provided by Digital Equipment Corporation (DEC), will allow a workstation to access CD-ROMs in the library and on the campus network via a $VT^{100}/_{200}$, a PC terminal window or via dial-up.

Hardware at least $\rightarrow$ \$230,000 + Software (for multiple users)

- NeXT equipment interface design \$??
- Programming time \$??
- \$4,000 for each additional NeXT unit.

ADVANTAGES: This server architecture allows easy access to multiple CD-ROMs simultaneously by faculty, staff, and students who are connected to the campus network at Notre Dame. Simultaneous access to many (29 x 14 = 406) CD-ROMs if maximally configured with the present technology. This option also allows existing users of the 31xx IBM terminals, used in the Libraries, to access UNLOC and to gain access to either the IBM mainframe or the CD server. Since this terminal access is in a pass-through mode, the ALA character set will not be modified. Users can be presented with a menu outlining their choices of the CD-ROM server, or the Libraries' online catalog or IBM mainframe. Passwords are enforceable at any stage of the process allowing the University to limit access of nonuniversity users to government produced CD-ROM products.

The modular construction of the access server and Starport permits functionality to be reassigned, different modules can be added or substituted, and software can be changed as needed. Passwords, menus, and configurations can be dynamically updated. Automatic time-of-day switch-overs can also be implemented to reconfigure access rights and methods dynamically, if appropriate.

DISADVANTAGES: Technology is at the cutting edge. This implies there will be technological changes in the near future. Techniques might improve and prices might decrease. It also implies that the University is at maximum risk! This system could be obsolete or not conform to standards in a very short time. The initial cost is high. Giving access to the CD-ROM readers to many users 24 hours a day brings a curse of potentially low reliability metrics for the CD-ROM reading devices. This scheme also requires the most extensive programming because it really represents a developmental system. Programming costs are not included in the estimated price of \$250,000.00.

Based on its information, the Committee viewed this option as the optimal configuration, and therefore, recommended:

(7) The Libraries, or University agent, should incorporate CD-ROM Server into the campus network. When developed, this can serve the campus and the local area.

(8) The University should continue to support Read-only, Anonymous FTP (file transport protocol), which facilitates access to data housed within the University. Additionally, the University should grant non-university users read-only access to appropriate files. This is particularly important for

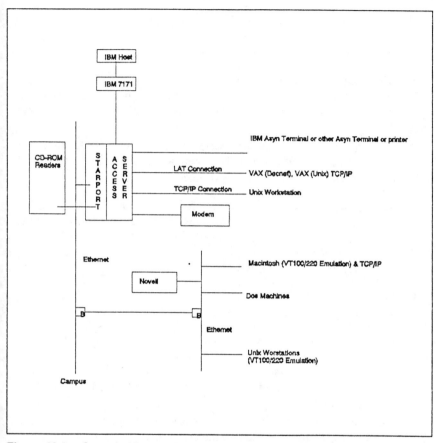

Figure 10-1. Generic View of Campus Networked CD-ROM Server.

government depository materials which must be made available to members of the general congressional district.

OPTION 4: This option is the same as Option 2, with the addition of a dedicated compute engine as part of the generic approach. There is a NeXT or any other TCP/IP front-end workstation with a NeXT or other compute engine in the middle and a Meridian data multiple disk server for the back end.

Hardware at least → $70,000 + Software.   Single user using another NeXT, IBM RS6000 or DEC VAX as a server, at least 14 CD-ROMs accessible without manual intervention.

- NeXT equipment interface design $??
- Programming time $??
- $4,000 for each additional NeXT unit.

ADVANTAGES: Same as for Option 2.

DISADVANTAGES: The cost of the computer engine outweighs the advantages of the architecture. Consequently, this is not a viable solution at the present time.

OPTION 5: This option uses a NeXT or any other TCP/IP front-end workstation interface, and a Meridian data multiple disk server as the CD-ROM server that connects the server to the IBM mainframe.

Hardware at least → $45,000 + Software   Single user at least 14 CD-ROMs accessible without manual intervention.

- NeXT equipment interface design $??
- Programming time $??
- Cost to interface to IBM mainframe—Unknown
- $4,000 for each additional NeXT unit.

ADVANTAGE: The Committee saw no advantage to this configuration given the overwhelming disadvantages.

DISADVANTAGES: Manufacturers do not appear interested in designing a hardware and software interface for CD-ROM directly to the IBM systems. This option is not a solution.

OPTION 6: This option mounts all necessary data online using a NeXT or any TCP/IP front end workstation which can communicate to the IBM mainframe which reads selected data from a CD-ROM for storage on IBM disk drives.

Hardware at least → $??? install additional Disk drives on the IBM mainframe.

- workstation to read CD data into the IBM mainframe disk farm $8,000.00
- NeXT equipment interface design $??
- Programming time $??
- $4,000 for each additional NeXT unit.

ADVANTAGES: This option resolves the problem of transferring information to the mainframe.

DISADVANTAGES: With the growing number of CD-ROMs becoming available, it is apparent that this is not an economical long-term solution.

LIBRARY ACCESS TO CD-ROMS

Once access is assured to the CD-based information, user assistance becomes paramount.

Assistance

For CD-ROMs accessed in the Libraries, reference service, coordination, and assistance will be the responsibilities of the staff in University Libraries.
Included in these responsibilities are:

- Familiarity with the content and arrangement of the data on the CD-ROM;
- Familiarity with basic software capabilities (e.g., "page-turning" and/or menu-driven software);
- Knowledge of basic searching, printing, and downloading capabilities; and
- Coordination and liaison activities within the University community concerning CD-based information.

The staff of the Libraries will not be expected to give assistance regarding data manipulation, statistical packages, or user-specified formatting. This type of specialized assistance will be provided by University Computing and/or the SSTRL.

The University Libraries has a strong service component. The Committee thought that the CD-based information deserved the same level of support as any other "format" of information. It recognized that if support for CD-based information were to be transferred to another campus unit, then the profession was limiting its future to that of print-based information—not a particularly growth oriented media in today's world. Libraries and librarians must incorporate CD-based information into the profession's purview or watch the profession atrophy and die. The committee, therefore, recommended:

(9)   The Library will provide reference service, on a par with traditional print-and-ink based formats, for CD-based information housed or accessed within the Libraries and contained in UNLOC.

Training

Training in the use of the CD-ROMs housed in the University Libraries will be the responsibility of the library staff. Instruction in advanced searching techniques may be offered by the Libraries, University Computing, SSTRL staff, or a combination of the above.

The University Libraries will have the prerogative of requiring formalized training prior to using some CD-ROM products. While untrained users will be allowed to access the products, assistance from the library staff will be limited. The time limit set for use of CD-ROM products will be strictly enforced with untrained users.

The University Libraries will have the prerogative of limiting assistance to patrons whose class assignments involving CD-ROMs have not been previously communicated to the University Libraries. The Libraries do not have enough staff to support one-on-one training of users. Arrangements for group training need to be made by both T & R Faculty and Library Faculties.

In the University Libraries' experience, electronic-based information requires additional reference assistance in order to use the medium effectively. Not only does the informational content still need explanation, but also the technology required to access the informational content needs explanation and modification. The following recommendations attempt to allow the library some latitude in requiring efficiencies to protect scarce resources—staff time:

(10)   Training in the use of the CD-ROMs housed in the Libraries will be the responsibility of the Libraries. Instruction in advanced search techniques may be offered by the Library, University Computing, SSTRL, or a combination of these.

(11)   The University Libraries will have the prerogative of requiring training prior to usage of some CD-ROM products and limiting the time available to untrained users.

(12)   The University Libraries retain the prerogative of limiting reference service and assistance provided to those classes which have not communicated with the University Libraries or pre-arranged training sessions.

Funding

The University Libraries will assume the funding responsibilities for the maintenance of equipment transferred to or purchased by the Libraries. Departments that wish to make equipment available will be asked to transfer the equipment permanently to the Library. All maintenance, repairs, and upgrades will become the responsibilities of the Libraries.

Training costs associated with the level of assistance provided by the Libraries and described in recommendation 9 will be the responsibility of the Libraries. Training desired by a department for a particular product beyond the level of the Libraries will become the responsibility of the requesting Department.

Initially, the incentive for making the Libraries responsible for all CD-ROM information on campus is the availability of trained staff to provide user support and extended hours of service. Housing of CD-ROMs in other locations does not allow for access or user assistance after 5:00 p.m., a peak time for students. While user support is the primary benefit, the user of CD-based information may require, in many cases, extensive training and assistance. Again, the authority to limit assistance needs to be in place, or else library reference resources may be overwhelmed.

(13)   The cost of maintaining the workstations and the funding for training the Library staff in CD-based information is the responsibility of the University Libraries.

SOCIAL SCIENCE TRAINING AND RESEARCH LAB, UNIVERSITY COMPUTING, AND THE TEACHING AND RESEARCH FACULTY

The Director of University Libraries is responsible for providing advice to the University Officer concerning information resources on campus. Therefore, the Committee makes the recommendation listed below about the roles that various campus units should play concerning information in CD-ROM format.

Where the role of the Libraries in accessing the CD-based information stops, that of the SSTRL, University Computing, and the T & R Faculty begins.

SSTRL is the most logical unit to assume a role in the use of CD-based information. Staff members are trained in the extraction, manipulation, validation, and analysis of the information contained in machine-readable format, including CD-ROMs. The expertise to assist students, faculty, and other users in the use of this information rests with them. The Committee recommended:

(14)   The University needs to develop the resources of the SSTRL to facilitate its role in assisting in the extraction, manipulation, validation, and analysis of machine-readable data, in particular CD-based information.

The University Computing staff members, as the computer experts on campus, should facilitate the accessibility of CD-based information and its movement to an appropriate workstation. The ability to mount and analyze the data rests with them. The Committee, therefore, recommended:

(15)   Access to the campus backbone from the library must become a top priority within the University. At a minimum, the Ground, 1st, and 2nd floors of the library need to be immediately "wired" to the campus network. University Computing needs to facilitate the movement of information from CD-ROMs to end users' workstations.

(16)   University Computing needs to provide access to CD-ROM based information via the campus backbone so computer labs on campus may facilitate the extraction, manipulation, and analysis of machine-readable

information housed within the University Libraries and other locations on campus. This may require appropriate high-end workstations capable of more sophisticated data analysis and manipulation.

The T & R Faculty has several roles which need to be clearly defined through department chairpersons. These roles include communication with the Libraries, provision of in-class training opportunities for students, and selection of appropriate use of CD-based information.

The T & R Faculty must communicate to the Libraries the need for, and uses of, machine-readable information. This could take the forms of recommendations for purchase, present faculty use of machine-readable information, and information about developments in specific academic fields or courses in the use of machine-readable information.

A critical need exists for close communication concerning class assignments requiring the use of CD-based information. This technology requires training in order to use the information efficiently and effectively. Use is not always intuitive to a user. Faculty need to work with the Libraries in planning for training when developing their syllabi and course timetables. Further, the faculty need to be aware that, in some cases, use of a print version (or the making of special arrangements for information to be extracted and printed from CD-ROM products, and placed on Reserve) is preferable to making an assignment to use CD-based information.

In communicating effectively about such assignments, the T & R Faculty can help the Libraries in providing efficient group instruction, thereby limiting one-on-one assistance now provided to users of CD-ROMs.

Based on these facts, the Committee recommended:

(17)   An issue of Access should be devoted to machine-readable information in the University Libraries with particular emphasis on CD-ROM information.

(18)   A special memo from the Director of Libraries should be sent to all department chairpersons regarding the utilization of CD-ROMs in the classroom and reiterating the issues covered in Access.

ADDITIONAL COMMITTEE SUGGESTIONS

The following are suggestions for the Director of University Libraries to communicate to departmental chairpersons regarding the utilization of CD-ROMs in the classroom.

The University Libraries is beginning to develop its capabilities to provide ready access to information received on CD-ROM formats. The technology to do this well is not yet in the marketplace.

Departments can facilitate the Libraries' ability to provide service to CD-based information by doing the following:

- Alert the Library Faculty, via the Reference Department, well in advance, about the nature and extent of CD-ROMs expected to be used for class assignments;
- Appraise the Standing Committee on Electronic Media about ongoing discussions in the profession or departments concerning use and publication of scholarly materials in CD-ROM or other electronic format;
- Notify the Reference Department if the material is available only in CD-ROM format or if the electronic aspects of information are the focus of the assigned class work;
- Plan into the syllabi and course timetable adequate training of students and other users, and other preparation time by the reference staff of the Library;
- Emphasize the use of printed materials as much as possible in the classroom and notify the Reference Department when materials needed for the classroom are available in printed and CD-ROM or other electronic format;
- Explore the possibility of having that portion of the information printed from the CD-ROM and placed in the Reserve Book Room if the material is available only on CD-ROM or if only a fixed portion of that material is required for student use;
- Consider purchasing PC and other equipment by the Academic Department and transferring the equipment, and the ownership and maintenance of this equipment, to the Library as part of the costs of electronic products. Library funding for computers and other equipment is limited. If the CD-ROM or electronic information is a high priority for the Department, then this option may expedite acquisition of the CD-ROM product.

In closing, Option 1, a high-end workstation, was established in October 1991 for exclusive use with government produced CD-ROMs. The first electronic product from an academic department with a "restriction of use" message will be entered into UNLOC soon. Some unforeseen benefits of the planning process are increased communications among individuals in departments and the Libraries and potential assistance in technical support for a grant proposal. The Libraries' administration is considering additional recommendations. The planning process has set in motion a procedure and perspective for integrating information resources throughout campus and for best serving the needs of the University's clientele.

Chapter Eleven

Florida Keys Community College*

Lawrence S. Berk

This case study examines the impact of technology on a Federal depository program in an academic library located in the smallest community college in Florida. The study identifies the dramatically improved access to Federal documents that online and CD-ROM technology have contributed. The emphasis of the chapter, however, is centered on detailing the fundamental challenges resulting from the introduction of new technology: increased pressure on staff and resources during a time of fiscal constraint; shift of activity from end-user to staff; need for new instructional programs; and difficulties involved in using new CD-ROM products. The challenge to integrate new technologies into the program of service is ameliorated by the benefits already realized by users of the documents collection.

The Library/Learning Resources Center of Florida Keys Community College became a participant in the Government Printing Office's depository program at the end of 1989. Located in Key West, the college is on the last island in a chain of tiny islands that extends over a hundred miles from the mainland into the Gulf of Mexico. The only other depository library in the 19th congressional district is 150 miles from Key West, at the University of Miami. The impetus for Florida Keys Community College, the smallest community college in Florida, to become designated a depository library was clear: Documents were virtually inaccessible to the citizens of Monroe County, and the program of service in the college Library/Learning Resources Center needed strengthening.

---

* Special thanks to Elizabeth Scholl, Documents Specialist, FKCC

It was understood from the start that the Library/LRC would request not more than 7 percent of the items available in the program. This was necessarily the case due to insufficient space and staff to handle any more. This was not viewed as a problem, since we had become dial-access members of OCLC the year before, and could interlibrary loan those documents that we did not have in our collection. Online technology had, in fact, given us easy access to all documents, and we were now able to retrieve them for our community rapidly. But we still had a number of issues to face; and technology—the impact of electronic media—has been an integral element in the problems we have encountered and the solutions we have found as we have implemented our program of service.

We knew what kind of collection we wanted. Our goal was to meet the informational needs of our constituents, and we enlisted the help of many community leaders in selecting our initial items. We focused on publications most related to the obvious needs of our community: all aspects of the marine environment, education, medicine and allied health, and a range of Federal programs. We were very careful because we were, quite literally, afraid of being overwhelmed. Not only were we very limited in the space we could devote to a new collection, but the director, while having nearly 20 years of experience in academic libraries, had no direct experience with Federal documents, and he was the only librarian on the staff of seven. He knew that the new electronic media were designed to provide not only easy access to large databases, but also to save space and long hours of clerical drudgery. He was reassured by colleagues at other depository libraries that the space he had allocated would be ample, and that an additional five to seven hours per week of staff time would certainly be sufficient. And our director, much to the dismay of his ever-increasingly energetic staff, was an occasional proponent of an unorthodox management philosophy: ready, fire, aim.

The next step was to attend an in-service workshop with the paraprofessional who was given the responsibility of managing the depository collection on a day-to-day basis. Those who are familiar with small academic libraries know that paraprofessionals must routinely perform duties viewed in larger libraries as exclusively the province of master's-level librarians. The deficit many para-professionals must deal with is the lack of a conceptual framework for the set of new duties and an unfamiliarity with the literature of library and information science. However, learning a new job, like learning anything else, is best accomplished by motivated learners actually doing what it is they are challenged to learn. We have found that a paraprofessional can excel at the day-to-day management of a small depository collection, including the provision of reference service, staff training, and the promotion of collection utilization. The key from the director's point of view is to delegate the responsibility to a capable employee, and to mean it.

It was not until the early months of 1991, more than a year after the Library/LRC was designated a participant in the Depository Program, that the program became fully operational. It might be of interest to note that it does appear that the space we were able to allocate to the depository collection is adequate, but the commitment of staff time to the program was underestimated. The paraprofessional in charge of the program gives it an average of at least eight to ten hours per week, and volunteers check in materials for approximately six hours per week. The director is involved on an as-needed basis for reference questions, policy issues, and CD-ROM and online applications. He devotes between one and two hours per week to the program.

The primary source of access to the collection is the GPO index available from SilverPlatter. The director made a videotape which demonstrates the fundamentals of searching the CD-ROM. Additionally, he teaches a 2-credit hour course, "Electronic Access to Information," whose primary focus is to introduce students to a range of CD-ROM products, including those from the GPO, and online services, including Dialog and OCLC.

The community this depository library serves is diverse. Key West is a small town with a cosmopolitan flavor, large hospitality and recreation industries, and a large military population; it should be noted that there are a disproportionately high number of people with very sophisticated informational needs living in Key West. It is said that there are more writers per capita in Key West than in any other city in the world. The rest of the Keys, however, are considered rural, and the primary industries are fishing and recreation.

The remainder of this chapter details this library's experience dealing with the new, rapidly proliferating information-handling technologies. The focus is on the use of GPO on SilverPlatter and the rapidly proliferating Sudoc CD-ROM products, and the chapter notes our use of online services.

ACCESS TO FEDERAL DOCUMENTS

Although we are a new depository without staff experienced with documents collections, we soon verified the legendary difficulties in using the *Monthly Catalog* for access to documents. The availability of CD-ROM products, such as GPO on SilverPlatter, provided a much-needed improvement, allowing the user to conduct searches of the *Monthly Catalog* database using logical operators; the capability for field-specific searches are another enhancement of the electronic version of this too. In fact, instruction in the use of this type of CD-ROM product has already been integrated into the course, "Electronic Access to Information." Unfortunately, no more than 15 students enroll in this course each semester. And so the obvious challenge presents itself: library staff must conduct the searches for most users of the Federal documents collection. In an effort to address this problem, an instructional videotape was made, and instructional handouts prepared; but patrons routinely do not want to take the time to learn how to use a new system, especially if they are unfamiliar with computers, as many still are.

Of the few possible answers to this problem, none are fully acceptable. We could insist that patrons take the time to learn to search GPO on SilverPlatter, which is even more problematic than it would otherwise be because we are unable to dedicate a workstation to GPO. We could redirect patrons to the *Monthly Catalog,* which we unfortunately but necessarily subscribe to on microfiche only, compounding the inhospitability of this tool for easy access to documents. Or, we could take queries and respond to them when staff have time. We find ourselves doing a combination of all of the above, as we continually remind ourselves that patience is indeed a virtue and that time will ameliorate this problem as more people become familiar with the use of electronic databases.

USING SUDOC CD-ROM PRODUCTS

A number of factors converge when we begin a discussion of how the new Sudoc CD-ROM products are being assimilated into our library. As a small academic library, our primary users are community college students and faculty. Very few of our primary users are involved in any research activity which extends beyond the requirements of the curriculum. Our program of service certainly extends to the community at large, especially in the area of Federal documents. However, it is the rare patron indeed that relies on our collection for research purposes; rather, most patrons are seeking a section of the *Federal Register,* a specific set of data elements of the census, the language of a section in the *Code of Federal Regulations* or the *Catalog of Federal Domestic Assistance,* a new bill in Congress, or directory-type information. ERIC documents are used, as are a number of medical sources. Occasionally, more demanding queries are made, and we do use online databases and interlibrary loan, and make referrals to our regional depository library. However, no significant pressure is placed on our collection for research purposes.

So that when a CD-ROM product like the *Toxic Chemical Release Inventory* arrives, so does a problem: An extremely demanding set of answers to manage for (what is to us) a virtually nonexistent set of questions. Who on our staff should install this program and learn to use it? Our paraprofessional documents specialist is also in charge of periodicals (420 subscriptions) and microforms, in addition to routine circulation/reference desk coverage and a variety of special projects. And if someone does install and learn the program, this staff member will also be responsible for the provision of special service to patrons who will not be able to use this tool by themselves.

Following Murphy's Law, we received a call about the *Toxic Chemical Release Inventory* from a local high school chemistry teacher doing graduate work for a master's degree. We attempted to install the program, but received error messages, such as "insufficient disk space," although the computer on which we were installing the program had more than one million bytes free. We called the number in the less-than-helpful manual, and the attendant at the number referred us to a hotline that took a message. As of this writing we are still awaiting a return call.

We then received the CD-ROM containing the *Congressional Record* for 1985, the first session of the 99th Congress. These discs were issued as one of the pilot projects sponsored by the Joint Committee on Printing. Nowhere in the accompanying *Tutorial and Reference Manual* were we informed that the new version of Microsoft Extensions was a requirement to run the software, so that a good deal of time was wasted in the installation process. It must also be noted that we received fewer than five total requests all year for information contained in the entire *Congressional Record*. An introductory course in political science is only occasionally offered on our campus. Still, we proceeded with the installation of the program; however, using the program was another matter. At least two hours were spent trying to make it work properly; the best we were able to accomplish was to search using the index, which is fine as long as one knows exactly what one is looking for. After two hours we gave up attempting to search using logical operators. We have the confidence to admit this, as we successfully teach students and community members how to use a variety of CD-ROM products. The accompanying 139-page manual is staggeringly long and anything but straightforward in its presentation. Unfortunately, we have very little choice but to place this tool on a shelf and leave it there for the time being. We simply do not possess the resources to integrate this tool into our program of service. When necessary, we still search the *Congressional Record* on Dialog. Most searches can be done rapidly and inexpensively. At this point, the director performs all Dialog searches. The only other Dialog databases searched with any regularity in support of the depository program are the *Federal Register* and occasionally the GPO *Publications Reference File*.

Fortunately, not all the new CD-ROM products are like the ones described above. It appears that the CD-ROM products disseminated by the Bureau of the Census are relatively user-friendly. The first product we tried was *County Business Patterns*, 1986 and 1987. The floppy disk has a one-screen readme file that is clear and simple. Three letters start the program, and even a novice can search this simple menu-driven program effectively, without so much as consulting the *Technical Documentation*, which is more of a reference manual dealing with the data itself, rather than how to search the database. While staff still have to set the patron up for searching, doing so with a product such as this is a pleasure—because it can be done easily, quickly, and well.

Even more useful to our community of users is the *County and City Data Book* on CD-ROM. This is also issued by the *Bureau of the Census* and, while somewhat more demanding to run than *County Business Patterns*, it is loaded and searched without undue difficulty; one does, however, need to refer to the technical documentation for this product in order to maximize use. Like other census publications, the data is in dBase format, and can be used in conjunction with dBase. It is important to note, however, that knowledge of dBase is not needed to search the database; use of dBase would be required if there were a need to generate reports for users. Frankly, as our library, like other small academic libraries, especially community college libraries, focuses on the support of instruction rather than research, we will continue to rely on the print version of the *County and City Data Book* and use the CD-ROM version only by special request, i.e., our own college's Office for Institutional Research—and even in this case we would be sure to determine that the electronic version of this tool is really needed. Clearly, the time and effort it would take to develop the requisite expertise to manipulate the data in this and similar tools into sophisticated dBase reports for researchers is prohibitive and unnecessary in our environment. In practice, such requests for service will be routinely referred to the regional depository library.

The last CD-ROM product discussed is the 1990 *Census of Population and Housing*. This is the simplest to run of all the programs we have received. The software is included on the CD-ROM disc, and all the user does is choose the CD-ROM drive and type "GO" to begin the program. The user is then presented with a menu and can easily locate needed data. The accompanying user guide elucidates all relevant material. If any CD-ROM product can be used as a model for a user-friendly electronic tool, this is it. Although demand for the data contained in the census is sporadic, it is nonetheless expected, and, with this CD-ROM, easily accessible.

From our perspective, it would be useful if the GPO and the Federal depository program could standardize the methodology of searching CD-ROM products disseminated by all Federal agencies. It is understood that searching bibliographic databases differs from searching statistical databases; however, the goal must be standardization, with clarity of documentation and simplicity of technique a must. Otherwise, the use of these tools will be confined to the largest depository libraries, and even those libraries will be hard-pressed to develop the requisite expertise to handle sophisticated informational needs.

WHERE TO FROM HERE?

The focus of this case study has been the experience of one small academic library, a new participant in the depository program, using technology, particularly CD-ROM products. However, we must take note of what is ultimately a much larger issue facing our library than how to manage the rapid proliferation of technology. The early 1990s economic recession has had a dramatic impact on our library and on many libraries throughout the country. How we manage in times of fiscal constraint is an issue that overwhelms the problems of managing innovative technologies, although the two are by no means unrelated. Although this case study cannot deal with an extended discussion of library management during times of fiscal constraint, it is essential to make a few observations.

When we decided to apply for designation as a Federal depository library, we had two staff members more than we have now. Due to staff attrition, we lost a part-time evening library assistant, and then, half of another full-time library assistant; and then we lost an assistant librarian, who joined the staff after we became a participant in the depository program, but whose presence somewhat ameliorated the underestimation of staff time that we were understandably encouraged to make by all members of the Federal depository community. In 1991, we were literally forced to closely study the efficacy of continuing our participation in the depository program. We reexamined our priorities and struggled to squeeze as much as possible from a shrinking budget and a smaller staff. We will do everything possible to explore ways we can survive as a depository library, because we are completely convinced of its central importance to what we are about as a library, as an academic community, and as a resource for all the citizens of the 19th congressional district, especially those living in our isolated county. If we can ride out the storm, as it were, we will be in excellent shape to add power to our depository program of service when the economy improves.

The struggles we face integrating emerging technologies into our program of service are much less frustrating than those we have just mentioned; however, this is not to minimize the demands on resources that are necessitated by advancements, such as CD-ROM and online services. Not only are these technologies moving more work to library staff—away from the end user for the time being, at least—but the use of these technologies requires large investment in microcomputer workstations, instructional programs, and the development of technical expertise without other experts always being locally available.

There has been no more exciting time for librarianship than the present. The impact of technology in times of resource scarcity is a challenge to our creativity, and this extends far beyond document librarianship. As librarians in a small academic library, we are of necessity generalists: We do it all. This has its satisfactions, to be sure, but it also has its limitations: We cannot do it all as well as we would like. And so we do the best we can. We struggle to learn Edlin so that we can rewrite config.sys and autoexec.bat files when a new version of CD-ROM software comes out, or something else in the system changes. We quickly learn the first names of our customer service representatives, and the ones servicing some of the CD-ROM products issued by the Superintendent of Documents are probably considering getting unpublished phone numbers. But how much better off we—especially those of us who are literally hundreds of miles from our nearest university or depository library—are as a result of these new electronic media! We now have access to information. However difficult it has been to deal with, it bears repeating: We have access to information.

Chapter Twelve

University of Florida Libraries

Pamela Lowe

This chapter describes the data and reference services offered by the University of Florida Libraries for its 1990 electronic census products. An overview of the types of services offered are described within the census services policy. Specifics as to how the policy is enacted are provided by sample dBase programs developed for the P.L. 94-171 CD-ROMs and by a description of the fee-based services offered for census products stored on magnetic tapes.

The University of Florida Libraries have a long tradition of providing access to and assistance in the use of data and information provided by the U.S. Bureau of the Census. The Libraries have served as a regional depository for U.S. Federal publications since 1962. In addition to printed and microform products, and now CD-ROM products, distributed to the depository program, the Libraries have been acquiring machine-readable data files on magnetic tape for academic use since the 1960s. The variety of formats that U.S. census material is distributed on and collected by the Libraries present complex challenges for the public services division of the Libraries. This chapter addresses the levels of data and reference services offered for census materials as well as provides specifics as to how the policy is enacted for its electronic products, CD-ROMs and magnetic tapes.

Preparation for the Libraries' receipt of 1990 decennial census products began in 1990 with the creation of a task force on Census Bureau Publications Service Issues. The task force recommended that the Documents Department be the primary public access point for census services, and that an advanced census unit be established to provide data and reference services for machine-readable census products. The census unit includes staff from the Documents Department, and the Humanities and Social Sciences Reference Department. Specific individuals comprising the census unit are the Machine Readable Data Files (MRDF) Librarian in the Humanities and Social Sciences Reference Department, the Assistant Chair to the Documents Department, and support staff from the Documents Department. The task force further recommended hiring additional staff, a programmer/analyst and a Library Technical Assistant (LTA), to assist with the demand 1990 census products would create.

The level of demand expected by the Libraries is voluminous. Historically, the Libraries have served government, business, and other group's census needs in the state of Florida. Whereas most other states have State Data Centers that assist patrons in accessing machine-readable census data, the University of Florida Libraries have traditionally filled this role in Florida. The State Data Center (SDC) in Florida distributes census data on magnetic tape to its affiliates and makes referrals, but it does not offer programming assistance. In order to assist patrons in gaining full access to machine-readable census data and information, the Library's Systems Office began offering programming services in 1971. Although this auxiliary service was formally discontinued in 1984, the demand for assistance in accessing electronically disseminated census data has not diminished. Between April and August of 1991, the census unit created over 200 machine-readable subsets from either the P.L. 94-171 CD-ROM or Summary Tape File 1A stored on magnetic tape. Moreover, a large but undetermined number of requests were serviced using the P.L. 94-171 CD-ROM in conjunction with the GO software.

Budget restrictions have prohibited the Libraries from hiring additional staff during the 1991/1992 year, specifically a programmer/analyst who would enable the Libraries to offer in-depth data and statistical analysis services. However, in lieu of full-scale programming services, the Libraries have maintained several types of assistance for machine-readable census products. The MRDF librarian has written dBase[1] programs, facilitating types of access to the census CD-ROMs that it is either impossible or impractical to use with only the GO software. Additionally, the Libraries have garnered the support of the Center for Instructional and Research Computing Activities (CIRCA), a computing facility on the UF campus. A programmer/analyst at CIRCA has assisted the Libraries by creating SAS[2] batch files that extract data stored on magnetic tapes. Census unit staff edit the batch files, creating printed output or machine-readable

---

[1] dBase is a database management software for microcomputers. The Census Bureau is releasing numeric data files on CD-ROMs in a dBase III format.

[2] SAS is a software system designed for data analysis. SAS software products allow information storage and retrieval, data modification and programming, report writing, statistical analysis, and file handling.

subsets on floppy diskettes. A description of the types of data and reference services provided for machine-readable census products is included in the next section of the chapter.

CENSUS SERVICE AT UF LIBRARIES

The following levels of census services, prepared by Gary Cornwell and myself, are based on a similar listing of "Levels of Data Service," prepared by Jim Jacobs for the 1990 ICPSR Management of Machine-Readable Social Science Information Workshop. Jacobs (1991) describes the levels of data service that an organization might provide its constituency. His resulting list is meant to help organizations identify what services are already being provided and to choose which other services to offer.

The following listing of census services (with an emphasis on electronic files and services) has a very similar scope. Its purposes are to: (1) identify services and procedures that the Libraries already have in place for acquiring and accessing census data, (2) identify computing services and advisory services that the Libraries should provide for census data, (3) identify those services that are best provided by the private sector and that the Libraries should not engage in, and (4) notify staff of services available at the Libraries for census materials.

Level 1. Pre-Acquisition of Census Material

The primary goal of activities at this level is to gather background information and make the administrative decisions necessary before acquiring census data. The UF Libraries have a long-standing commitment to the acquisition of census material and consequently many of these decisions have already been made. However, the introduction of new electronic formats for the 1990 census have raised questions such as "Who else is providing census services?" "What computers and software are required to access these new electronic products" and "How much and what level of staff is necessary to service these products?" The Libraries are currently working with other agencies within the state to identify the level of census services that are being offered elsewhere. At the same time, the Libraries have reaffirmed their commitment to acquiring census data by the purchase of computer hardware, through the centralization of census activities within the Documents Department, and by the reassignment of staff to work with census files.

Level 2. Acquisition of Data

The Libraries have a well-established mechanism for the acquisition, processing, and preservation of data tapes and accompanying technical documentation.

Many of these products are received through the State Data Center, while others are the result of special purchases. Beginning with the 1990 census, the Libraries will receive a wide range of information on CD-ROM via the depository library program. Additionally, many data files from the 1990 census are available through the Census-BEA Bulletin Board.

Level 3. Distribute Access to Data

All data files and accompanying technical documentation received by the Libraries are cataloged and listed in the Library's online catalog, LUIS (Library User Information System). As a result, all State University System (SUS) faculty, staff, and students (as well as anyone with dial-up access to LUIS) can easily learn what products are available at the UF libraries. Additionally, due to the Libraries long-standing commitment to servicing census data numerous referrals and requests are made to the Libraries for census information each month.

Level 4. Computing Services

The library provides layers of computing services, allowing multiple access avenues. The following options are a combination of services already in place and recommendations for the future:

A. Patrons may access the Census CD-ROMs themselves utilizing the Libraries' equipment. The Main Library maintains equipment in the public area of the Documents and Reference Departments. Equipment in non-public areas of both departments may be used via an appointment. Patrons who access census CD-ROMs may use the GO software provided by the Census Bureau or dBase provided by the library. TIGER/Line files may be accessed via various software packages provided by the Documents Department.

B. Census unit staff may create machine-readable subsets on disk from the CD-ROMs for patrons. The patron must supply their own floppy disks or reimburse the Libraries at a later time. TIGER/Line data for single counties may be downloaded to floppy disks in ASCII format. P.L. 94-171 data as well as 100% data (when released on CD-ROM) may be subsetted and downloaded to floppy disk in either dBase, ASCII delimited with blank, or Lotus 1-2-3 wks format. The patron may request data for any geographic level (county, tract, place, block group, or block), however, all data fields for the requested area will be given. The census unit will not provide specialized subsets by limiting the number of fields or searching for specific data values. Data extracts created from a CD-ROM will be free to the patron, however census unit staff are under no obligation to provide the data within any specified time period.

C.   Current census data can be downloaded or printed using the GO software with the CD-ROMs or from the Census-BEA Bulletin Board in a rapid, straight forward manner. Similarly, 1980 census data can be retrieved via the Florida State University's (FSU) 1980 Online Census Bulletin Board. In most cases, these sources are used for data requests requiring only one or two numbers. Information obtained from bulletin boards or printed copies of tables from CD-ROMs are usually mailed to the patron free of charge.

D.   In addition to procurement of CD-ROMs, the Libraries archive census material on magnetic tapes in the Libraries' Systems Office. Patrons may request usage of magnetic tapes at the Reference Desk. If the use of machine readable datasets are appropriate, a referral form is completed. The patron takes the referral form to the Systems Office where the patron will be given the volume and serial numbers needed to access the tapes at the North East Regional Data Center (NERDC). The Systems Office is responsible for transporting magnetic media to and from NERDC.

E.   Retrieval of census data from magnetic tapes is provided on a cost-recovery basis by the census unit. Printouts of data tables for any geographic level can be produced via SAS batch files. Additionally, Florida census data can be downloaded from magnetic tapes in an ASCII format for any geographic level.

F.   Additional data services, such as searching for user-specified values (e.g., geographic areas that have a black population greater or lesser than 50% of the total population for that area) or comparison of 1990 machine-readable data with machine-readable data products from previous censuses, are not currently available within the Libraries. This service is recommended and is dependent upon hiring staff with the requisite computing skills.

Level 5. (Data) Advisory Service

Once data have been acquired staff should be available within the library to offer consultation with regards to the data. This service is limited to assisting patrons with technical documentation/codebooks and to helping them interpret data structures.

Level 6. Advisory Services (Analysis)

This level of service is designed to advise users in such areas as appropriate statistical procedures for analysis of data or writing statistical programs. Services such as interpreting results of statistical analysis fall into this category.

This service is handled within the university environment by the computing facilities or by individual colleges and departments.

Level 7. Analytical Services

This level of service does everything for the user. Staff would analyze data as requested and deliver finished output to users requesting products such as charts, graphs, measures of significance, and cross-tabulation of variables. This service is best handled by individual consultants or businesses.

dBASE APPLICATIONS FOR P.L. 94-171 CD-ROMS

The majority of 1990 census requests to date have been serviced using dBase with the P.L. 94-171 CD-ROM. Census data stored on CD-ROMs are the same data that in previous censuses were only available on magnetic tapes. The Census Bureau provides access software, GO, on each CD-ROM. Although it is not necessary to use dBase with the CD-ROM, dBase provides options for data retrieval and manipulation that are not possible with the GO software. The GO software is impractical when the patron needs the data in a format allowing data manipulation or if the quantity of information requested is great. A typical data request at UF might involve downloading all of the tract records for Dade County, Florida. The researcher may prefer the data in its raw data format, i.e., column and rows, in order to manipulate the data. He or she may also request the data in a format that is easily used with a particular software package, perhaps Lotus 1-2-3. While it is possible with the GO software to give the researcher printouts or a copy of the tables in an ASCII format, it would take one person the better portion of a day to retrieve Dade county's 264 tracts with the GO software. dBase can be easily utilized to retrieve all 264 tracts in about ten minutes. Also, dBase permits the transfer of data from a dBase format into one of six other formats, including the Lotus worksheet format (wks).

dBase programs are frequently used at the Libraries in order to generate subsets of large amounts of data on to floppy diskettes. Many of the Libraries' clients, such as planning agencies, health care facilities, county and city school boards, businesses, and researchers, need census data in its original raw data structure. However, they do not need all of the data for the state. Patrons are usually interested in just the records that pertain to a single city, county, or group of counties. In order to service researcher's requests, dBase programs were developed to produce subsets of user specified geographic locations from the CD-ROM, downloading only the data records requested to a floppy disk.

The dBase programs utilized at UF are written as modules, a collection of smaller programs. Included in the next section of the chapter is the primary command file called filemenu and three other command files, fltract, flblk, and flsum that are connected to the the primary command file through the dBase statement, DO CASE.[3] The command files are commented. Comment lines begin with an asterisk and explain the general purpose of the program. Additionally, notes within parenthesis to the right of the program statements are included to explain the function of that particular statement. Statements within parenthesis should not be included within the programs; they are not legitimate dBase comments, but were only included in this chapter to clarify program statements in a line-by-line mode for the reader.

SAMPLE dBASE PROGRAMS

FILEMENU.PRG

```
*Primary module, named FILEMENU.
*This program manipulates P.L.94-171 data,
*retrieving records for user-specified geographic locations.
*
SET ESCAPE OFF
SET TALK OFF
SET BELL OFF
*SET COLOR TO W/N, N/W, B
*
*The following statements draw a menu on the screen. The user is
*instructed to enter a number that reflects their choice. If the user
*wants tract data, they would choose 5.
*
DO WHILE .T.
    CLEAR
    @ 1,25 SAY [Please Choose Geographic Level]
    @ 3,5 SAY [1. STATE...retrieves data for the state.]
    @ 5,5 SAY [2. COUNTY...retrieves data for one county.]
    @ 7,5 SAY [3. COUNTY SUBDIVISION...retrieves all subdivision for one county.]
    @ 9,5 SAY [4. PLACE...retrieves data for one place.]
    @ 11,5 SAY [5. CENSUS TRACTS/(BNA'S)...retrieves all census tracts within a
    county.]
    @ 13,5 SAY [6. BLOCK GROUPS (BG'S)...retrieves all block groups within a
    county.]
    @ 15,5 SAY [7. BLOCKS...retrieves all data for one county.]
    @ 17,5 SAY [8. SEARCH BY SUMMARY LEVEL ONLY!]
```

---

[3] The DO CASE statement is a series of IF-ENDIF statements. It allows a condition to be tested. If the condition is true, the immediately following command is executed.

```
    @ 19,5 SAY [0. EXIT]
*
STORE 0 TO SELECTNUM
    @ 21,33 SAY "select"
    @ 21,42 GET SELECTNUM PICTURE "9" RANGE 0,8
    READ
*
*The DO CASE statement directs dBase to begin the next module or exit
*the program. If the user chose 5 for tract data, dBase would issue
*the command, DO FLTRACT.
*
    DO CASE
    CASE SELECTNUM = 0
    SET BELL ON
    SET TALK ON
    SET ESCAPE ON
    CLEAR ALL
    CLEAR
    RETURN
*
    CASE SELECTNUM = 1
        DO FLSTATE
    CASE SELECTNUM = 2
        DO FLCO
    CASE SELECTNUM = 3
        DO FLCODIV
    CASE SELECTNUM = 4
        DO FLPLACE
    CASE SELECTNUM = 5
        DO FLTRACT
    CASE SELECTNUM = 6
        DO FLBLKGR
    CASE SELECTNUM = 7
        DO FLBLK
    CASE SELECTNUM = 8
        DO FLSUM
    ENDCASE
ENDDO
RETURN
*EOF: FILEMENU.PRG
```

FLTRACT.PRG

The next module, FLTRACT, requests that the user enter the FIPS code for the county of interest. The resulting subsetted file, FLTRACT.DBF, will be created on the C drive.

*FLTRACT.PRG searches for tract records for a user-specified county.
*The following variables are used within the program: ISUM and ICNTY.
*ISUM holds a value of 140; it will be used to find records in the dBase field,
*SUMLEV,[4] that have a value of 140. ICNTY will hold the value of the FIPS[5]
*county code the user enters; it will be used to find records in the dBase
*field, CNTY, that have the value entered by the user.
*

```
CLEAR ALL               {Closes any open files.}
SET DEFAULT TO D:       {Sets path to CD-ROM drive }
USE PL9417FL            {Opens P.L. 9417FL file.}
SET INDEX TO PL9417FL   {Opens index.}
SET TALK OFF
SET BELL OFF
   DO WHILE .T.
      CLEAR             {Clears the screen.}
      ISUM = "140"      {ISUM is a variable.}
      ICNTY = SPACE (3) {ICNTY is a variable.}
*
```

*The following statement prompts the user to enter the FIPS county code for
*the county of interest. The READ statement stores the value entered into
*ICNTY.
*

```
   @ 06,10 SAY "Enter county FIPS code (CNTY):" GET ICNTY
      READ
CLEAR                   {Clears the screen.}
GO TOP                  {Goes to the top of the file.}
*
```

*The next statement, SEEK ISUM, searches for the value held in the
*variable, ISUM. The record pointer will be at the first record with
*the SUMLEV value of 140.
*

```
SEEK ISUM
```

*The next three statements comprise a loop. The record pointer will skip to
*the next record until the value held in ICNTY matches the value in the
*dBase field CNTY.
*

```
DO WHILE ((.NOT. EOF()) .AND. (SUMLEV = ISUM) .AND. (CNTY <>
ICNTY))
```

---

[4] SUMLEV is a dBase field name on the P.L. 94-171 CD-ROM that holds the summary level sequence value. The summary level sequence value is a code that designates the geographic level of the record.

[5] FIPS (Federal Information Processing Standards) codes are assigned for varing geographic levels. FIPS codes used in the census are explained in the technical documentation accompanying data files and in *Geographic Identification Code Scheme* (1983).

```
SKIP
ENDDO
*
```
*The next three commands instruct dBase to copy the records with the
*matching SUMLEV and CNTY values to the file c:fltract.
```
*
IF ((.NOT. EOF()) .AND. (SUMLEV = ISUM) .AND. (CNTY = ICNTY))
COPY TO C:FLTRACT WHILE SUMLEV = ISUM .AND. CNTY = ICNTY
ENDIF
CLEAR ALL              {Closes all open files.}
SET DEFAULT TO C:      {Sets path.}
USE C:FLTRACT          {Opens file, fltract.}
*
```
*The next statement counts the number of records subsetted, and stores
*the value into the variable named total.
```
*
STORE RECCOUNT() TO total
*
```
*The next two statements display the number of records on the screen.}
```
    @ 13,13 SAY [The number of records copied = ]
    @ 13,45 SAY total
WAIT                   {Requires a key to be hit to continue.}
CLEAR                  {Clears the screen.}
BROWSE                 {Displays the active file.}
CLEAR ALL              {Closes all open files.}
RETURN
*EOF:FLTRACT.PRG
```

FLBLK.PRG

The next module, FLBLK, produces a subset all of the data records for a user-specified county. Many counties are too large to fit on a single floppy disk. In such case, the data are compressed using a utility, like PKZIP.[6] If the county is still too large for a single floppy, the DOS command, BACKUP,[7] can be used to copy the data to multiple diskettes.

FLBLK.PRG requests that the user enter two county FIPS codes. The first code entered should be for the county requested. The second code should be the next highest county FIPS code within the state. The program will download those records of the county that have a SUMLEV value of 050, 060, 140, 700, 710, 720, 730, 740 and 750.

---

[6] PKZIP is a utility that reduces the size of a file.

[7] BACKUP is a DOS command that can be used to copy files and directories to multiple diskettes; it prompts the user for new diskettes.

```
*FLBLK.PRG subsets data records pertaining to a single county.
*This program uses the index to identify the record number of the first
*record of the county requested and the record number of the first record
*of the next county stored on the CD-ROM. It then downloads to the file called
*FLBLK all of the records beginning with the first logical record number of
*the county of interest up to the logical record number of the next county
*stored on the CD-ROM.
*
CLEAR ALL
SET DEFAULT TO D:
USE PL9417FL
SET INDEX TO PL9417FL
SET TALK OFF
SET BELL OFF
SET SAFETY OFF
   DO WHILE .T.
      CLEAR
      ISUM = "050"
      ICNTY = SPACE (3)
      ICNTY2 = SPACE (3)
   @ 05,10 SAY "Enter the FIPS code for the county of interest:" GET ICNTY
   @ 07,10 SAY "Enter the next highest FIPS County Code:" GET ICNTY2
      READ
CLEAR
GO TOP
SEEK ISUM
DO WHILE ((.NOT. EOF()) .AND. (SUMLEV = ISUM) .AND. (CNTY <>
ICNTY))
   SKIP
ENDDO
IF ((.NOT. EOF()) .AND. (SUMLEV = ISUM) .AND. (CNTY = ICNTY))
   STORE VAL(LOGRECNU) TO IREC1
ENDIF
SEEK ISUM
DO WHILE ((.NOT. EOF()) .AND. (SUMLEV = ISUM) .AND. (CNTY <>
ICNTY2))
   SKIP
ENDDO
IF ((.NOT. EOF()) .AND. (SUMLEV = ISUM) .AND. (CNTY = ICNTY2))
   STORE VAL(LOGRECNU) TO IREC2
ENDIF
CLOSE INDEX
CCOUNT = IREC2 - IREC1
GOTO IREC1
COPY TO C:FLBLK NEXT CCOUNT
CLEAR ALL
```

```
SET DEFAULT TO C:
USE FLBLK
STORE RECCOUNT() TO total
@ 13,13 SAY [The number of records copied = ]
@ 13,45 SAY total
WAIT
CLEAR
BROWSE
CLEAR ALL
RETURN
*EOF:FLBLK.PPG
```

FLSUM.PRG

The next module, FLSUM, downloads records that match the summary-level code entered by the user. This program is useful to download all county summary records or all place summary records within a state. 050 is entered to retrieve county records; 160 is entered to retrieve place records.

```
*FLSUM.PRG searches for records that have a user-specified summary level
*value.
CLEAR ALL
SET DEFAULT TO D:
SELECT 1
USE PL9417FL
SET INDEX TO PL9417FL
SET TALK OFF
SET BELL OFF
SET SAFETY OFF
  DO WHILE .T.
    CLEAR
    ISUM = SPACE (3)
    @ 04,10 SAY "Enter summary level (SUMLEV):" GET ISUM
    @ 06,10 SAY "Leave blank to exit."
    READ
    IF ISUM = "END"
    RETURN
    ENDIF
CLEAR
GO TOP
SEEK ISUM
DO WHILE (.NOT. EOF()) .AND. (SUMLEV = ISUM)
  COPY TO C:FLSUM WHILE SUMLEV = ISUM
ENDDO
CLEAR ALL
SET DEFAULT TO C:
SELECT 2
```

```
USE C:FLSUM
STORE RECCOUNT() TO total
    @ 13,13 SAY [The number of records copied  = ]
    @ 13,45 SAY total
    WAIT
CLEAR
BROWSE
CLEAR ALL
RETURN
*EOF:FLSUM.PRG
```

Any of the above programs can be edited to work with P.L. 94-171 data for any State. In order to use the above programs with other state's P.L. 94-171 data, edit the USE and SET INDEX TO commands. For example, statements, such as USE PL9417FL and SET INDEX TO PL9417FL, would be changed to USE PL9417AL and SET INDEX TO PL9417AL if Alabama data were required.

TAPE SERVICES

In addition to CD-ROM services, the Libraries offers several services to patrons who require access to data stored on magnetic tapes. The Systems Office within the Libraries archives and processes the tapes for library and patron use. Patrons may access the tapes themselves free of charge. The following additonal services are provided on a fee-basis: (1) The Systems Office within the Libraries provides tape copies, (2) census unit staff will create user-defined subsets in an ASCII or SAS format, and (3) census unit staff will provide standardized printed output of data tables for any geographic level in Florida.

Tape copies are provided by the Systems Office with a 3-day turn-around period. Fees charged to patrons for tape copies recover all incurred costs associated with the service, including labor, data processing, supplies, and accounting and administrative fees. Fees charged for services provided by the census unit are designed to recover data-processing costs only. Labor costs are not recovered since the services provided are considered within the general domain of the reference department. The rationale is based on the typical fee structure used by many institutions for online services where the patron is charged for telecommunication costs, but not for the librarian's time and effort. Popular requests include subsetting all of the data for a particular county in an ASCII format to floppy disks or providing a printed copy of all data tables from Summary Tape File 1A for census tracts within a particular county. The standard fee to download a single county from magnetic tape in an ASCII format is $23.25. The charge includes a $10.00 data retrieval fee designed to pay for computing costs, an $11.00 fee for copying the technical documentation, a $1.60 charge for the cost of the disk, and the balance recovers postage and sales tax. A printout of census tract data for a single county can range anywhere from $15.00

to $25.00 depending on the size of the county. The fee reflects a $10.00 data retrieval fee, plus CPU and printing charges incurred, and postage and sales tax. The $10.00 data retrieval fee for printed reports is designed to cover overhead data processing costs, such as failed jobs, as well as recover costs from patrons who do not pay their bills.

The tape services provided by the census unit are possible due to a cooperative venture between the Libraries and the Center for Instructional and Research Computing (CIRCA). A programmer/analyst at CIRCA provides the census unit with SAS batch files. The census unit edits the programs to the patron's specifications and submits the program on the campus mainframe. The SAS setups used by CIRCA were originally acquired from the SASPAC-L file server, and adapted to work with Florida data. John Blodgett at the Urban Information Center, University of Missouri, has loaded SAS setups designed to work with the STF1A data on the SASPAC-L list.[8] The INTERNET address of SASPAC-L is UMSLVMA.

CONCLUSION

The University of Florida Libraries serve a highly diverse clientele whose needs for census data range from requests for a single data table to requests for large quantities of data covering several geographic areas. The variety of formats that the Census Bureau releases data on allows the Libraries several options for providing data services. The Libraries have successfully integrated advanced data and reference services for machine-readable data into the public services division of the Libraries. Many requests have successfully been answered using the census CD-ROMs in conjunction with dBase programs. Other requests have been serviced with magnetic tapes. Due to the release of numeric data on CD-ROMs and the cooperation between the campus computing facilities and the Libraries' census unit, public service librarians have developed new programs for servicing electronic products that were previously handled by computer specialists within the Systems Office or the campus computing center.

REFERENCES

Geographic Identification Code Scheme. Washington, D.C.: Bureau of the Census, (1983).

Jacobs, Jim. "Providing Data Services for Machine-readable Information in an Academic Library: Some Levels of Service," *Public Access Computer Systems Review*, 2 (1991): 144–160.

---

[8] SAS-PAC-L is the name of a file server that is located at the UMSLVMA Internet address; it contains modules, MVS job streams, to convert STF1 data to SAS datasets

CONCLUSION

Chapter Thirteen

Management Issues

Jan Swanbeck

The sudden deluge of electronic products and services received by depository libraries has forced managers to make important decisions often without adequate time to review the successes of other libraries. This chapter describes the manager's dilemma, presents lobbying strategies for documents librarians attempting to garner scarce resources, and outlines the major decisions facing administrators of depository libraries.

Almost overnight, Federal depository libraries have become involuntary test sites for the myriad of new electronic products and services distributed via the depository program, including CD-ROMs, floppy disks, and electronic bulletin boards. After years of debate concerning the public's right to information stored electronically electronic products and services are suddenly flooding depository libraries. Regional depository libraries, which receive 100% of the items distributed via the depository library program, will have received by the end of 1991 close to 200 CD-ROMs. This is astounding given that as recently as 1989 this format was described as "a promising form of storage" for government information (Sanchez, 1989, p. 135). Zink (1990, p. 51) advocated a cautious approach to this format warning that "too few institutions have reviewed the implications of CD-ROM before making their purchases." Depository libraries did not and do not have the luxury of reviewing the CD-ROMs prior to receipt.

One positive result of the current state of chaos will be the useful management information generated by depository libraries. Library administrators faced with a statutory obligation to provide access to this depository information are making organizational decisions without any models of what does and does not work. Their successes and mistakes will serve as models for those more fortunate administrators who have the luxury of planning.

HOW DID THIS HAPPEN?

Back in the late 1970s, the Government Printing Office (GPO) proposed to distribute a number of its publications in microfiche format citing that it was cheaper to produce and mail, it took up less space, and it enabled the GPO to distribute more information. However, in the final analysis, GPO's decision to distribute documents in microfiche had absolutely nothing to do with enhancing access to information but rather with GPO's budget and rising costs of printing and mailing. The bottom line for publishing in CD-ROM format is again cost. Agencies have quickly recognized that it is an inexpensive way to disseminate an enormous amount of data. Because this format decision is made at the agency level, unlike the well documented microfiche conversion project, documents librarians have no input concerning appropriate software, documentation, etc. Indeed, there are already many examples of CD-ROM products being distributed via the depository library program without documentation or agency produced software.

MANAGER'S DILEMMA

The manager's dilemma began with what I term, "*Infotrac* mentality" CD-ROMs in the minds of many became synonymous with *Infotrac*, an easy to use index to magazine articles and one of the first CD-ROM products to hit the library market. *Infotrac*, with its simplistic keyword searching protocol, was quickly embraced by library patrons across the country. Thus, the announcement that CD-ROMs would be distributed via the depository program generated a positive response from the library community. Managers, lulled by "*Infotrac* mentality," welcomed the arrival of this format so loved by their patrons. The arrival of Census Test Disk 2 immediately dispelled the *Infotrac* myth. This CD-ROM contained data, not the bibliographic citations to which librarians were accustomed. In fact, the CD-ROMs that the Census Bureau distributes provide the very same data as contained on some of their magnetic tapes. And, like their tape counterparts, programming is necessary to extract datasets. This suddenly presents the manager with a myriad of problems. Where will they be located? Who is responsible for providing service? What level of service will be provided? If programming is involved, should the library charge? What is the responsibility of regionals towards the selectives? Furthermore, CD-ROMs represent only one example of the electronic products and services being distributed via the depository program. How do you provide public access to an electronic bulletin board? What do you do with floppy disks? Clearly, there are at this point in time more questions than answers for managers attempting to fulfill their statutory obligation to provide free public access to information distributed to depositories in electronic format.

SOLUTIONS IN THE LITERATURE

Understandably the literature, as yet, provides scant assistance to managers. However, a few articles clearly articulate the problems involved in coping with these new electronic formats. Hernon and McClure (1991) outline the issues relating to the provision of access to electronic census information via the depository program. Of particular interest are the five characteristics of technologies that depository library librarians cite as critical to the provision of information in electronic format (Ibid., p. 60):

- Be reasonably priced (fit within the library budget and technology needs);
- Be end-user friendly;
- Not be too sophisticated, e.g., require extensive staff training and constant use to maintain search skills;
- Require minimal staff intervention; because the staff are very busy, end users must be able to function on their own with minimal staff assistance; and
- Be compatible with other library equipment.

These characteristics were derived from a study done by Hernon and McClure for the Bureau of the Census to assess the role of the depository library program in the dissemination of electronic census products in the year 2000. Therefore, the results generated by this important study had no impact whatsoever on the development of the 1990 products and services. Ironically, many documents librarians would contend that the 1990 electronic census products received, thus far, meet none of the above characteristics. This is particularly frightening in that the study concludes that "technologies that do not meet the above-mentioned five characteristics are perhaps better left to providers other than depository libraries" (Ibid., p. 60).

Zink (1990) stresses the need to evaluate and plan for new CD-ROM products. He goes on to make the important point that "the use of automation where the public directly confronts technology has generally increased the need for user assistance" (Ibid., p. 54). This point is addressed in more detail by Bunge (1991) in his article on CD-ROM stress.

Jacobs (1990) outlines the problems faced by libraries attempting to provide access to government bulletin boards. His long-term solutions like, the scenarios offered by Hernon and McClure (1991), are of no immediate value to documents librarians currently coping with the electronic products and services received through the depository program.

Several useful articles have appeared in the literature on the topic of training for CD-ROMs. Allen (1990, p. 89) summarizes the literature in this area and states that "there does not appear to be agreement as to which is the best methodology to use for CD-ROM training."

Another issue of concern to managers is levels of service. Jacobs (1991) describes specific levels of data service which organizations might provide to their constituency. Olsen presents a more general overview of service issues associated with providing information in electronic format using Cornell's Mann Library as a model (see Arms, 1991); Olsen's study is a chapter in the book *Campus Strategies for Libraries and Electronic Information*, which describes the development work of selected institutions of higher education which are on the cutting edge in the area of providing access to electronic products and services.

COOPERATION: THE FIRST STEP

Depository collections historically have functioned as a library within a library, in that both the processing and servicing of the collection are done by the documents department staff. The pros and cons of this approach have been debated at length. But the reality of this organizational structure is that it presents major obstacles to the provision of access to electronic information. The key to success in absorbing these new technologies is first and foremost, cooperation. A documents department must seek the assistance of a variety of units within and outside the library in order to cope successfully with the onslaught of electronic products and services now being distributed via the depository program. The loading of tapes into a library's online catalog serves as a useful example of how a documents department must merge its activities with the rest of the library. At a minimum, such an endeavor requires the involvement of the cataloging department, systems department, acquisitions department, and circulation department.

How does a documents librarian garner the necessary cooperation to manage these new technologies? This is not an easy question to answer. There are serious obstacles to be overcome, the greatest of which is the documents librarian's lack of status within the organizational structure. The position responsible for the documents collection is usually at the level of department head or lower. Thus, the need to provide access to depository material in electronic format must be articulated up the chain of command. The fact that bibliographic records for depository collections are just now being added to online catalogs is a clear indicator of the lack of success of the part of documents librarians in making their needs known to the library administration. It also points up where access to government information traditionally falls within the priorities of libraries.

The staggering equipment start-up costs presents another serious obstacle. The GPO, in its recently issued recommended minimal technical guidelines for depository libraries, listed the minimum cost for the necessary hardware and software as $3,100 ("Recommended Minimum Technical Guidelines for Federal Depository Libraries," 1991). The current downturn in the economy coupled with escalating subscription costs seriously weakens the position of the documents department attempting to claim its share of the library resources to purchase necessary equipment and software for the new electronic products and services. Most libraries have developed long-range plans and determine annual allocations according to priorities set in the planning process. Providing access to government information in electronic format was not a priority in any library until the past year. As a result, in order to support these new products and services libraries must divert resources from critical activities, such as collection development, at a time when budgets across the country are shrinking drastically.

In the past, documents librarians have used the statutory responsibility to provide immediate access to depository materials as a tool to convince administrators of the need for more staff, space, and equipment. Periodic inspections by GPO staff served to reinforce the requests of documents librarians. Unfortunately, the law governing the depository library program does not yet address electronic information. In addition, the GPO has provided no guidelines for libraries attempting to service these new electronic formats. Nor is it clear how electronic products and services will be addressed in the inspection process.

STRATEGIES FOR DOCUMENTS LIBRARIANS

Given the obstacles cited above, what strategies can a documents librarian employ to garner the support and cooperation needed to provide access to depository electronic products? One powerful weapon now in the hands of documents librarians lobbying for cooperation is the distribution of census data to depositories in electronic format. Current census information is essential to the work of a wide variety of people in government, business, and academia. These users want the data as quickly as possible and have in the past bypassed the library in their attempts to retrieve data either before they are published in hardcopy or because they were not available in printed format. Electronic formats make census data available sooner and provide more data than ever before. Documents librarians can make good use of this "sooner and more" argument when lobbying their administration for the necessary equipment. For example, on the campus of the University of Florida, at least three units were identified as having done fee-based programming for 1980 census data. Arranging a meeting with these units and the library administration to discuss census services at our university resulted in the library's assuming the lead role for the 1990 census. This meeting had direct, positive results for the documents department as well. It emphasized to the directors the importance of census data on campus and was instrumental in the immediate purchase of a computer powerful enough to provide a high level of service.

The "sooner and more" argument applies to other electronic products, such as the National Trade Data Bank, Import and Export Data, the National Health Interview Survey, and the DOD Hazardous Waste Inventory. "Only" is another powerful argument; it will become increasingly more useful as important sources are published only in CD-ROM format.

The fact that depository materials are free is another lure for cooperation. Some academic librarians unable to access TIGER/Line files have co-opted the geographic information system (GIS) skills and necessary equipment from geographers on campus. The geography professors, in turn, are delighted to receive these expensive products ($250/disk; 46 disks) at no cost. Similarly, users of census data accustomed to paying for data extraction from the magnetic tapes will welcome the opportunity to download data for free from CD-ROMs for manipulation using dBase on a personal computer in their home or office.

Love of and implicit trust in information received electronically is yet another lobbying tactic. Any reference librarian would agree that users will almost always go to an index on CD-ROM rather than its paper counterpart. This is especially true in an academic environment where CD-ROM workstations function as magnets to a generation raised on computers.

DECISIONS

Assuming that the documents librarian is able to convince the library administration of the need to provide access to government information received in electronic format, the next step involves making several management decisions regarding location, levels of service, fees, and training.

Location

The first decision to be made, and by far the most crucial, is the location of the depository electronic products within the library. The choice of location is inextricably tied to the determination of which unit will assume responsibility for providing service for these products. A key factor in determining primary servicing responsibility should be technical expertise; that is, which area of the library has the necessary hardware and software skills to provide access to electronic information. Yet, there still remains a need for subject expertise to interpret the information. Placing these products in an area dedicated to electronic information is logical in terms of consolidation of equipment and staff.

However, there are equally valid arguments to be made for keeping all government information, regardless of format, in a central location serviced by documents experts.

The ideal solution to the location/servicing dilemma is to create a service point which offers some combination of technical skills and subject expertise. At the University of Florida, this was attained by reassigning the Machine Readable Data Files Librarian who has the requisite programming skills to the documents department. The result is a wonderful symbiotic relationship. She relies on the documents staff's knowledge of census terminology and the printed products, and the department, in turn, makes use of her knowledge of SAS and dBase in order to offer a high level of service. Other libraries are creating new positions which require the combined skills. The July/August 1991 issue of *American Libraries* contained an ad for a "Documents Librarian/Federal Technology Specialist." This was followed by a vacancy announcement for a "Government Documents/Data Services Reference Librarian." Both positions *required* experience with microcomputers.

There are also important floorplan considerations in selecting the location of depository electronic products and services. Zink (1990) reports that CD-ROM workstations take up over 40 feet of floor space. Depository libraries, especially regionals, already facing severe space shortages will have to sacrifice precious stack or seating areas. This is further complicated by the need to have the stations adjacent to or very near a service desk for both the convenience of the staff as well as the security of the equipment. In addition, there must be adequate electrical wiring and a phone line for online access to bulletin boards.

Instead of placing the equipment in a public service area, the decision may be made to place a workstation in a separate office, thereby providing the user with a place to work undisturbed. This is particularly desirable for patrons or staff using the more complex products, such as the TIGER/Line files. It would also ensure that the public area workstations would not be tied up by the downloading or processing of data, which can take hours at a time. Clearly, this is a costly option and one that would depend on the level of service offered by the library.

Another location decision must be made concerning electronic bulletin boards. The key question is whether or not to place this service in a public area. For many libraries the location of an appropriate phone line will be the sole consideration. Libraries considering making bulletin boards available to the public should keep in mind that currently the library must bear all telecommunication costs. In addition, users must be familiar with communications software. A further consideration is the potential to tie up a public area workstation for extended periods of time. Also, based on the comments on Govdoc-L, the documents list server, librarians are experiencing many problems accessing bulletin boards. It, therefore, seems prudent not to locate modems in a public area until a more user friendly and less costly mode of accessing bulletin boards is available, such as that proposed by Jacobs (1990).

Levels of Service

Decisions regarding the level of service offered by a library are dictated by the size of its budget and the expertise of its staff. Clearly, only those libraries having adequate resources to purchase the requisite hardware and software, as well as having the resident technical expertise, will be able to provide a high level of service for the emerging depository electronic products. As a result "those few libraries that are able to provide in-depth reference service are being overwhelmed with the number of referrals they are receiving" ("Service Levels at Depository Libraries," 1992, p. 31).

Library administrators must make decisions as soon as possible as to what specific services a library is prepared to offer in order to provide access to depository electronic products and services. These decisions should result in written guidelines which describe in detail the services the library can offer to assist the patron in the use of depository electronic information. It is important that the guidelines also include a list of services that the library cannot provide. Additionally, the library should attempt to identify alternative libraries, individuals, or businesses that are able to provide these services.

At the low end of the service spectrum, the library can decide simply to make these products available to any patron having the equipment and expertise to access the information. The library would check out the product in much the same way that one circulates a hardcopy document. This is the only option available to libraries committed to providing the information but lacking the necessary equipment and/or technical skills. This is also a viable option for specialized products, such as the TIGER/Line files. Use of these CD-ROMs requires familiarity with GIS software as well as equipment not included in GPO's minimal technical guidelines.

An intermediate approach to servicing these products is to provide the necessary hardware and software to "read" the information and to rely on the expertise of the patron to perform any manipulation of the data or text. This level of service is appropriate for a library whose staff lacks the necessary hardware and software skills. It can also serve as a temporary servicing policy for libraries whose staff are in the process of self education or for libraries in the process of attempting to hire or co-opt the necessary technical skills.

At the upper end of the spectrum lie services such as downloading datasets, programming, and the creation of maps. These are services traditionally provided by State Data Centers on a fee basis. Logically, many libraries rather than attempting to duplicate these services continue to refer patrons to their State Data Center. Yet, patrons in some parts of the country have free access to this same information because their local depository library is able to offer an exceptionally high level of service. This inequity of access is so against the grain of depository librarians that a workgroup within the American Library Association's Government Documents Round Table's (GODORT's) Federal Documents Task Force developed a discussion paper on the topic of service levels. One scenario identified by the group proposes the formation of geographic networks whose individual members would develop expertise in and assume responsibility for a specific subject or electronic product. The work group members also see networking as a possible method of more equally distributing the burden of providing access to information in electronic format as well as ensuring its availability to a broader segment of the general public at no cost ("Service Levels at Depository Libraries," 1992).

Fees

Without doubt, the most emotionally charged decision a manager must face concerning depository electronic information is whether or not user fees of some type are appropriate. For example charging for programming associated with census data on magnetic tapes is an accepted practice. These same data now are distributed via the depository library program in CD-ROM format, but complete access to the data still requires programming in dBase. Does the fact that the data are distributed via the depository library program prohibit the library from imposing a user fee for programming time? The answer to this question would appear to be "yes" according to GPO's General Counsel, who states that "Depository libraries are prohibited under existing law from charging the public for accessing Government information supplied under the aegis of the Depository Library Program" (Zagami, 1991, p. 387). Given this prohibition, few, if any, libraries can afford to offer this service. Ironically, libraries unable to provide free access to depository electronic information must refer patrons to entities which charge for programming.

One option available to libraries providing in-depth service is to charge not for the programming but for the floppy disk onto which the data have been downloaded. The same would be true of information obtained by printing data or text from a CD-ROM or bulletin board. In this instance, the library would charge for the paper much like a photocopy charge for an interlibrary loan transaction. While these options seem to defy the philosophy of the public's right to this information, dwindling budgets are forcing libraries to consider such strategies.

Related to the issue of user fees is that of clientele. The library's administration must clearly define the clientele to be served. If some sort of charge is to be levied, a decision must be made as to whether it will be a uniform charge or a charge determined by the status of the patron. Again it is important that these decisions be clearly stated in the library's service guidelines.

Training

The issue of training is overwhelming for depository libraries attempting to provide access to electronic products and services. The library must decide how to train staff, who will train staff, what staff will be trained, and to what level will staff be trained.

Decisions concerning how to train and who will train will vary greatly according to the organizational structure of the library, the in-house expertise, and the level of service offered by the library. As mentioned previously, the literature does offer several useful articles on this subject.

A more difficult process for a library is determining for which staff and to what level training will occur. Presumably all public service staff of that unit having primary service responsibility for depository products in electronic format will be targeted for some level of training. In addition, a library may choose to train staff at other service points. For example, it would be extremely useful to provide minimal training to the reference staff if the documents department services the electronic products. This would greatly enhance the quality of referrals.

Assuming that all public service staff of the unit receive training the next question is to what level. At issue here is whether all staff should be trained at the same level or should individual staff be assigned servicing responsibility for a particular electronic product. The ideal is to have all staff trained to an equally high level and be familiar with all hardware and software housed in the department. Given the recent deluge of government information in electronic format this expectation is unrealistic. The latter option of assigning responsibility for a product is appealing but is only viable for well-staffed departments. For small service units, the broader geography-based networking approach described earlier seems to be the only workable solution for the short term.

CONCLUSION

The sudden deluge of electronic products and services via the depository library program caught the library world by surprise. As a result, administrators have had to cope as best they can with the complex issues surrounding the provision of access to this electronic information, weighing the urgency of their statutory obligation against the reality of their shrinking budgets. Lacking the luxury to plan libraries have been forced to make the decisions described in this chapter without the benefit of successful models. In fact, depositories have become models for the rest of the library community. A review of GPO's newsletter *Administrative Notes* or Govdoc-L quickly points up how successful documents librarians have been in absorbing the new terminology of electronic information. The initial frustration of documents librarians is being replaced by the excitement of success. Documents librarians, unlike any other segment of the library community, have banded together in a collective effort to absorb technology.

An important result of this sudden influx of electronic products and services will be a stronger than ever push to re-examine the depository library program. Clearly, individual libraries are not capable of providing a high level of service at this point in time. Even regional libraries cannot be expected to assume this burden. Some form of networking must emerge to counter the current inequities of access to government information in electronic format.

REFERENCES

Allen, Gillian. "CD-ROM Training: What Do the Patrons Want?," *RQ*, 30 (Fall 1990): 88–93.

Arms, Caroline, ed. *Campus Strategies for Libraries and Electronic Information*. Rockport, MA: Digital Press.

Bunge, Charles A. "CD-ROM Stress," *Library Journal*, 116 (April 15, 1991): 63–64.

Hernon, Peter and Charles R. McClure. "Electronic Census Products and the Depository Library Program: Future Issues and Trends," *Government Information Quarterly*, 8 (1991): 59–76.

Jacobs, Jim. "Providing Data Services for Machine-Readable Information in an Academic Library: Some Levels of Service," *Public Access Computer Systems Review*, 2 (1991): 144–160.

_____. "U.S. Government Computer Bulletin Boards: A Modest Proposal for Reform," *Government Publications Review*, 17 (1990): 393–396.

"Recommended Minimum Technical Guidelines for Federal Depository Libraries," *Administrative Notes*, 12 (August 31, 1991): 1-3 *(GP3.16/3–2:12/19)*.

Sanchez, Lisa. "Dissemination of United States Federal Government Information on CD-ROM: An Issue Primer," *Government Publications Review*, 16 (1989): 133–144.

"Service Levels at Depository Libraries," *Documents to the People*, 20 (March 1992): 31–32.

Zagami, Anthony J. "Memorandum: 'Cost Sharing' for the Dissemination of Government Information in Electronic Formats," *Government Information Quarterly*, 8 (1991): 387–391.

Zink, Stephen D. "Planning for the Perils of CD-ROM," *Library Journal*, 115 (February 1, 1990): 51–55.

Chapter Fourteen

Documents Librarianship: Present and Future

Diane H. Smith

This chapter discusses the present status of Federal documents librarianship and its outlook for the future. Analyzing the environmental forces at work in the present depository program, the chapter presents probable roles for document librarians in the future. The chapter ends with a blueprint for change in the education and training for documents librarians.

A recurring theme in the literature of management and strategic planning is the concept that a business must accurately identify its industrial niche in terms of its ever changing environment. If this is not done, the business is doomed to eventual failure. An example frequently given of this industrial myopia is the ice industry that flourished in the first part of the 20th century. Viewing their business as one of simply providing ice to homes rather than one of keeping food cold, the industry neglected to notice the steady development of the refrigeration industry. Eventually this oversight led to the industry's demise.

If care is not taken, this analogy may hold true for the profession of documents librarianship. Today librarianship as a whole is on the brink of tremendous change; change accelerated by technology, political, and economic realities, and societal expectations.

In many ways the forces that will affect documents librarians are harbingers of pressures that will rock the entire profession. How Federal document and depository librarians react to these changes will determine their place in the profession in the future. At the outset it should be noted that there may be a significant difference in the future between a "Federal documents librarian," or one who is an expert in locating Federal information, and a "Federal depository librarian," or one who manages a depository collection. This chapter discusses the current situation, assesses the future for each of these types of librarians, and lays out a survival strategy for documents librarianship.

PRESENT STATUS OF DOCUMENTS LIBRARIANSHIP: THE 1990s

Environment

Documents Librarians' Skills and Characteristics—An Inventory. The professional skills exhibited by the depository community range from great proficiency to a passing knowledge of resources and publications. This broad spectrum of skills is reflective of the very nature of the depository system and is to be expected given the size of the program. Some depositories are very large, selecting the majority of publications available and investing a significant amount of library resources into these collections. Other libraries choose only a limited number of materials, with the role of the "depository librarian" being an additional responsibility assigned to a staff member whose primary job focus is in another library activity. Nonetheless, five generalities can be made about the profession and its competencies, based on the body of literature produced by its professionals, on research that has been conducted to study the performance of documents librarians, and on anecdotal evidence.

First and foremost, Federal documents librarians have been obsessed since the establishment of the program with bibliographic control. This comes as no small wonder given the varying levels of commitment that the Federal government has provided to this activity over the years. The lack of standard bibliographic control, in conjunction with the fact that few libraries had cataloging units willing and able to take on the amount of material being accessioned, resulted until very recently in home grown classification systems and processing routines; endless indexes/abstracts to help locate information; and constant harping on the GPO's mistakes in cataloging/classifying. A quick scan of library literature up to 1989 shows that the number of articles dealing with bibliographic control and indexing clearly outnumbered most other topics of interest at a rate of four to one.[1]

---

[1] In looking at Schorr's (1988) comprehensive bibliography of literature concerning documents librarianship, one finds 567 entries dealing with bibliography, abstracts, and technical services, compared to 40 entries on administration, 128 on collection development, 185 on the depository program, 117 on microform issues, 161 on public services, 48 on teaching, and 372 on information policy.

A second general attribute of depository librarians is the professional skill that has been developed in the area of collection maintenance and processing. This trait is easily attributable to the fact that document formats and classifications have often defied normal library practices. Constant shifting, reshelving, refiling, and processing of materials that are not usually bound, and are frequently flimsy and small, have added to this concern. The sheer amount of material that a selective depository might be receiving has also added to the situation. Managing the timely processing of materials and their disposition becomes a major focus in most large selective depositories. GPO regulations requiring selectives to maintain titles for a set number of years and making weeding a labor-intensive and consultative endeavor have only exacerbated the situation.

The third generalization about depository libraries and their staffs is the fact that research and observation imply that the reference service given to document collections is less than optimum. McClure and Hernon's study (1983) on the accuracy rate of reference service in depository libraries clearly implies that better negotiating skills and a broader knowledge of the varying sources available in depository collections need to be developed.

A fourth trait of depository librarians is that they have only recently begun to embrace computer technology in comparison to their other colleagues in reference and technical services. This characteristic is evidenced by the small number of articles in the literature of documents librarians dealing with all facets of technology (Schorr, 1988); from research investigating the use of online services by documents librarians (Ibid.); and by the fact that only recently have some depository librarians managed to have document holdings included in their OPAC's (Smith, 1990).

The final common characteristic of depository librarians has been their intense interest in Federal information policies. The depository community has long been a staunch proponent of the rights of the citizenry to have access to Federal information. This interest has been played out repeatedly in the last 20 years in articles, in political action and awareness campaigns that the American Library Association's Government Documents Round Table has undertaken, and in the activities of the Depository Library Council to the Public Printer.[2] This central concern for information policy, in concert with the move of the Federal government to automate more of its publishing activities, has forced the Federal depository library community to demonstrate a growing desire for government information in electronic formats, even though few of them are prepared at the moment to deal with the data. Regardless of their abilities to use these resources successfully, this insistence that Federal information policy for depositories

---

[2] Refer to back issues of *Documents to the People (DttP)* and transcripts of Depository Library Council meetings for evidence of this.

include electronic formats will be a major factor contributing to the evolution of documents librarianship in the near future.

Depository Libraries in the 1990s. Just as in the case of documents librarians, there are general characteristics that describe the majority of depository libraries throughout the United States. These characteristics are: fiscal constraints; lack of technical skills throughout the staff; slow absorption of technology; and few partnerships with the varied computing organizations within their community.

There can be little doubt that the 1990s will be a time of strict budget control in academic, Federal, state, and public libraries. Even those institutions known for large endowments will be keeping an accounting eye on library activities. Library directors will need to justify each service offered and spiraling costs associated with any technological innovations. In the setting of the 1980s Smith (1990) found that large academic depositories did not fare well in getting support from administrators for their collection and automation. In the 1990s, the continuation of depository status could easily come under very close scrutiny should costs begin to exceed perceived benefits.

In most libraries today it is not unusual to find a staff that is, by and large, "computer illiterate." This lack of knowledge runs throughout libraries, with the inevitable exception that each institution has one or two hackers who are the people called whenever a problem occurs. Although this appears to be a sweeping generalization, the rampant problems that have been witnessed in the installation of privately and publicly produced CD-ROM products and in the implementation of library online catalogs point to a sizeable gap in knowledge that needs to be addressed across the profession as a whole.

Few libraries in the United States are early adaptors of technology for the delivery of information. The reality is that fiscal conservativism in conjunction with low technology knowledge levels have not created an environment in which technological risk taking is appropriate or actively encouraged. A handful of library directors in academic settings have begun to develop partnerships with the computing bodies on their campuses precisely because these entities do have the necessary technical knowledge and can leverage computing equipment from major vendors. These risk-taking directors see the growing need to intertwine library and information services on campus. However, this is a trend that is just beginning and it will be some time before it is the norm.

Government Information Policy in the 1990s. Not only will financial matters be of keen interest to library directors during the 1990s, but they will be of primary significance to the Federal government. In the past the Government Printing Office was a key player in the process of government information dissemination and is developing strategic plans to continue this role. According to Robert Houk (1991, p. 7), the present Public Printer:

> GPO's future mission will be to assist Congress and Federal agencies in the creation and replication of information in a cost-effective manner, and to provide

efficient and effective means for disseminating and using that information for the public.... It will, however, require that GPO embrace and advance the use of electronic technologies, methods, techniques, and strategies to accomplish that mission.... The emergence of print-on demand technologies, in particular, is likely to be a key factor....

At the same time Federal agencies are investigating the use of electronic bulletin boards, databases, and CD-ROM's as means of disseminating information in a cost-effective manner. There is no reason to believe that this trend will slow down in the 1990s; rather, there may likely be an accelerating upward growth.

Against this financial backdrop of information dissemination there is yet another information policy being played out: The political questions of autonomy and cost-effectiveness for Federal agencies printing and dissemination programs. In the 1980s and early 1990s unrelenting pressure by the Office of Management and Budget and the private sector has forced a continual justification of free government information dissemination. Limited economic resources and rapidly changing technologies will sustain these pressures on the GPO and its depository program in the coming decade.

Finally, one disturbing aspect of the Federal policy to computerize government information creation, storage, and dissemination is the apparent lack of forethought about the potential obsolescence of the machinery necessary to mount the data. Recent press releases concerning the usability of mid-20th century census data have highlighted this fact.[3] The importance of developing an information dissemination plan that includes the guarantee of usable archival data will need to be addressed as the technologies spin forward at an ever increasing rate.

Computing, Scholarship, and Society in the 1990s. Significant changes in scholarship and publishing are predicted for American society in the 1990s. The initial signs of these changes are seen in discussions concerning the National Research and Education Network (NREN). The possibilities for collaborative research among researchers; electronic publishing; and instantaneous access to materials located at other locations all become an attainable reality with the development of such a national research network. Similarly work in the area of printing on-demand, as seen by the Xerox DocuTech system, have tremendous ramifications for society and libraries.[4] These developments in electronic publishing, networks, and data storage all indicate that the traditions and practices of libraries may need to change substantially, if libraries wish to survive in some form other than a paper archive.

---

[3] In 1991 a major story was carried by the syndicated presses focusing on the problem of archiving machine data. The concern was that although the data had been archived during the 1950-1970s, the computing equipment to run the data had not, thus making the data not useable now.

[4] For a brief description of DocuTech see Gherman (1991). Other descriptions are available in recent library literature concerning the pilot Xerox project being undertaken at Cornell University to preserve crumbling mathematics texts through this technology.

At the same time that the infrastructure and technology are developing, the level of expectations and knowledge of the American population about computing is also rapidly evolving. The continual development of icon-based system interfaces and the penetration of computing into all facets of jobs and education indicate an acceptance of computer technology that is pervasive in society. As experience with computers grows, it is not unreasonable to assume that expectations of information retrieval will also grow.

Clash of Realities in the 1990s

In the past year the deluge of CD-ROM products into the depository system has underscored the conflict in which documents librarians find themselves: Caught between a professional ethic to provide quality information service and the realities of fixed budgets and staff capabilities. However, the Pandora's box of Federal electronic resources has been opened, and there is no way to stuff the informational resources back in the box—even if one wanted.

The present depository system was never intended to handle electronic data. Rather, it was designed in a time in which physical access to publications was the only way to guarantee a citizen's access to government information. This was the primary reason behind having a depository in every congressional district. However, the premise for this type of physical access crumbles in the face of telefacsimile machines, high-speed national networks, and printing on demand. The need for 1,400 constantly growing depository collections located throughout the country dissolves. A drastic restructuring of the depository program, in light of printing, computing, and networking advances is inevitable. With these new technologies the real reason for the depository program, providing citizens with timely and free access to government information, can become a reality. It is crucial that the depository and documents librarians not make the same mistake as the ice manufacturers. The "industry" of documents librarians is providing access to Federal information, regardless of its physical location; the "industry" is not developing a collection of paper and electronic government publications.

THE FUTURE OF DOCUMENTS LIBRARIANSHIP—
INTO THE 21ST CENTURY

Having discussed the present and the past, it is worthwhile to take a look at the probable environment which the future holds for depository librarians and their collections. These predictions are based on general library and computing literature.

Society in the 21st Century

By the year 2000 it is not unreasonable to assume that most educated and working Americans will be comfortable with computers. This will naturally occur as education becomes more heavily dependent upon computer technology for teaching in K-12, as well as at the university level. This change will not be evident only in the younger section of the population. The "greying" population, spearheaded by the babyboomer generation, also will have become competent with these technologies through their occupations and professional connections. Understanding and using computer technology will become an expected skill, similar to using a telephone. A national network for the transmission of data will exist. The development of wide area information servers (WAIS) will have progressed to the point that people will be able to identify and use resources available through the network.

Libraries in the 21st Century

Libraries will be connected to the national networks and easily transmit articles from collections to users. The question of physical access versus bibliographic access will have become moot. The quality of a library will be determined not by the size of its collection, but rather by its ability to serve its users with needed sources, whether that is a section of a book, an article, a dataset, a quote, or a bit of information in a cost-effective and efficient manner.

The Federal Depository System in the 21st Century

For a number of reasons the depository system will evolve into a structure different than what presently exists. First, there will be a significant decrease in the number of selective depositories. In all likelihood, only a limited number of regional depositories will remain. This streamlining of the system will occur for a variety of reasons. The costs of being a depository during the 1990s compared to the benefits accrued will force many out of the system. It will be a simple economic decision made by library directors within the financial straits of the time. Similar to the cuts presently being made in journal collections, the lapse of depository status will be viewed as an economic necessity for the library to survive. Second, the continued phenomenon of privatizing and commercializing government information resources will cut into lean library budgets. As the government seeks to cut its dissemination costs, cost-sharing between libraries and the GPO will become the norm. This trend, in conjunction with the increased expenses resulting from cost-sharing for depository operations will force a number of libraries to leave the program. At the same time that this shakeout is occurring in the library sector of the program, the Federal government will have taken a serious look at the printing and distribution costs incurred in the maintenance of the program. The existence of the NREN in conjunction with individual agency databases available through the network, will decrease the need for the GPO depository system. Fewer publications will be printed for general distribution; rather, there will develop a "print on demand" capability. Continued pressure to privatize information sources will continue as the Federal government struggles to balance its budget.

New and Old Rules for Documents Librarians in the 21st Century. With the streamlining of the GPO depository system there will be a natural decrease in the number of true "depository librarians." However, this may not mean a decrease in the need for documents librarians. Rather, it implies that the primary role of a documents librarian will evolve from one of being a custodian of a depository collection temporarily lent by the Federal government to a role that is more proactive in helping patrons locate needed information. It is ironic that the reference and automation skills that will be needed most in the future are the ones least cultivated and discussed now in the literature.[5]

The primary role of a documents librarian will be as an expert on the information that the government gathers and "publishes," rather than as an expert in locating and processing a physical document. Even now the evolution of the depository librarian from the bibliographic focus to a reference focus is seen in data and from anecdotal evidence from libraries that have included government records into their OPAC's, as found by Smith (1990). The ability to perform a reference interview, find the needed sources, and advise patrons on statistical interpretation and manipulation will all be essential skills. The development of artificial intelligence software and wide area information servers for resources on the network to aid users in locating their own information will be important challenges for this group of librarians. Naturally, instructional skills in dealing with a broad spectrum of users will also facilitate these jobs.

Collection development for documents will take on an added dimension in this environment. In order to provide patrons with needed information, the library will need to either purchase or gain access to data which once came "free" via the depository program. Now that "free" is no longer an option, greater care will be exercised in developing the non-electronic collection of Federal publications. The retrospective collections which will exist throughout the country will probably remain in the libraries (since it is unlikely that the government would want them back) and they will need to be managed. Skills in older bibliographic resources will be necessary, but these skills will be used with the frequency with which the indexes to the Serial Set are now consulted.

---

[5] For evidence of this one only needs to scan the primary journals of documents librarianship: *Government Information Quarterly, Government Publications Review,* or *DttP.*

The political role that documents librarians have undertaken in the last two decades will continue to be an important aspect of their jobs. Preserving the *safety net* for government information will fall naturally to documents librarians, who have traditionally viewed their roles as one of proponents of free and open access to information. It will be important for these librarians to maintain a watchful eye on the archival quality of electronic government files, including both the software and the hardware necessary to use the information stored.

BLUEPRINT FOR THE SURVIVAL
OF DOCUMENTS LIBRARIANSHIP

The future of documents librarianship is totally dependent upon the Darwinist principle of adaptation to a changing environment. The first step in this process is to recognize that technology will force transformations in the coming century. If clinging to the past depository structure is the choice of action, then the field of documents librarianship will be left the task of being the archivist for paper and microform products produced in the 19th and 20th century. If, on the other hand, the profession realizes that there need not be as many "depository libraries" in the future, then the natural transformation of "documents librarians" into "government information specialists" can transpire.

In order to adapt to these changing times new skills will be needed, both by librarians entering the profession and by those with years of experience. First and foremost will be the need to improve reference skills. As simplistic as that is on the surface, it is a weakness now of the profession and as the number of resources available for consultation expand and change in format, the need for a solid reference background will be essential. Improving reference skills will need to be expanded far beyond the standard bibliographic identification and quick fact finding skills that presently exist. The documents librarian will need to become a government information consultant for the user, pointing out the possible options, and helping to interpret data, as well as locating sources for information.

As a second training step documents librarians will need to have a solid foundation in data manipulation and in the use of statistical software programs. The reality is that as more data are stored in computer format, they are more easily manipulated, studied, and used for hypothesis testing, correlation analysis, and cross-tabulation. At present, this type of statistical knowledge is very limited in the library profession as a whole. If these skills are not developed by documents librarians, it is guaranteed that another professional group will develop them to help patrons use government data.

Along a similar line, documents librarians will need to acquire a working knowledge of mainframe computer and microcomputer usage. Expecting the Federal government to choose a limited mode of information delivery methods is unrealistic given the options available in the marketplace and given the Office of Management and Budget's insistence on cost-saving procurements. Agencies will choose their information delivery options based on budgetary constraints and how the products will deliver their information. Harping for standards in informational databases, products, and user-interfaces is unproductive when dealing with an industry that has not developed to the point of creating and abiding by its own industrial standards. Developing a good working relationship with computing professionals will be essential in developing these statistical and computing skills. Cross-training with the staffs responsible for computer files will help in attaining these skills.

The ability to perform collection analysis and user needs studies will be extremely important in the coming years. The ability to justify the acquisition of one product, be it in paper or electronic form, will be essential. Again, this is a skill that has had short shrift in the documents profession, because of the very framework of the depository program. However, with the unraveling of that structure, this will be an important attribute for documents librarians.

Finally, advocacy and lobbying ability will be necessary skills for documents librarians to assure the continuation of a national policy of free Federal information dissemination. If the price of democracy is "eternal vigilance," then an important role for the documents profession will be as an advocate for the continual dissemination of information under the evolving national depository system. The further development of these skills will be essential for the successful documents librarian of the future.

REFERENCES

Gherman, Paul. "Point of View," *The Chronicle of Higher Education,* 37 (August 14, 1991): A36.

Houk, Robert W. "Technology and Its Future Effect on the Government Printing Office," *Administrative Notes,* 12 (July 31, 1991): 1–10 (*GP3.16/3–2:12*)

McClure, Charles R. and Peter Hernon. *Improving the Quality of Reference Service for Government Publications.* Chicago: American Library Association, 1983.

Schorr, Alan E. *Federal Documents Librarianship, 1879–1987.* Juneau, Alaska: Denali Press, 1988.

Smith, Diane H. "Depository Libraries in the 1990's: Whither, or Wither Depositories," *Government Publications Review,* 17 (1990): 301–324.

Contributors

Duncan M. Aldrich is Head, Government Publications Department, Library, University of Nevada, Reno (Reno, Nevada 89557-0044). He is the international and state documents librarian and has responsibility for managing electronic products. He chairs the ALA/GODORT Legislation Committee.

Laura Bayard is Head, Catalog & Database Maintenance, Hesburth Library, University of Notre Dame (Notre Dame, Indiana 46556-5629). Most frequently, she works in technical services, although once she was acting head of a selective depository collection in an academic library.

Lawrence S. Berk, former Director, Library/Learning Resources Center, Florida Keys Community College, is now at Ulster County Community College, MacDonald/Dewitt Library, Stone Ridge, New York 12484. He was educated at Hunter College (A.B., 1968) and the University of Kentucky (M.S.L.S., 1972). Throughout his career, he has combined various types of librarianship with equally various teaching positions. Among other professional activities, he has developed a network of special education library centers in South Australia, has been a special education teacher in the inner city, and has taught library science, English composition, and poetry workshops in colleges, prisons, and schools. His interest in library technology deepened while working at the SUNY-Albany libraries. He has spent most of his career, however, as a director of community college libraries, focusing on innovative programming.

Myrtle Smith Bolner is Head of the Business Administration/Government Documents Department, Louisiana State University Libraries, Baton Rouge, Louisiana 70803. For her work as editor in upgrading the GPO/MARC tapes (Marcive tapes), she and her co-editors received the 1990 ALA/GODORT/CIS "Documents to the People" Award. She is the co-author of *Books, Libraries, and Research* (Kendall/Hunt, 1979, 1983, 1987) and *Library Research Skills Handbook* (Kendall/Hunt, 1991). She has contributed articles to professional journals, including the *Louisiana Association Bulletin* and *Government Publications Review.*

Diane Calvin is Government Publications Librarian, A.M. Bracken Library, Ball State University, Muncie, Indiana 47306-0160. She received her B.S. and M.L.S. degrees from Emporia (Kansas) State University. She co-authored a *Government Information Quarterly* article on developing a government publications collection development policy. She is a member of the American Library Association and the Government Documents Round Table.

David A. Cobb, formerly the Map & Geography Librarian at the University of Illinois, is now Head, Harvard Map Collection, Harvard College Library, Cambridge, Massachusetts 02138. His educational background includes a B.A. and M.A. in History, University of Vermont, and a M.L.S. from Indiana University. He has been with the University of Illinois since 1973 and has held previous positions at Indiana University and the University of Vermont. Mr. Cobb has guided research grants awarded by the Office of Education, National Endowment for the Humanities, and the Mellow Foundation. Among his publications are two editions of the *Guide to U.S. Map Resources, Checklist of Printed Maps of the Middle West to 1900: Illinois,* and *New Hampshire Maps to 1900.* His current research includes the impacts of technology and electronic information on library services, and library preservation. He is editing a volume on the mapping of the U.S. national parks.

Gary Cornwell is Federal documents librarian at the University of Florida Libraries (George A. Smathers Libraries, University of Florida, Documents Department, Library West, Gainesville, Florida 32611). He recently completed two terms as Chair of the ALA/GODORT Cataloging Committee and currently serves as the Chair of the ALA/GODORT Statistical Measurement Committee. He is a member and Chair of the Depository Library Council. He has conducted several workshops and made numerous presentations regarding the online processing of Federal documents.

Stephen M. Hayes is an Associate Librarian for Reference and Public Documents Librarian at the Hesburgh Library, University of Notre Dame (Notre Dame, Indiana 46556-5629). As the depository librarian since 1974 and an active member of GODORT (including past chair and the fulfillment of many committee assignments), he has been interested in government information and in providing the public with access to that information for many years. His chapter provides the insights gained from his position as chair of the Standing Committee on Electronic Media at the University of Notre Dame.

Peter Hernon, Professor at Simmons College (300 The Fenway, Boston, Massachusetts 02115), teaches courses related to government information, information policy, research methods, evaluation of library services and programs, and statistics. He received his Ph.D. from Indiana University and has authored 26 books and more than 75 articles. He is the founding editor of *Government Information Quarterly* (Greenwich, CT: JAI Press) and has conducted research for various Federal government agencies.

Janita Jobe is Documents Librarian, Government Publications Department, Library, University of Nevada, Reno (Reno, Nevada 89557-0044). She oversees Federal government information and serves as regional librarian for Nevada. Ms. Jobe currently serves on the ALA/GODORT Membership Committee and chairs the ACRL/ANSS Bibliography Committee.

Thomas Kinney is Assistant Head of the Systems Office at the University of Florida Libraries (18 Smathers Library, George A. Smathers Libraries, University of Florida, Gainesville, Florida 32611), where he coordinates and supports library-wide automation projects. He has published articles and given presentations on a variety of library automation topics, including access to machine-readable government information, telecommunications strategies for academic libraries, and online catalog user interfaces.

Claire T. Loranz is Documents Librarian at Wellesley College Library, Wellesley, Massachusetts 02181 (INTERNET: cloranz @lucy.wellesley.edu). She is a 1969 graduate of the Graduate School of Library and Information Science, Simmons College.

Pamela Lowe, was Machine-readable Data Files Librarian, University of Florida Libraries, Gainesville, Florida. She now resides in Fort Collins, Colorado 80525 (4501 Boardwalk Drive, #Q162).

Harold B. Shill is Head, Division of Library and Information Services, Pennsylvania State University, Harrisburg (Heindel Library, Middleton, Pennsylvania 17057). Previous to assuming this position in 1991, he was Evandale librarian at West Virginia University, Morgantown. He holds degrees from Rutgers University and the University of Maryland, and earned his Ph.D. in political science from the University of North Carolina. He has been active in state and national library associations and has testified before congressional committees. He also serves on the editorial board of *Government Information Quarterly*.

John A. Shuler is the Head of the Documents, Maps, Microforms Department, Case Library, Colgate University, Hamilton, New York 13346. He received a B.A. degree in Urban Planning/Geography from California State University, Long Beach, and a M.L.S. from the University of California, Los Angeles. He serves as Reviews Editor for *Government Information Quarterly*, chairs the Government Information Technology Committee of the American Library Association's Government Documents Round Table, and chairs the New York State Library Association's State Documents Committee. He also teaches the graduate governments and information course at Syracuse University's School of Information Studies. Mr. Shuler is currently working on a book titled *The U.S. Government Printing Office: Challenge and Change in the Age of Information*.

Diane H. Smith is Chief, Humanities and Social Sciences, at The Pennsylvania State University (E308K Pattee Library, University Park, Pennsylvania 16802). Previous to assuming this position, she was the head of documents and maps at Pennsylvania State University. She has been the chair of ALA/GODORT and the Depository Library Council to the Public Printer. She has written many articles on the depository program and documents librarianship.

Jan Swanbeck is Chair, Documents Department, University of Florida Libraries (George A. Smathers Libraries, University of Florida, Documents Department, Library West, Gainesville, Florida 32611).

Author Index

Subject Index